booksonline

Read SAP PRESS online also

With booksonline we offer you online access to leading SAP experts' knowledge. Whether you use it as a beneficial supplement or as an alternative to the printed book – with booksonline you can:

- Access any book at any time
- Quickly look up and find what you need
- Compile your own SAP library

Your advantage as the reader of this book

Register your book on our website and obtain an exclusive and free test access to its online version. You're convinced you like the online book? Then you can purchase it at a preferential price!

And here's how to make use of your advantage

1. Visit www.sap-press.com
2. Click on the link for SAP PRESS booksonline
3. Enter your free trial license key
4. Test-drive your online book with full access for a limited time!

Your personal **license key** for your test access including the preferential offer

tai6-u9ng-pbw2-zyve

SAP NetWeaver® Process Integration

 PRESS

SAP PRESS is a joint initiative of SAP and Galileo Press. The know-how offered by SAP specialists combined with the expertise of the Galileo Press publishing house offers the reader expert books in the field. SAP PRESS features first-hand information and expert advice, and provides useful skills for professional decision-making.

SAP PRESS offers a variety of books on technical and business related topics for the SAP user. For further information, please visit our website: www.sap-press.com.

Mandy Krimmel and Joachim Orb

SAP NetWeaver® Process Integration

Bonn • Boston

Galileo Press is named after the Italian physicist, mathematician and philosopher Galileo Galilei (1564–1642). He is known as one of the founders of modern science and an advocate of our contemporary, heliocentric worldview. His words *Eppur se muove* (And yet it moves) have become legendary. The Galileo Press logo depicts Jupiter orbited by the four Galilean moons, which were discovered by Galileo in 1610.

Editor Maike Lübbers
English Edition Editor Kelly Grace Harris
Translation Lemoine International, Inc., Salt Lake City, UT
Copyeditor Ruth Saavedra
Cover Design Jill Winitzer
Photo Credit Masterfile/Royalty Free
Layout Design Vera Brauner
Production Editor Kelly O'Callaghan
Assistant Production Editor Graham Geary
Typesetting Publishers' Design and Production Services, Inc.
Printed and bound in Canada

ISBN 978-1-59229-344-5

© 2010 by Galileo Press Inc., Boston (MA)
2nd Edition 2010, updated and revised
German edition published 2010 by Galileo Press, Bonn, Germany

Library of Congress Cataloging-in-Publication Data
Krimmel, Mandy.
   SAP NetWeaver process integration / Mandy Krimmel, Joachim Orb. — 1st ed.
      p. cm.
   Rev. ed. of: SAP exchange infrastructure.
   Includes bibliographical references and index.
   ISBN-13: 978-1-59229-344-5 (alk. paper)
   ISBN-10: 1-59229-344-1 (alk. paper)
   1. Enterprise application integration (Computer systems)   2. SAP NetWeaver.
 3. Business enterprises — Computer networks. I. Orb, Joachim. II. Title.
   HF5548.4.R2.K75 2010
   658.4'038028553--dc22

                  2010002865

Contents at a Glance

Contents

Introduction

With SAP NetWeaver Process Integration (PI), SAP provides a product for cross-system process integration; that is, for the exchange of messages between components and applications. SAP NetWeaver PI is not an adapter, but a component of SAP NetWeaver with an open architecture that enables you to integrate a wide range of SAP and non-SAP systems within and outside your enterprise's boundaries. Given the diversity of systems installed in today's enterprises and the increase in cross-enterprise communication, the need for support in this area is greater than ever before.

SAP has considered these requirements with the implementation of the new release for process integration. The comprehensive enhancements in Web service application support and the enhancements in the SAP NetWeaver PI runtime made it particularly necessary to revise this book, which was published in 2004, on the basis of SAP NetWeaver PI 7.1. You should note that where it is not expressly mentioned, this book applies to SAP NetWeaver PI 7.1 (enhancement package 1).

Release

This book is a revised and extended edition of the book *SAP Exchange Infrastructure*, which SAP PRESS published in 2004 for Release SAP XI 3.0. It is aimed at readers who want to facilitate the initial steps with SAP NetWeaver PI and at readers who have already gained experience with SAP Exchange Infrastructure and want to obtain an overview of enhancements and the new options of SAP NetWeaver Process Integration. The first part describes the functions and most important concepts of SAP NetWeaver PI. The second part presents scenarios that customers using SAP NetWeaver PI have implemented. Note that, in this book, expressions such as developer and consultant refer to both male and female developers and consultants.

Target group

Chapters 1 and 2 are essential for understanding all subsequent chapters. **Chapter 1** provides an overview of SAP NetWeaver, on the levels of process modeling, on the basic principles of process integration with

Functions and concepts

SAP NetWeaver PI, and on demo examples that are used throughout this book. **Chapter 2** introduces you to the first steps in SAP NetWeaver PI and in Enterprise Services Builder in particular.

Chapters 3 through 5 concentrate on design and development with SAP NetWeaver Process Integration, independently of a specific system landscape. **Chapter 3** deals with the design of collaborative processes; **Chapter 4** discusses service interfaces, messages, and proxy generation; and **Chapter 5** provides in-depth knowledge on all aspects of mapping.

Chapter 6 summarizes everything discussed in the previous chapters: It describes how you configure the cross-system process for a specific system landscape, based on the developments made at the logical level. The order in which topics are addressed reflects the chronological order of the corresponding steps in an SAP NetWeaver PI integration project.

Logically speaking, **Chapter 7**, which deals with SAP NetWeaver PI runtime, could also be read concurrently with all of the other chapters. Here, you get to know the Integration Server and the Integration Engine, the Advanced Adapter Engine, the Web service and proxy runtime, and the monitoring tools. **Chapter 8** completes the first part of the book with its description of the *business process management* cross-component, which marks the transition from stateless to stateful communication.

Scenarios
To illustrate how SAP NetWeaver PI is applied in a business context, the second part of the book examines three customer scenarios that have been implemented with SAP NetWeaver Process Integration. We selected typical scenarios and believe that scenarios that are similar to our examples can be applied at other enterprises. Naturally, the scenarios are not intended to be merely examples, but to also be technically demanding, each focusing on a specific function of SAP NetWeaver PI.

Chapter 9 describes how the BPM cross-component is used as part of an SAP NetWeaver PI scenario. **Chapter 10** shows how the business-to-business features of SAP NetWeaver PI help connect a Customer Relationship Management (CRM) system to an electronic marketplace over the Internet. **Chapter 11** presents the implementation of a Web service call for checking addresses against a boycott list in an SAP Business-Objects Global Trade Services application.

The revision of this book could not have been done without the support of many people who, directly or indirectly, were involved in writing or checking the manuscript. We are also indebted to the following colleagues from SAP NetWeaver PI development and solution management who found time to proofread sections from their specialist areas and resolve open questions: Vladimir Dinev, Vanessa D'Silva, Frank Oliver Hoffmann, Susanne Rothaug, Michael Schmitt, Ilya Stepanov, Martin Tewes, Akitoshi Yoshida, and Alexander Zubev. Special thanks go to Stefan Proksch and Maike Lübbers and the entire team at Galileo Press for their valuable support.

I, Mandy Krimmel, would like to thank the entire SOA Quality Engineering team for their cooperation, valuable comments, and organizational support, particularly Felix Ratschow for the review of the chapter on services registry. Special thanks go to Andreas Quenstedt and Christian Lienert, who supported the revision of the book during their working hours.

Also, I would like to thank Gabriela Teufel from Boehringer Ingelheim, who agreed on the presentation of the Web service scenario of her business area in this book. I would also like to thank Dennis Kropp from HANN & KROPP Consulting for the design and implementation of the various process models and the precise and comprehensive documentation work of the objects created for the scenario.

I, Joachim Orb, would like to thank Peter Ludwig and Joachim Mette for their organizational support and Boris Rubarth, Christian Geldmacher, Stephan Schluchter, and the entire SAP NetWeaver Regional Implementation Group (RIG) for their valuable remarks about content.

I would also like to thank Matthias Allgaier, Thomas Grosser, Ülo Kontor, Robert Reiz, Alan Y. Smith, and Xiaohui Wang for their support in both organizational and content issues. Thanks also go to Mr. Detlef Schulz from iWay Software for his critical review of Chapter 10, and to Dr. Klaus-Ulrich Meininger from the Linde Group for allowing us to include a scenario from his business area.

Mandy Krimmel and **Joachim Orb**

Acknowledgments

Starting with SAP NetWeaver, this chapter describes the focus and components of SAP NetWeaver PI.

1 Overview

SAP NetWeaver Process Integration (SAP NetWeaver PI) is just one component of the SAP NetWeaver technology platform, which is summarized briefly in Section 1.1. Section 1.2 clarifies at which level you can integrate processes with SAP NetWeaver PI, and Section 1.3 introduces you to the world of process integration.

1.1 SAP NetWeaver

An enterprise's competitiveness generally depends on whether it can manage quality and cost considerations to achieve a profit within a reasonable period of time. In the past, enterprises could achieve a competitive advantage simply by accelerating their existing processes. In recent years, however, another success factor has emerged: the ability to react to changes in the market and within an enterprise. Such changes require you to adapt the existing processes in your enterprise and integrate your organizational units (including employees) into new organizational structures. The necessary changes have direct implications for the existing IT landscape of your enterprise. Therefore, one of the major challenges facing the IT sector today is enabling enterprises to react quickly and flexibly to constant changes and demands.

The SAP NetWeaver product groups gather various technological concepts and previous SAP platforms. The focus of SAP NetWeaver is the integration of people, information, and processes in one solution. Figure 1.1 shows an overview of the capabilities of SAP NetWeaver. This book covers the *enterprise services repository* and *processes areas*, but it only discusses the business process management (BPM) aspects that are relevant

The integration challenge

to SAP NetWeaver PI (namely *cross-component* BPM). The components of SAP NetWeaver and the capabilities that they address are discussed below.

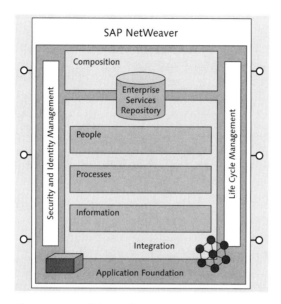

Figure 1.1 Capabilities of SAP NetWeaver

Application
platform

SAP NetWeaver Application Server (currently release 7.1 enhancement package 1 of SAP NetWeaver AS) is the basis of all SAP applications and constitutes the *application foundation* area in the figure. The core of SAP Web AS is the "old" SAP Basis, which offers the recognized advantages of the ABAP development and runtime environment, including reliability, scalability, and operating-system and database independence. SAP NetWeaver AS supplements these fundamental aspects with technologies such as the SAP Java 2 Platform, Enterprise Edition (J2EE) Engine and the Internet Communication Manager (ICM), which handles Internet requests and distributes them to the individual components. Furthermore, SAP NetWeaver AS supports a wide range of technical standards such as HTTP(S), SMTP, WebDAV, SOAP, SSL, SSO, X.509, Unicode, HTML, XML, and WML.

The SAP products SAP NetWeaver Process Integration and SAP NetWeaver Composition Environment (SAP NetWeaver CE) form the basis for optimized process management for process chains:

▶ **SAP NetWeaver Process Integration (SAP NetWeaver PI)**
SAP NetWeaver PI acts as a data hub for SAP and non-SAP systems. Simply put, it's SAP's answer to the problems of enterprise application integration (EAI), which were previously tackled by using, and often combining, products of all types from different vendors.

▶ **SAP NetWeaver Business Process Management (SAP NetWeaver BPM)**
SAP NetWeaver Business Process Management supports the development, management, and implementation of cross-system and cross-organizational business processes and is delivered within the scope of SAP NetWeaver CE. Its development environment supports the standard BPMN (*Business Process Model Notation*) and covers the requirements of process developers and of business process experts and process architects.

▶ **SAP NetWeaver Business Rules Management (SAP NetWeaver BRM)**
Within a flexible and reactive business management system, business rules are often subject to change. To fulfill these dynamics, these rules should not be "hidden" in source code by developers, but be created and managed transparently by a business user. SAP NetWeaver Business Rules Management provides the tools required for this. Because the functionality of SAP NetWeaver BRM is particularly significant for SAP NetWeaver BPM, it's also delivered with SAP NetWeaver CE.

Before the dawn of the Internet and distributed systems, the problem for users was finding information about a particular topic. The challenge facing them now is filtering out what is relevant from the mountain of information available. The task of the IT sector is to find a solution to meet the requirements arising from this problem, which are often summarized under the term *information management*. SAP NetWeaver meets these requirements via the following components:

▶ **SAP NetWeaver Business Warehouse (SAP NetWeaver BW)**
SAP NetWeaver BW, an *online analytical processing OLAP)* system,

holds and retrieves data from SAP and non-SAP systems to enable differentiated information analysis by management (data warehousing). In addition to real-time data extraction and reporting options using MS Excel, SAP NetWeaver BW also offers Web-based reporting.

▶ **Knowledge management component**
The knowledge management component enables you to handle unstructured data. Its main functional areas are content management and the collaboration rooms of SAP NetWeaver Portal as well as TREX (Search and Classification Engine). The goal of knowledge management is to enable access to enterprise-internal information, which is stored, for example, on file servers, web servers, and WebDAV servers, and to provide tools to browse, classify, and structure the information. You can then use this information in SAP NetWeaver Portal, for example.

▶ **SAP NetWeaver Master Data Management (SAP NetWeaver MDM)**
Consolidated master data management across system boundaries is becoming ever more important in the complex arena of information management. Many enterprises have heterogeneous IT landscapes, not least because of the wide range of new SAP applications. All systems within these landscapes have to access the same master data; for example, business partners, address information, or products. This has resulted in many complex distribution processes aimed at ensuring the consistency of this data.

People integration | Lastly, we must not forget the employees of these enterprises, who, together with their colleagues, work with applications on a day-to-day basis. They, too, are constantly developing and changing areas and need a particular selection of applications, or tailored access to these applications, depending on their function. SAP NetWeaver provides the technical solutions to meet these requirements via the following components:

▶ **SAP NetWeaver Portal**
SAP NetWeaver Portal provides an enterprise's employees with a central point of access to the applications of various backend systems, tailored to an employee's user roles. They access not only applications, but also information from the intranet and Internet with single sign-on (SSO), using a uniform user interface of their web browser. SAP NetWeaver Collaboration (see below) and knowledge manage-

ment (see above) are integrated into the SAP NetWeaver Portal and give employees access to structured information and their personal network.

► **SAP NetWeaver Collaboration**
Good internal communication is an important success factor for an enterprise. The challenge facing us here is that interdependent teams, and even employees within a team, often work in different buildings, towns, or even countries. SAP NetWeaver Collaboration has various tools to support the exchange of information: virtual rooms, discussion forums, and wikis. Moreover, you can integrate commonly used third-party tools (such as MS Exchange and WebEx) in SAP NetWeaver Collaboration.

► **SAP NetWeaver Mobile**
Employees who spend a lot of time away from the office as part of their jobs need access to relevant information when they are on the move. A service technician, for example, needs access to information regarding the availability of spare parts. In the SAP NetWeaver framework, SAP NetWeaver Mobile is the technical basis for mobile applications of this type. To support as many mobile devices as possible, SAP NetWeaver Mobile has a platform-independent runtime for these applications. Synchronized access to data from one or more backend systems supports, among other things, encryption, compression, synchronous and asynchronous data exchange, user-specific data replication, and conflict management. Also, SAP NetWeaver Mobile has a sophisticated development environment and a central administration and deployment tool.

These main components are supplemented by *security and identity management* for cross-system user management and *lifecycle management,* which extends the existing *transport management system* (TMS) to all SAP NetWeaver components.

1.2 Levels of Process Modeling

As mentioned in the previous section, the main factor for today's enterprises in gaining competitive advantage has less to do with their ability to accelerate their processes and more to do with the flexibility necessary to adapt their processes to ever-changing requirements. What are these processes? There are many possible answers to this question, even within a single enterprise.

Process types

To avoid misunderstandings, let's start by examining Figure 1.2, which shows an overview of process types within SAP systems, starting at the top with the more business-oriented level and progressing down to the execution of processes. At each level, you work with the model corresponding to that particular level of abstraction:

▶ SAP enterprise modeling applications by IDS Scheer supplement SAP NetWeaver with process modeling at the business level. SAP enterprise modeling applications enable you to model the whole process architecture of an enterprise, strictly from the business perspective, without referencing technical objects. You use this conceptual architecture model to describe the process strategy of your enterprise.

▶ At the next level, you use one or more scenarios to describe the configuration of the business process, right down to the individual process steps. The process descriptions at this level are within the SAP Business Suite and enable you to derive customizing activities, navigate to the component in SAP systems, and define relevant information for monitoring (for example, threshold values). This way, you obtain a presentation of the process from the transactional perspective. For this purpose, SAP Solution Manager works with reference processes, which you configure during implementation by using Customizing. You can synchronize process models between SAP enterprise modeling applications and SAP Solution Manager.

▶ In parallel, you describe the *cross-system* process execution using SAP NetWeaver CE and SAP NetWeaver PI. This enables you to connect processes within applications in a flexible manner. *Integration scenarios* and *integration processes* (in SAP NetWeaver PI) and *processes* (in SAP NetWeaver BPM) are used not only for the enterprise-internal, but also for the cross-enterprise process control.

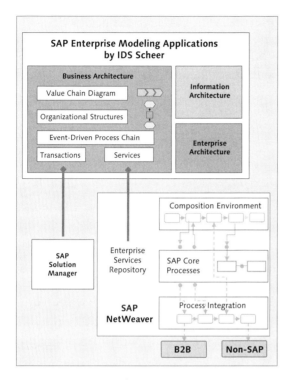

Figure 1.2 Overview of Process Types in SAP NetWeaver and ARIS

Together, the joint solution of SAP NetWeaver and SAP enterprise modeling applications contains a universal and integrated description of the process architecture — from the business model to implementation of the process by SAP Solution Manager to the implementation of executable cross-system processes in SAP NetWeaver PI and SAP NetWeaver CE and cross-application processes within a system in SAP Business Workflow.

This book focuses on process integration using SAP NetWeaver PI. The terms *integration process* and *integration scenario* pertain to the development objects for describing a process. When it's necessary to refer to the real process that the models describe, we differentiate them from the existing development objects by using the term *collaborative process*. The next section covers the basic concepts of SAP NetWeaver PI.

1.3   Process Integration with SAP NetWeaver PI

Connected systems

If you visited the data processing department of any modern enterprise of considerable size and looked at the hardware and software it uses, you would probably notice that the solutions deployed are derived from more than just one software provider. Software solutions are becoming increasingly more interconnected, partly because cost considerations prevent enterprises from replacing entire software solutions and partly because enterprises build their complete solution based on their individual requirements. Furthermore, enterprises want to use software to automate cross-enterprise business transactions.

Enterprises have long been able to integrate a wide range of systems within a system landscape. A range of middleware technology is available for exchanging data between these systems. At first glance, the simplest solution would appear to be point-to-point connection of the various applications and systems. However, as the number of different systems increases, so does the complexity of the overall system landscape, and you would be well-advised by any computer engineer to never change a running system. Because the information regarding the integration of the applications is distributed across the various systems, it's extremely difficult to get an overview of the overall implementation. Therefore, making changes after the initial implementation is laborious, time-consuming, and expensive.

Shared collaboration knowledge

This is where SAP NetWeaver Process Integration (SAP NetWeaver PI) comes into play — by making integration knowledge available at a central location. This means you don't have to search through all of the systems to find the relevant information; rather, you can access this information at a central location (*shared collaboration knowledge*). This is discussed in more detail in Section 1.3.2, Design and Configuration. However, to give you a better idea of the cross-system scenarios supported by SAP NetWeaver PI, we assume that the required integration objects (mappings, interfaces, and so on) already exist, and the next section examines the SAP NetWeaver PI runtime.

1.3.1 Communication Using the Integration Server

The central component of the SAP NetWeaver PI runtime is the Integration Server, which receives and forwards messages of the application systems. The Integration Server uses a message format based on the Extensible Markup Language (XML), which has become the standardized exchange format on the Internet. Additional standards and tools based on the XML standard exist that make working with XML even easier, such as XML Schema, XSLT, and XPath. XSLT (Extensible Stylesheet Language for Transformations), for example, enables you to define mappings required when two communication parties use different message structures.

Moreover, the XML standardized format makes it easier to connect to non-SAP systems. Once data from a non-SAP system has been converted to XML using an adapter, it's a simple step to convert the data to other XML formats for other receivers. However, defining mapping pairs for all different systems isn't recommended.[1] This is where the Integration Server comes into play: In SAP NetWeaver PI, all communication parties use it to exchange messages.

Various *engines* work together on the Integration Server (see Figure 1.3):

▶ Integration Engine
The Integration Engine receives messages using the XI message protocol and performs central services such as routing and mapping for received messages. The XI message protocol is based on the World-wide Web Consortium (W3C) note, SOAP Messages with Attachments. As of SAP NetWeaver AS 6.40, SAP systems support this protocol directly using the proxy runtime and a local Integration Engine. Therefore, in this case, no adapters are required for communication with the Integration Engine on the Integration Server.

▶ Adapter Engine
You use adapters to connect other systems to the Integration Server. Apart from the IDoc adapter and the plain HTTP adapter, all adapters run on the Adapter Engine, which provides central services for mes-

XML

Engines on the
Integration Server

---

1 If there were *n* different systems, you would need $n*(n-1)/2$ different mappings.

saging, queuing, and security handling. Each adapter converts calls or messages from a sender into the XI message format for the Integration Engine. Conversely, the adapter receives messages from the Integration Engine and converts them for the receiver. You only need to convert the message protocol for communication with the Integration Server, and not for every combination of application systems. In this way, you can use SAP NetWeaver PI to exchange messages with a wide range of systems.

▶ **Business Process Engine**
Put simply, the adapters and the Integration Engine are limited to forwarding a message to the receiver or receivers and, if necessary, executing a mapping. Once a message has been sent successfully to the receiver, message processing is complete. The Business Process Engine now extends this Integration Server function to include *stateful* message processing: The engine processes a process model and, if necessary, waits for other messages before continuing with execution. Chapter 8, Integration Processes, addresses this fundamental enhancement.

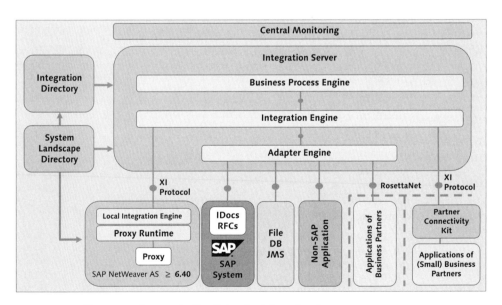

Figure 1.3 Communication Using the Integration Server

To process messages, the Integration Server accesses information from an Integration Directory and the System Landscape Directory. Before the next section takes a more detailed look at these components, let's concentrate on communication using adapters and the proxy runtime.

SAP ships SAP NetWeaver PI with adapters for enterprise-internal and cross-enterprise communication. It would, however, be unfeasible for SAP to provide an adapter for every type of third-party application. Therefore, SAP relies on partners to develop additional adapters for these applications. SAP then offers these adapters to customers via a reseller agreement and is responsible for the first-level support for the adapters. The partners are responsible for second-level and third-level support and use the same support system as SAP.[2] As of SAP NetWeaver Exchange Infrastructure (XI) 2.0, SAP has been able to offer adapters in this way, to integrate applications from Siebel, PeopleSoft, and Oracle; for example, Adapter Engine and Adapter Framework.

Adapter strategy

There are several installation options for the Adapter Engine. As shown in Figure 1.4, you can install the Adapter Engine either centrally on the Integration Server (recommended) or noncentrally. Both the central and non-central Adapter Engine and the Partner Connectivity Kit are based on the *Adapter Framework* with the core functions for adapter communication. This framework supports the Java Connector Architecture (JCA) standard and thus provides the foundation for the aforementioned development of new resource adapters. Section 6.4.1 in Chapter 6 discusses how you configure the adapters of the Adapter Engine centrally. The configured adapters then take on the inbound and outbound processing on the Integration Server for the Integration Engine, according to the respective protocol. The J2SE Adapter Engine is pre–SAP NetWeaver XI 3.0 and is of interest in only a few special cases.

If you want to process messages statelessly — that is, without the participation of the Business Process Engine — within the framework of your scenarios, we recommend processing them using only the *Advanced Adapter Engine* (AAE). Here, the adapters are directly connected for the

Advanced Adapter Engine

---

2 For more information about third-party adapters, see SAP Service Marketplace at *http://www.sdn.sap.com/irj/sdn/nw-soa* via Mediation, Reliable Transport and Connectivity • Third-Party Adapter.

inbound and outbound messages. The AAE provides services for routing and mapping. Processing via the Integration Engine isn't required; this is done by the AAE's messaging system. Because this type of processing usually entails higher performance, it's SAP's recommended variant for scenarios that require routing and/or mapping.

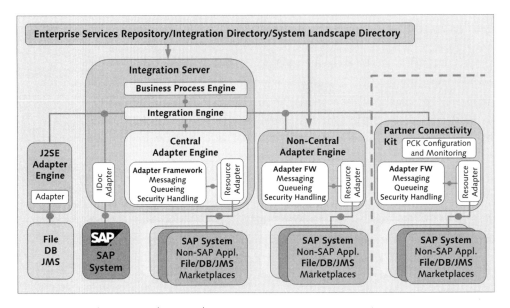

Figure 1.4 Adapter Architecture

Direct communication In addition to the processing of messages via engines, SAP NetWeaver PI also provides the option of *direct communication* as of release 7.1. Of course, the direct communication between sender and receiver provides an even higher processing speed. Nevertheless, this option initially appears to provide an impairment from the architecture perspective, because it entails all of the problems of a point-to-point connection. However, the direct communication within the scope of SAP NetWeaver PI provides some benefits compared to the classical point-to-point connection: Even though messages are exchanged directly at runtime, the connection is configured centrally. Moreover, the exchange of messages is monitored by the central monitoring of SAP NetWeaver PI. The direct communication therefore combines the benefits of the point-to-point connection (performance) and the centralized communication (central configuration and central monitoring). Also, the disadvantages of direct communication directly result from the architecture concept: They don't provide the option either of mapping or of routing, nor can you process messages statefully. Figure 1.5 summarizes the possible variants for processing messages using SAP NetWeaver PI.

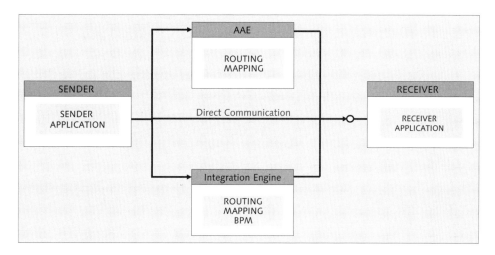

Figure 1.5 Communication Variants

What do you require in order to implement the message exchange using the Integration Server or the Advanced Adapter Engine? To explore this question, let's first look at the implementation in the application systems. There are several common implementation features, even though implementation varies according to the system platform. The idea is similar to remote function calls (RFCs): Communication with another system is encapsulated using an interface, whose parameters are converted into a message. However, the significant difference here when compared to RFC is that SAP NetWeaver PI always requires two interfaces for communication: one interface on the sender side and one interface on the receiver side. At first glance, this may appear to be a disadvantage, but it's actually an advantage over RFC, because sender and receiver interfaces don't have to match exactly.

Figure 1.6 shows a message exchange schematically from the perspective of the application. On the sender side, the application calls an outbound interface to transfer the data to the PI runtime (an adapter or the proxy

Outbound and inbound

29

runtime). The SAP NetWeaver PI runtime uses the parameters of the interface to generate a request message, which the Integration Server can process.[3] Before the message reaches one of the process engines, the message header merely contains specifications about the sender and does not yet have any receiver information. If you think back to the goal mentioned previously — that is, to use sender-receiver assignments to access information at a central location rather than searching through all application systems — this immediately makes sense. The receiver of a message is determined in the process engine, which makes this decision on the basis of configuration data from the Integration Directory. On the outbound side of the engine, an adapter or the proxy runtime must convert the request message into a call. It does this by calling an inbound interface at the receiver, which implements the inbound processing of the application.

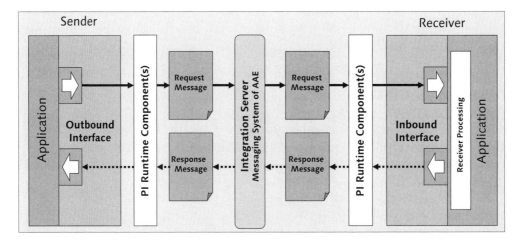

Figure 1.6 Communication via Interfaces

Synchronous and asynchronous With *synchronous* interfaces, the return parameters of the inbound interface determine the response message that the sender is waiting for before continuing the application. With *asynchronous* interfaces, the application does not expect a response. Here, the message exchange is complete

---

3 Section 7.1.1, Basics, in Chapter 7, looks at the structure of such messages.

after processing at the receiver. This *mode* must be the same for the outbound and inbound interface.[4]

In a real scenario, the outbound and inbound interface can be all manner of things; for example, an RFC, an IDoc, or a proxy (we will examine the differences in more detail below). The configuration for determining the receiver is based on the assumption that such interfaces exist. If this isn't the case (for example, when exchanging messages using the file, JMS, or JDBC adapter), you simply work with an invented name for the nonexistent outbound interface. What is important is that outbound and inbound interfaces separate (potential) senders and receivers. If the parameters of the interfaces for message exchange don't match, you map them to each other using a mapping. This *loose coupling* enables different senders and receivers to communicate with each other. In particular, it enables you to assign such interfaces to one another when one side of the communication cannot or must not be changed; for example, when using a proxy as the outbound interface, which calls an RFC in an SAP system of release 4.6C. In this case, the RFC has the role of an inbound interface.

Loose coupling

The message exchange within the scope of direct communication is correspondingly easier. In this case, two systems communicate directly with one another via the Web services runtime without any intermediate Integration Server or Advanced Adapter Engine. Because neither routing nor mapping is possible here, sender and receiver must be closely linked, and the parameters of the interfaces must correspond for the message exchange. This is referred to as *close coupling*.

Close coupling

As you've already seen, SAP NetWeaver PI provides you with various communication variants:

Proxies and adapters

▶ You can use *proxies* to exchange messages directly or via the Integration Engine.

▶ You can use *adapters* to send messages via the Integration Engine or the Advanced Adapter Engine.

---

4   As of SAP NetWeaver XI 3.0 SP5, you can use a synchronous-asynchronous bridge within an integration process to forward the request message of a synchronous call.

These two approaches have a fundamental difference, as shown in Figure 1.6. You develop interfaces that are to be connected to the Integration Server using an adapter in the application system. Proxies, on the other hand, are objects (classes, methods, and data types) generated from a language-independent description. The underlying goal is, again, to make all information relevant to integration available at a central location, and the interfaces for message exchange are undoubtedly part of this information. To achieve this goal, SAP NetWeaver PI works with a central *Enterprise Services Repository*, where you save interface descriptions, for example. For interfaces, there are two different development approaches:

- **Inside-out development**
  When using adapters to connect systems, you develop the interfaces for message exchange as you normally would in the application system (or they may already exist there). You then import the interface descriptions from the application systems to the central Enterprise Services Repository. SAP NetWeaver PI allows this import for RFCs and IDocs. If you have the message structure in WSDL, DTD, or XSD format, you can import this structure to the Enterprise Services Repository as an external definition.

- **Outside-in development**
  SAP provides a programming model with SAP NetWeaver PI, which you use to define language-independent *service interfaces* in the Enterprise Services Repository. You can then use proxy generation to create either ABAP or Java proxies in application systems.

Figure 1.7 shows both approaches in an example: An ABAP proxy calls a Java proxy, an IDoc, and an RFC. Proxy communication development starts with objects in the Enterprise Services Repository, and adapter communication development starts in the application system. In both cases, you can centrally access the interface description in the Enterprise Services Repository. This separation of the description and the implementation enables you to use the interface description to develop mappings in parallel with the implementation in the application systems. Chapter 4, Service Interfaces, Messages, and Proxy Generation, examines interface development in more detail.

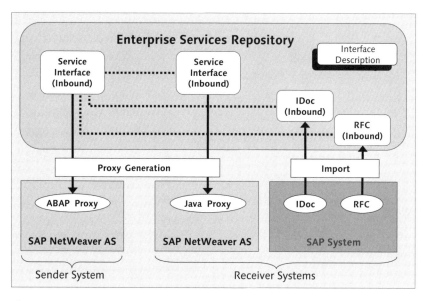

Figure 1.7 Proxy and Adapter Communication (Example)

In addition to service interfaces, there are numerous other objects that are important for the implementation of a cross-system process and that you develop centrally in the Enterprise Services Repository. Now that you've learned about the runtime and some fundamental aspects of it, the next section takes you back to the beginning of development.

1.3.2 Design and Configuration

The Integration Server, the Advanced Adapter Engine, and the Web services runtime need the technical address of a receiver to be able to forward messages. These addresses are dependent on the specific system landscape, but you can describe the collaborative process between the applications at the logical level without this information. Therefore, SAP NetWeaver PI divides the implementation of the collaborative process into the following phases:

▶ **Design time**
At design time, you describe the message exchange between applications (not between systems), based on the collaborative process to be

implemented. You can then derive the required interfaces and mappings.

▶ **Configuration time**
Put simply, at configuration time you assign systems to the applications and configure the message exchange. You not only reference existing objects from the design, but also supplement this information according to the requirements of a scenario; for example, with security settings.

Implementation phases
Figure 1.8 shows the different phases. The *Enterprise Services Builder* is the central tool of SAP NetWeaver PI, and you use it both at design time and when configuring the collaborative process in a specific system landscape. The Enterprise Services Builder creates *design objects* in the Enterprise Services Repository and *configuration objects* in the Integration Directory. At runtime, the Integration Server and the Advanced Adapter Engine access the configuration in the Integration Directory to process inbound messages. Moreover, the Enterprise Services Builder saves executable design objects directly on the Integration Server or the Advanced Adapter Engine to be able to execute them at runtime (mapping programs, for example).

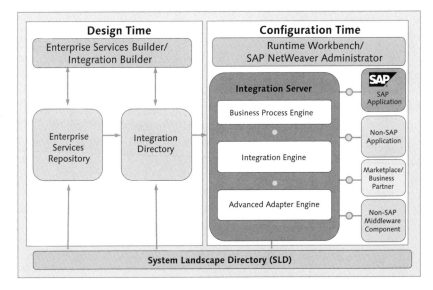

Figure 1.8 Implementation Phases

To illustrate the implementation of the collaborative process, let's compare it with the construction of a car. At design time, you use the Integration Builder to develop the design of the car. The design references the parts that you'll need to build the car later. The design also leaves some individual options open for the customer. The color and the horsepower of the car, for example, are specified in the purchase order. At configuration time, the car is built according to a specific purchase order, and, if everything is done correctly, it will drive once finished.

Before we provide you with an overview of design and configuration time, let's look at the advantages of this architecture:

Advantages

▶ The basic philosophy of SAP NetWeaver PI (unlike the construction of a car) is to make all information and objects required to integrate the applications available at a central location. No matter how many applications you want to integrate, you always use the Integration Builder to call the information from the Enterprise Services Repository or Integration Directory.

▶ At design and configuration time, you first define the collaborative process at the logical level, ignoring the technical details. Accordingly, at configuration time, you distinguish between logical and technical routing: Logical routing determines the logical receiver, whereas technical routing determines the technical address of the receiver. This separation means you don't have to change your whole design and configuration if technical addresses change; for instance, in the event of a server change.

With regard to this last point, SAP NetWeaver PI uses the System Landscape Directory (SLD), which is where you save products, software components, and business systems for the logical level and technical systems for the technical level. Among other things, you can use the SLD to determine which technical systems are installed in your system landscape, which of these are assigned to a business system for a cross-system scenario, and which products and software components are installed in this system. Chapter 3, Designing Collaborative Processes, discusses products and software components, and Chapter 6, Configuration, discusses technical and business systems.

System Landscape Directory

This concludes the basics and overall concept of SAP NetWeaver PI. If you feel there are still pieces of information missing that prevent you from understanding the complete SAP NetWeaver PI picture, don't worry. The various areas of SAP NetWeaver PI are all interconnected, and it takes time to get a hold of this topic. In the next several chapters, you need only identify the individual components in their context to comprehend the material. Chapter 2, First Steps, is an introduction to the SAP NetWeaver PI tools and presents a demo example to give you some practical experience.

However, let's first take a look at the different design and configuration objects. The Integration Builder is the tool for creating and managing objects, and these objects are stored in the Enterprise Services Repository and Integration Directory. To clarify whether a particular section relates to design or configuration time, it's often assumed that you are working directly in the Enterprise Services Repository or in the Integration Directory. Don't let this confuse you: In both cases, you access the objects by using the Integration Builder.

Design Objects in the Enterprise Services Repository

Figure 1.9 shows an overview of the main design objects in the Enterprise Services Repository. Each design object is assigned to a software component version, which you must import from the SLD beforehand. The software component version clarifies to which product and which application the objects are assigned. This enables you to control which design objects are shipped with an application from the Enterprise Services Repository. Design objects are shipment objects, whereas the objects of the Integration Directory must be configured at the customer site.

Graphical editors The Integration Builder provides graphical object editors to enable you to edit objects. The sequence of the design objects in the figure corresponds to a usage hierarchy; the Integration Builder supports both top-down and bottom-up development. Because the design objects are based on XML standards, there are export and import functions to enable you to use definitions in tools outside the Integration Builder as well and vice versa. For example, instead of using graphical mapping in the Integration Builder, you can import XSLT or Java mapping programs to the Enterprise Services Repository and use them. For interface development, this example shows only the outside-in approach.

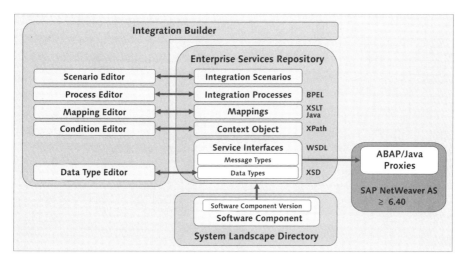

Figure 1.9 Design Objects and Editors in the Integration Builder

Configuration Objects in the Integration Directory

The configuration in the Integration Directory determines the message processing at runtime. Figure 1.10 illustrates this relationship. The routing rules (receiver determination and interface determination) determine the receiver and whether mapping programs from the Enterprise Services Repository are to be executed. You use collaboration profiles to describe the technical options of the sender and receiver. Together with collaboration agreements between a sender and the Integration Server or between the Integration Server and a receiver, you can derive the inbound and outbound processing of the Integration Server and the logical routing. We discuss this in more detail in Chapter 6, Configuration. You can specify just systems as the receiver or an integration process executed by the Business Process Engine of the Integration Server. You use this integration process to relate messages to each other on the Integration Server.

For the processing of messages using the Advanced Adapter Engine, in the Integration Directory you use the *integrated configuration*. It combines inbound processing, receiver determination, interface determination with mappings, and outbound processing in one configuration object (Figure 1.10).

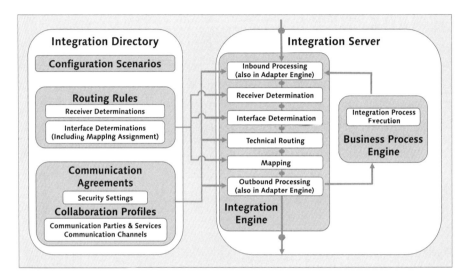

Figure 1.10 Configuration of Message Processing

For simplicity, the figure shows only the essential services. Moreover, the figure represents only the logical process flow of message processing. The directory data, for example, isn't actually read directly from the Integration Directory, but from a cache.

This chapter provides you with an overview of how to access the tools in SAP NetWeaver PI. The Enterprise Services Builder, Services Registry, and Integration Directory are of central significance here. SAP also gives you demo examples, which guide you step by step through the technical concepts and tools.

2   First Steps

The features of SAP NetWeaver Process Integration (SAP NetWeaver PI) can be divided into several task areas, each of which has corresponding user roles. Users require these roles to perform the tasks in their respective areas. Before discussing the SAP NetWeaver PI tools in detail, we list the various task areas and refer you to the chapters in this book that cover these areas:

▶ **Administration**
An administrator sets up the various SAP NetWeaver PI tools and is responsible for system monitoring and user management. Because these tasks are closely linked to the installation of SAP NetWeaver PI, it's advisable for the administrator to be involved in the installation process.

▶ **Technical configuration**
The configuration of the SAP NetWeaver PI runtime components is referred to as the *technical* configuration. It includes setting up the Integration Engine, the Advanced Adapter Engine, and the individual adapters. This configuration depends on the components used in the current system landscape. Consultants or administrators perform configuration independently of the design and configuration of the collaborative process.

This book does not cover the installation or administration of the tools. Sections 7.1 and 7.2 in Chapter 7 introduce the technical configuration of the Integration Engine and the Advanced Adapter Engine. For further information on the installation and technical configuration, refer to the

Installation Guide on SAP NetWeaver Process Integration 7.1 at the SAP Service Marketplace at *http://service.sap.com/instguidesNWPI71* and the chapter configuration of SAP NetWeaver in the SAP Help Portal at *http://help.sap.com*. This book focuses on the following task areas:

▶ **Design**
This area includes the design of collaborative processes by a development or consultant team. Chapter 3, Designing Collaborative Processes, first describes the organizational steps of this development and then addresses the modeling of the collaborative process using integration scenarios. This description provides the basis for an examination of the objects required to integrate the applications: service interfaces (Chapter 4), mappings (Chapter 5), and integration processes (Chapter 8). These objects, which you create at design time in the Enterprise Services Builder, are referred to as *process integration (PI) content*. The service interfaces from the Enterprise Services Builder can also be published and consumed as Web services. These steps of storing and classifying Web services in the *Services Registry* (Chapter 2, Section 2.1.2) and consuming Web services in calling applications (Chapter 4) are also part of the design area.

▶ **Configuration**
This area consists of the configuration of collaborative processes by a development or consultant team. You configure inbound and outbound processing, logical routing, technical routing, and mapping for a particular business-to-Business (B2B) scenario or system landscape. Chapter 6 discusses this topic. This task area also includes the maintenance of configuration data for the IDoc adapter.

▶ **Monitoring**
This area consists of the monitoring of collaborative processes at runtime. This includes monitoring of the message flow (with respect to throughput, for example) and analysis and further processing of messages that have not been processed (status tracking). The monitoring of processed IDocs and RFCs in the corresponding adapters also belongs to the monitoring task area. Section 7.3, Proxy Runtime, in Chapter 7, discusses this in more detail.

There is a seamless transition from the configuration of the collaborative process to the technical configuration (an administrative task). For example, the IDoc adapter must access metadata that describes the structure of an IDoc. Which IDocs are to be processed depends on the collaborative process (and therefore is part of the configuration, which is the task of a consultant). To access the metadata of an IDoc, there must be an RFC connection to the system that wants to send or receive the IDocs (this in turn is part of the technical configuration, which belongs to the administrator's task area).

SAP NetWeaver PI 7.1 consists of Java and ABAP-based applications. Table 2.1 shows the authorizations that you need to access the functions of SAP NetWeaver Process Integration. They are related to user roles and correspond approximately to the aforementioned task areas. These are composite roles, and each references a single role for accessing the Java applications and a single role for accessing the corresponding ABAP transactions. Users must be assigned only the composite roles. This automatically gives them access to the ABAP and Java tools. Before logging on to the SAP NetWeaver PI design and configuration tools, each user must first change his initial password by logging on to the ABAP side or one of the web browser–based Java applications; for instance, NetWeaver Administrator or Runtime Workbench. Other options for assigning authorizations for users of the SAP NetWeaver PI design and configuration tools are addressed at the end of Section 2.1.1, Enterprise Services Builder and Integration Builder.

User roles

Role	Task Area
SAP_XI_DISPLAY_USER	This role groups together the display authorizations for all SAP NetWeaver Process Integration tools
SAP_XI_DEVELOPER	Design
SAP_XI_CONFIGURATOR	Configuration
SAP_XI_CONTENT_ORGANIZER	Tasks related to the organization and structuring of the content of the Enterprise Services Repository and the System Landscape Directory that are not usually performed by developers, for example, the maintenance of software components
SAP_XI_MONITOR	Monitoring
SAP_XI_ADMINISTRATOR	Administration and technical configuration

Table 2.1 User Roles in SAP NetWeaver PI

Once a user has logged on to a client in an SAP system, a user menu that corresponds to the roles assigned to the user is displayed. To start the Java-based applications, you need a user at the client in which the Integration Engine is configured as the Integration Server (this is discussed in more detail in Chapter 7, Section 7.1.1, Basics). Once you've done this, you can use the Start Integration Builder transaction (Transaction SXMB_IFR) to call the SAP NetWeaver PI start page in the web browser and log on to the Java applications by using the ABAP user.

Figure 2.1 shows the SAP NetWeaver PI start page in the SAP system LU1. From here, you can call the Enterprise Services Builder (for design), the Services Registry (for managing Web services), the Integration Directory (for configuration), the System Landscape Directory (for describing the system landscape), or the Runtime Workbench or SAP NetWeaver Administrator for SAP NetWeaver PI for monitoring.

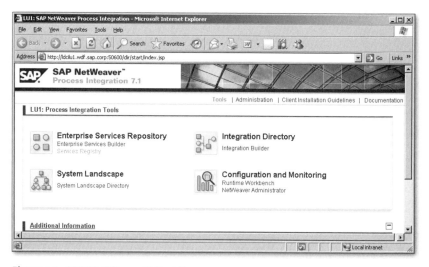

Figure 2.1 SAP NetWeaver PI Start Page

Chapter 3, Section 3.1, Development Organization, and Chapter 6, Section 6.1, Describing Systems and Communication Components, describe the System Landscape Directory in more detail. The next section describes the Enterprise Services Builder, the Services Registry, and the Integration Directory. Chapter 7, Section 7.3, Proxy Runtime, discusses the two monitoring tools.

2.1 Introduction to the SAP NetWeaver PI Design and Configuration Tools

The Enterprise Services Builder and the Integration Builder are the central tools for designing and configuring collaborative processes with SAP NetWeaver PI. The storage and classification of service interfaces that are published as Web services is done in the Services Registry.

2.1.1 Enterprise Services Builder and Integration Builder

Both Java applications use the same *graphical user interface* (GUI) framework and are started using Java Web Start (for information about installing Java Web Start, see the Client Installation Guidelines on the SAP NetWeaver PI start page). The libraries of the two applications are saved on the Integration Server after you install SAP NetWeaver PI. When you start the applications for the first time, Java Web Start transfers the required libraries to your PC by HTTP and starts the Java application. You can also change this HTTP connection (and all other internal HTTP connections of the Enterprise Services Builder and the Integration Builder) to the HTTPS protocol.

The Java applications have their own logon dialog box. The user and password pertain to the client of the SAP system in which the Integration Engine is configured as the Integration Server. If single sign-on (SSO) is activated for the system, you only have to log on to the Java applications once. You can then call any subsequent sessions without having to reenter your user and password. You can change to logon language at any time via the menu path TOOLS • PERSONAL SETTINGS. In addition to settings for the navigation and the search function, you also determine the original language for the documentation of objects.

Logon and personalization

Figure 2.2 shows the Enterprise Services Builder that is used for designing the collaborative processes. The tabs on the left side are for object navigation and for managing change lists. The respective object editor is displayed on tabs on the right side (in this case the mapping editor). To compare several objects, select the Detach Window icon in the top-right corner of the object editor (⊞). In addition to the navigation tree options, you can use the blue arrows in the main menu of the Enterprise

Navigation

Services Builder to navigate forward and backward in the navigation history, which remembers the sequence in which you've opened objects.

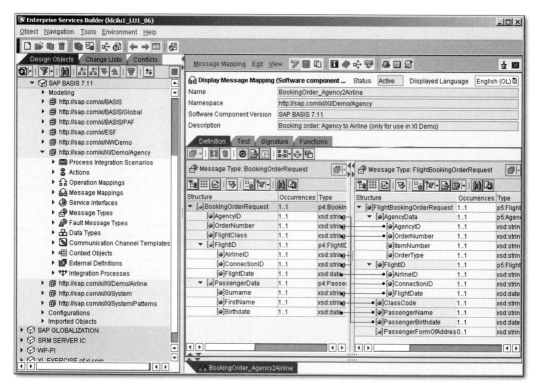

Figure 2.2 Enterprise Services Builder

Because the Enterprise Services Builder and Integration Builder user interfaces for design and configuration are based on the same GUI framework, you operate them in the same way in both cases. There are differences, however, with regard to the object types and their organization. Before you can use the Enterprise Services Builder to create objects at design time, you need a software component version, which you import from the System Landscape Directory (see Section 3.1.2, Organizing Design Objects in the Enterprise Services Repository, in Chapter 3). Configuration objects, on the other hand, are not assigned to software component versions and can be grouped using *configuration scenarios* or in folders (see Section 6.1.2, First Steps in the Integration Directory, in Chapter 6). The differences in the object types mean that they must be handled differently during copy or transport procedures. The following discusses how to edit objects in the two Java applications and, where applicable, points out differences between the Enterprise Services Builder (design) and the Integration Builder (configuration).

Editing and Managing Objects

To create a new object, select OBJECT • NEW in the main menu, select the object type, and enter at least the required attributes. Required attributes are marked with a red asterisk (*) in the dialog box. If you use the context menu in the navigation tree to create objects, some input fields are populated with certain information derived from the position of the object in the tree; for instance, the object type and, in the Enterprise Services Repository, the software component version and namespace.

Once you've saved an object, the Enterprise Services Builder and the Integration Builder generate a new object version (status: Being Processed) and add it to a user-specific change list. Change lists simplify object management in the following ways:

Change lists

▸ While an object is being edited in a change list, the changes are visible only to the user making the changes. The change list still has the Open status. This enables you to edit several objects in a change list and then make all changes visible to all Enterprise Services Builder or Integration Builder users (status: Active) by releasing the change list. The change list is then closed. You can display older object versions by selecting <OBJECT> • HISTORY in the respective object editor menu.

▸ If the user doesn't yet have a change list, the Enterprise Services Builder or Integration Builder automatically creates a new standard change list. Every user can create additional change lists. You can also reassign change lists of other users to yourself.

▸ In the Integration Builder, you release change lists to activate changes for runtime.

▸ In the Enterprise Services Builder, the change lists are grouped by software component version. If objects belong to the same software component version, you can move them between different change lists by using drag-and-drop. Dependent objects are moved as well.

Object references
and copies

As is clear from the last point, software component versions are important for organization in the Enterprise Services Builder: They represent the smallest shippable unit. Limitations on object references and behavioral considerations when copying design objects stem from the requirement that objects that belong together must also be able to be shipped together. For example, the Enterprise Services Builder does not permit references between interface objects from different software components, because at least one interface must be shipped with all its dependent objects (message and data types) as a unit. Otherwise, a customer can end up with an interface definition, but cannot access the structure of the message. The Enterprise Services Builder differentiates object reference types to account for these shipping implications. Similar to hyperlinks (in this case the object reference) in an HTML document (in this case the referencing object), the Enterprise Services Builder saves the references of an object to another object either relatively or absolutely to a software component version:

▶ **Relative object reference**
In this case, the reference in an object becomes invalid as soon as you copy the referencing object to another software component version. There is a good reason for this in interface objects, as mentioned above. Therefore, all object references between interface objects are relative. If you copy an interface object to another software component version, you can copy all dependent interface objects as well.

▶ **Absolute object reference**
In this case, the reference in an object is still valid, even when you copy it to another software component version.

Object check and
processing log

In the Enterprise Services Builder, references are defined as absolute or relative. To check all relative object references after an object has been copied, select <OBJECT> • CHECK in the object editor menu. If objects are missing in the current software component version, these are listed in the processing log of the check function.

Figure 2.3 shows an example: The FlightSeatAvailabilityQuery message type was copied to the software component version DEMO 2.0. The reference to the FlightSeatAvailabilityQuery data type has therefore become invalid. The processing log at the bottom of the editor screen shows the results of the check; that is, that the Enterprise Services Builder cannot find an active version of the FlightSeatAvailabilityQuery data type in the software component version, DEMO 2.0.[1] When change lists are released, the processing log can contain a range of messages relating to different objects. You can navigate directly from the log to the object in the list. You can show or hide the processing log by clicking on the icon circled in Figure 2.3.

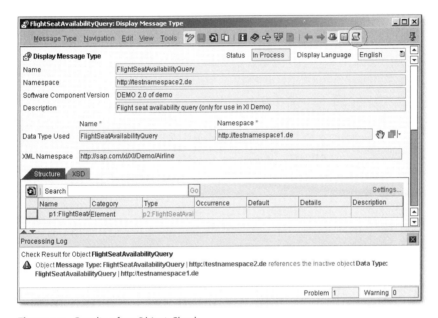

Figure 2.3 Results of an Object Check

Conversely, object references enable you to determine where an object is used. The Enterprise Services Builder and the Integration Builder provide a where-used list in the object editor for this purpose. You use this where-used list to identify either the direct user or the indirect (transitive) user. You can also search for objects:

Object search and where-used list

▶ The search function in the toolbar of the navigation tree enables you to search for texts from the selected position in the navigation tree.

---

1 The object check also considers the underlying software component version. This is discussed again in Section 3.1, Development Organization, in Chapter 3.

You can use the wildcard * to mask any number of text characters and the wildcard ? to mask exactly one character. If the text is found, the tree is expanded and the corresponding node selected. If the search is unsuccessful, it's performed again, starting at the top structure node.

▶ The search help (main menu OBJECT • FIND) enables you to use search requirements to search for objects in the Enterprise Services Repository or the Integration Builder. Examples of search requirements are header data (object type, software component version, namespace, name), changed on, changed by, and other object-dependent attributes. The latter enable you to select service interfaces by mode (synchronous or asynchronous), for example. In the extended search, you can logically link the search attributes.

So far, the focus has been on the basic functions of the design and configuration tools of SAP NetWeaver PI. To understand the concepts of SAP NetWeaver PI and the corresponding tools, it's helpful to use examples. SAP ships design objects and demo applications, which you can configure with the Integration Builder. Section 2.2 presents the demo examples, but first let's look at how authorizations are assigned in the Enterprise Services Builder and the Integration Builder and at the dependencies that exist between the these two tools and the other SAP NetWeaver PI components.

Authorizations

Access to objects is determined by the roles assigned to the ABAP user. As shown in Table 2.1, there is one role for assigning display authorizations, one role for design, and one role for configuration. The SAP_XI_CONTENT_ORGANIZER role exists for certain activities relating to the organization of SAP NetWeaver PI content in the Enterprise Services Builder (for example, the import of software component versions), because only selected users (and not all developers) perform such activities. To add additional access rights for particular object sets, select TOOLS • USER ROLES in the menu and create additional roles. The Enterprise Services Builder or the Integration Builder transfers activated roles to the SAP User Management Engine, which you use to assign the roles to user groups on the Java side. In the default setting, there are no restrictions on access to particular object sets in the two SAP NetWeaver PI tools. The user roles that you transfer to the SAP User Management Engine limit the existing authorizations to a selected group of people.

During configuration in the Integration Builder, you reference design objects in the Enterprise Services Builder. However, there are no references the other way around. To accelerate access to objects, the following caches exist:

▶ **Runtime cache**
At runtime, the Integration Engine or the Adapter Engine must access configuration objects, mapping objects, and integration processes of the Enterprise Services Builder or the Integration Builder. The Integration Builder activates object versions in the runtime cache. The cache is updated whenever you activate a change list in the Integration Builder or a change list in the Enterprise Services Builder that contains mapping objects or integration processes. To check whether the cache has been informed of changes, select ENVIRONMENT • CACHE STATUS OVERVIEW in the Enterprise Services Builder or Integration Builder main menu. You can analyze the content of the runtime cache in the Integration Engine client by calling Transaction SXI_CACHE.

▶ **SLD cache**
The Enterprise Services Builder and the Integration Builder access information about software components, business systems, and technical systems in the System Landscape Directory (SLD). This cache is updated every time the SAP NetWeaver PI tools are restarted. Alternatively, you can declare the data in the cache invalid by selecting ENVIRONMENT • CLEAR SLD DATA CACHE in the main menu.

Now that you've learned about the two tools for designing and configuring collaborative processes, the following section briefly discusses a tool for the central management of service interfaces that are published as Web services: the Services Registry.

2.1.2 Services Registry

Both service interfaces created at design time in the Enterprise Services Builder and all other Web services available in the system landscape can be described and classified as Web services at a central position in the system landscape using the Services Registry. Therefore, the UDDI-based Services Registry centrally provides information on available services and references to its metadata. The services can be published as modeled, activated, or deployed services, for which no configuration exists yet, and as completely configured services, which can be called directly. In the latter case, the Services Registry provides all information that is required by the calling application to call the Web service.

Options for publication

By default, after installation the Services Registry contains Web services that exist on the Java server on which the Services Registry runs. However, you can also publish all service interfaces that are provided in the Enterprise Services Builder as Web services in the Services Registry. The publication of the services in the Services Registry can be carried out using different approaches:

▸ From the Enterprise Services Builder, you can publish the *Web Service Description Language* (WSDL) descriptions of the modeled service interfaces directly via a publishing function in the Services Registry; then they are available as *modeled Web services* in the Services Registry.

▸ The Web services that are developed in the Java and ABAP development environment can be published directly from the development environment. These implemented Web services are displayed as *activated* or *deployed* Web services in the Services Registry.

▸ You can configure the Web services using the Integration Builder, the Web services configuration in the SAP NetWeaver Administrator, or via the SOA Manager (Transaction SOAMANAGER); all of these tools provide the option of publishing *configured Web services* in the Services Registry.

▸ All of these Web services can be published directly from the Services Registry. In this case, the Services Registry actively obtains the Web service description from the tool or system in which you modeled, implemented, or configured the Web service.

Classifying web services

All web services published in the Services Registry can be classified according to specific criteria to facilitate the search for certain web services. Here you can use classification systems provided by SAP or create additional ones. The classification systems contain different values to which you can then assign the web services.

In the Services Registry, you can now centrally search for Web services that exist in the system landscape. Start the Services Registry via the Services Registry link in the SAP NetWeaver PI start page. You can use the Web service name, the status of the Web service (modeled, activated/deployed, configured), and the system in which the Web service is configured as search criteria. In the advanced search, the previously discussed classifications are also available. Figure 2.4 shows the result of a simple search in the Services Registry.

Searching web services

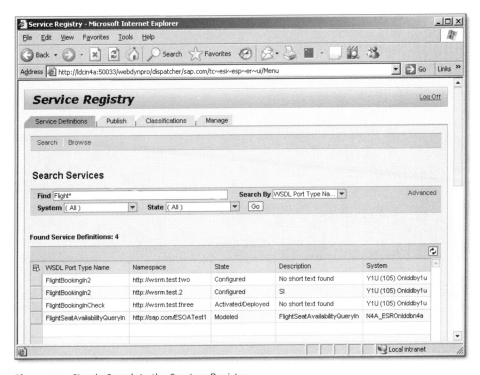

Figure 2.4 Simple Search in the Services Registry

In this example, we searched for Web services whose names start with Flight. The search finds four Web services: a service that is modeled in the Enterprise Services Builder, an activated Web service from the ABAP development environment, and two Web services for which configurations are already available. For these configured Web services, in addition to the WSDL, the Web service description, you are also provided with the target address of the service endpoints, which you can use to call the Web service. For the FlightBookingIn2 Web service in Figure 2.5, two service endpoints were configured via which you can address this Web service.

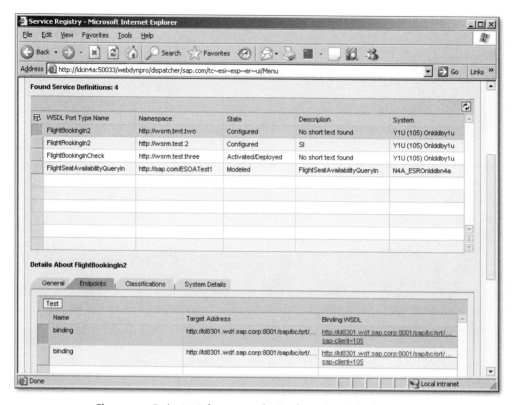

Figure 2.5 Endpoint Information of a Configured Web Service

Mass configuration A central Services Registry not only provides the advantage of searching for available Web services at a central point, but also allows you to use the services stored in the Services Registry to define the runtime configurations for multiple Web services at the same time. In this configuration, which is also referred to as *mass configuration* of Web services, you group multiple Web services and assign these service groups to configuration profiles in the SAP NetWeaver Administrator; these profiles include the settings for the Web service runtime (for instance, the authentication method and the settings for the transport security).

2.1.3 Web Service Navigator

You can test configured Web services using the Web Service Navigator. From the Services Registry, you can also start the WS Navigator for existing service endpoints directly by clicking on the Test button. The Web service is then called with the target address stored in the service endpoint. Figure 2.6 shows the result of the Web service call of the FlightSeatAvailabilityQueryIn service interface. In the WS Navigator, the results are displayed both in a web browser–based interface and in XML format that is used for the communication. Moreover, you can view the complete HTTP reply in addition to the results.

Testing Web services

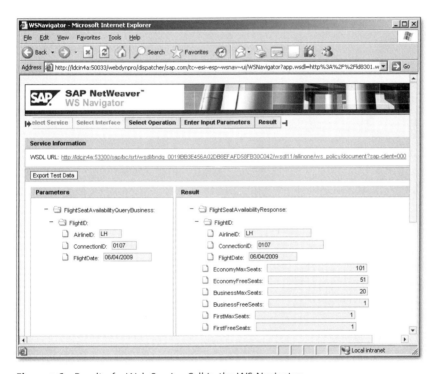

Figure 2.6 Result of a Web Service Call in the WS Navigator

To consume the Web services from the Services Registry in an application, that is, to be able to use and call the application, you have the option to address the Web service description from the Services Registry directly from the Java development environment and to use it for the implementation of a calling application. In the ABAP development

Consuming Web services

environment, this option will not be available until SAP NetWeaver 7.30. Chapter 4, Service Interfaces, Messages, and Proxy Generation, discusses the generation of service providers and service consumers in more detail.

SAP provides the *Enterprise Services Workplace* (ES Workplace) as a central option to view descriptions of all services provided by SAP, to test them, and to evaluate them for use in your own applications. You can find the ES Workplace at *http://sdn.sap.com* via the menu path SERVICE-ORIENTED ARCHITECTURE • EXPLORE ENTERPRISE SERVICES • BROWSE THE ES WORKPLACE.

After this introduction to the SAP NetWeaver PI design and configuration tools, the next chapter describes the individual subareas of SAP NetWeaver PI. The demo examples discussed in the next section will help you understand how to use SAP NetWeaver PI in practice.

2.2 Simple Use Cases and Demo Examples

SAP ships demo examples as part of SAP NetWeaver PI. You can use simple use cases, demo examples, and additional exercise tasks to set up, implement, configure, and execute basic communication scenarios. As is typical in a shipment of a cross-system SAP application, the SAP NetWeaver PI content in the Enterprise Services Builder and the example applications are part of the shipment, and you have to configure the scenarios yourself in the Integration Builder. The scenarios enable you to become familiar with SAP NetWeaver PI and perform tests; they are not intended for productive use. Detailed documentation is available on the configuration and execution of the individual scenarios.[2]

Simple use cases
The *simple use cases* are very simple, easy-to-configure sample scenarios that — based on a scenario with one sender and one receiver — gradually integrate a second receiver and a payload-based routing and mapping with the scenario. The scenarios can be configured both for the message processing by the Integration Server (Chapter 7, Section 7.1)

---

[2] For further information, refer to the SDN at *https://www.sdn.sap.com/irj/sdn/ soa-servicebus* via the menu path GETTING STARTED • GETTING STARTED DOCUMENTS.

and directly via the Advanced Adapter Engine (Chapter 7, Section 7.2). In the second case, the message processing, routing, and mapping take place directly in the Advanced Adapter Engine.

With the demo examples, SAP provides a complete application scenario that presents large parts of the SAP NetWeaver Process Integration functions as examples. Because the first part of this book refers to the demo example, you now obtain a more detailed overview of the demo examples. To ensure that users can understand the demo examples without having detailed business knowledge, we based them all on the communication between a travel agency (as the vendor of flight tickets) and three airlines (which sell their tickets through the travel agency). The flight data model has been used successfully in many SAP technology courses, and because booking a flight is something that most people have personal experience with, SAP NetWeaver PI uses this experience as an example with which to demonstrate cross-system communication. Note, however, that the goal of the examples isn't to mirror reality, but to demonstrate the central concepts of SAP NetWeaver PI, so not all aspects of this application scenario reflect how SAP NetWeaver PI is used in the real world. For example, the demo examples are based on the assumption that the travel agency books flights directly with the airlines. In reality, travel agencies use a central booking system for their flight bookings.

Application scenario

The design of the demo examples does not stipulate a particular number of airlines. However, the documentation for configuring the demo examples is based on the assumption that exactly one travel agency exchanges messages with three airlines. Figure 2.7 shows the scenario for this standard configuration. The applications that communicate using SAP NetWeaver PI are usually part of different products; for instance, SAP Customer Relationship Management (CRM) and SAP Advanced Planning and Optimization (APO). However, to keep the logistical effort involved in shipping the demo examples to a minimum, the demo example applications are implemented on SAP NetWeaver Application Server 7.1; this means that they are available on all systems based on SAP NetWeaver Application Server 7.1. Furthermore, in the standard configuration, the roles of travel agencies and airlines are performed by different clients of the same SAP NetWeaver system. SAP does not provide any support for scenarios that differ from the standard configuration.

Standard configuration

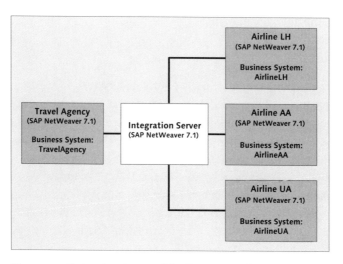

Figure 2.7 System Landscape of the Demo Examples

The documentation for the demo examples describes the general configuration steps for all of the examples and the specific configuration steps for each example. The documentation also describes how to execute the examples.

Design objects of the examples

The design objects required to integrate the travel agency application and the airline application are shipped with SAP NetWeaver PI 7.1. Table 2.2 gives an overview of the examples shipped with *enhancement package 1*. These objects are located in the Enterprise Services Builder in the SAP BASIS 7.11 software component version. The aforementioned logical separation of the travel agency application and the airline application is reflected in the Enterprise Services Builder. All design objects that belong to the travel agency application are located in the *http://sap.com/xi/XI/Demo/Agency* namespace, and those that belong to the airline application are in the *http://sap.com/xi/XI/Demo/Airline* namespace. Design objects that don't belong to a particular application (such as integration scenarios, integration processes, and mapping objects) cannot always be assigned uniquely to one of the communication parties. The demo examples are based on the assumption that the airline application provides certain services, which form a complete integration scenario together with the travel agency application. Therefore, all such design objects are defined in the namespace of the travel agency. The available design objects form the basis for executing the demo examples for test purposes. Furthermore, you can use the design objects to examine how the content of the Enterprise Services Builder is structured, how various object types are used in the Enterprise Services Builder, and the dependencies between the design objects.

Integration Scenario	Communication Types (→ Asynchronous; ↔ Synchronous)
Checking flight seat availability (CheckFlightSeatAvailability)	ABAP proxy ↔ ABAP proxy ABAP proxy ↔ RFC ABAP proxy ↔ web service
Booking a single flight (SingleFlightBooking)	ABAP proxy → ABAP Proxy ABAP proxy → IDoc ABAP proxy → web service
Booking connecting flights (MultipleFlightBooking)	ABAP proxy → ABAP proxy (via an integration process) ABAP proxy → IDoc/ABAP proxy (via an integration process)
Distributing booking order data (DistributeBookingOrderInformation)	ABAP proxy → file system

Table 2.2 Demo Examples of SAP Enhancement Package 1 for SAP NetWeaver PI 7.1

Based on the demo examples, two additional exercises are used to describe a scenario for canceling a flight booking that extends the scenarios delivered with the demo examples. The exercises describe all tasks, both design and configuration tasks, that you must perform to implement a complete scenario. You create design objects, such as data types, service interfaces, message mappings, and integration processes, and generate and implement ABAP proxies; this forms the basis for the configuration in the Integration Builder.

Additional exercises for the demo examples

This brings us to the end of the introductory chapters of this book. In the next chapters, you get to know the individual areas of SAP NetWeaver PI in more detail.

To design a collaborative process, you need a range of objects that are all related to each other. This chapter looks at how SAP NetWeaver PI organizes these objects and how you use them to design a collaborative process.

3 Designing Collaborative Processes

As described in Chapter 1, Overview, SAP NetWeaver PI distinguishes the design, configuration, and runtime phases to manage the complexity of collaborative processes. The term *collaborative process* means a cross-system process from the real business world; for example, the process for booking flights between travel agencies and airlines. The requirements of the process determine which design objects you need.

Definition

Before you can start the implementation, you make certain organizational steps or settings. Section 3.1, Development Organization, describes these organizational steps. The design of the collaborative process is closely linked to the planning and organization of the implementation, and describes which components exchange messages with each other. You model the collaborative process in the Enterprise Services Builder using *integration scenarios*. These scenarios provide you with an overview of the message exchange and group the objects created at design time together semantically.

3.1 Development Organization

In every type of software development project, you are faced with the challenge of grouping development objects and organizing them into appropriate units. For example, you may want to have a particularly high level of reusability or minimize the communication between individual components. It is an important feature of SAP NetWeaver PI that all objects involved in message exchange are centrally available. Therefore, regarding organization of objects, two general object types must be differentiated:

▶ **All design objects in Enterprise Services Repository**
Because you use this content to describe and implement the collaborative process, these objects are collectively referred to as *process integration content*.

▶ **Development objects in the application systems of applications that use SAP NetWeaver PI to exchange messages**
Examples are Java and ABAP classes, consumer and provider proxies generated by SAP NetWeaver PI, ABAP programs, and other development objects that implement the actual application logic (such as updates when a message is received).

Software
components

Of course, these objects belong together semantically and must be grouped together again for shipment of the cross-system application. The next two sections describe how this is done: Section 3.1.1 discusses the organization of products in the SAP System Landscape Directory, and Section 3.1.2, Organizing Design Objects in the Enterprise Services Repository, shows how you use this information in SAP NetWeaver PI.

3.1.1   Describing Products in the Software Catalog

An application is a piece of software that is installed or can be installed in a system. It can be updated and provides interfaces to enable other applications to access or transfer data. A cross-system application uses multiple systems and products. It helps both SAP and the customer get an overview of all systems and the components installed in these systems. SAP stores this information centrally in the SLD:

▶ It saves the information about the software that you can install in a system in a *software catalog*. SAP differentiates between *products* and *software components*. Software components can be shipped but don't have to be executed. The executable product consists of software components. We discuss this in more detail later in this section.

▶ The SLD also contains information about the systems that make up the system landscape in which the software is or can be installed. Because the system landscape is defined at the customer site, system data is of interest only at configuration and runtime. We discuss this in more detail in Section 6.1, Describing Systems Communication Components.

In SAP NetWeaver PI, products and software components belong to design time, and system landscape data belongs to configuration time. Don't let the product name System Landscape Directory confuse you. The SLD is relevant for the whole of SAP; therefore, the differentiation usually made between repository and directory in SAP NetWeaver PI does not apply.

System Landscape Directory and SAP NetWeaver PI

At the beginning of a software project, management defines a product's the software components. The SLD imports the relevant information to the software catalog. Initially, this catalog is just a list of *installable* software components. When a product is installed, the software components are assigned to a technical system in the SLD and thus become installed software components. We should also mention that different versions of products and software components can exist. For example, the product SAP CRM has product versions, SAP CRM 5.0 and SAP CRM 7.0, which you can find in the software catalog.

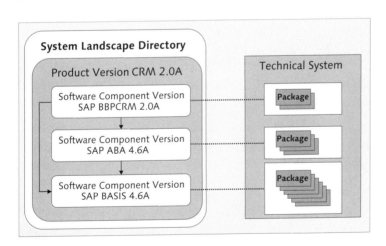

Figure 3.1 Software Component Versions and Packages

Figure 3.1 shows an example of product version SAP CRM 2.0A. It consists of three interdependent software component versions:

▸ SAP ABA 4.6A uses SAP BASIS 4.6A. Software component versions such as SAP BASIS 4.6A are referred to as *underlying* software component versions.

▸ SAP BBPCRM 2.0A uses SAP ABA 4.6A and SAP BASIS 4.6A.

Use relationship

This *use relationship* enables objects from underlying software component versions to be reused. Furthermore, a software component version can be used in different product versions. The actual functions for a product are developed in the application system. Developers work with packages[1] to divide the functions of a software component version into smaller units. In short, a customer never installs individual software component versions in a system; instead, an executable version of a product is installed. Developers, on the other hand, are more likely to work with software component versions, because they represent the smallest shippable unit. For example, SAP ships support packages on the software component version level, and not on the package level.

SAP provides information about the available SAP software in the software catalog in the SLD. Customers can add their own software components and products as third-party products. The SLD thus simplifies the administration of a customer's system landscape and provides a basis for describing the components that communicate using SAP NetWeaver PI. In Section 3.2, Modeling the Collaborative Process, you'll learn how to use this description as a basis to model the communication between components and what to do if these components are outside your own system landscape.

3.1.2 Organizing Design Objects in the Enterprise Services Repository

You use the Enterprise Services Builder to edit all of the design objects of your collaborative process. The responsibility for organizing this content lies with selected employees, called *content managers*. To perform the necessary steps, these content managers need special authorizations that go beyond normal developer authorization. Just as in development in the application systems, the design objects must be shippable and there-

---

1 Software logistics on SAP NetWeaver AS offers additional development units, which are not discussed in detail here.

fore must be assigned to software component versions. The software component versions of interest are those that belong to the products for which you want to implement cross-system communication. The content manager imports these software component versions via the menu path OBJECT • NEW • WORK AREAS • SOFTWARE COMPONENT VERSION • IMPORT FROM SLD in the main menu of the Enterprise Services Builder. After import, the software component versions are displayed in the navigation tree in alphabetical order. Displaying all of the software component versions would unnecessarily complicate the overview.

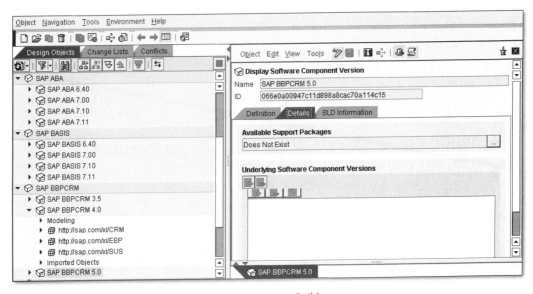

Figure 3.2 Software Components in the Enterprise Services Builder

Figure 3.2 shows the navigation tree of the Enterprise Services Builder in the central Enterprise Services Repository. The top level shows the software components, the next level shows the imported software component versions, and the level below that shows the namespaces. The content manager creates these namespaces after the import of the software component version to prevent naming conflicts between Enterprise Services Repository objects. Therefore, they are also referred to as *ESR* namespaces. You use ESR namespaces to identify design objects at different places in SAP NetWeaver PI: in the Enterprise Services Repository, in the Integration Directory, in application systems, and in the message

Namespaces

header. Because SAP NetWeaver PI uses the XML standard, there is also a range of other namespaces in addition to the ESR namespaces:

► RFC and IDoc descriptions that have been imported to the Enterprise Services Repository each have a fixed, cross-software-component ESR namespace.

► For messages and data type enhancements, you can assign an XML namespace as an alternative to the ESR namespace. Sections 4.3.1, Using Message Types Across Components, and 4.3.2, Enhancing Partners' and Customers' Data Types, in Chapter 4 discuss this topic in more detail.

► In message monitoring, you'll find internal namespaces in the message; for example, for the message format.

Folder   Folders enable you to sort objects within a namespace. The use of folders within the Enterprise Services Repository is based on the logic of file systems. For example, you can create further subfolders within a folder.

Versioning   Unlike ESR namespaces, software component versions aren't used to uniquely identify the object and are relevant only for shipment and versioning at the software component level. Once the development of a software component version is complete, content managers import a new version of the software component to the Enterprise Services Builder. It can use the Transfer Design Objects function (in the Enterprise Services Builder in the Tools main menu) to transfer the design objects of the previous version. To do this, they must first create the same namespaces in the new software component version that were in the old version. Software components with different versions can therefore use the same namespace.

Object references   The division of the product into software components has repercussions. Objects that are dependent on one another should be in the same software component version. Otherwise, you cannot be certain that a shipment to the customer is complete. For this reason, the Enterprise Services Builder warns users if they try to create the same namespaces in different software component versions, because the objects of a namespace are usually closely related. The Enterprise Services Builder also limits the options for object references. For example, interfaces in the Enterprise

Services Repository consist of different subobjects. To ensure that all of these interface objects are in the same shipment unit, an interface object can only reference interface objects of the same software component version or an underlying software component version. Therefore, you cannot select any other software component versions in the input help in the Enterprise Services Builder. Such references are valid only within this context. You can copy objects to another software component version, but the object references become invalid. On the other hand, in cross-component communication, you can't avoid referencing objects in different software component versions. For example, a mapping is basically located between two components (see Chapter 5, Section 5.2, Preconfiguration and Testing of Mapping Programs, for more information). In this case, the Enterprise Services Builder references the other objects *absolutely*, that is, the software component version is specified explicitly in the input help. These references remain valid when the objects are copied.

Because the concepts presented here also apply to other areas of software logistics, we discuss them in the next section. However, it isn't necessary to read Section 3.1.3 to understand Section 3.2, which looks at modeling collaborative processes using integration scenarios and process components.

3.1.3   Object Versioning and Transport

You've already seen that versioning occurs at the software component level. Versioning also exists at the object level (design objects in the Enterprise Services Repository and configuration objects in the Integration Directory) in the form of user-specific change lists. When an object is initially saved, a new object version is created, which is added to the change list. When users activate their list, this version of the object in the list is closed. All changes are then visible to all other users in the Integration Builder. One particular feature of this concept is that it enables the release of changes in the configuration collectively for the runtime environment in the Integration Directory.

Design objects are developed in a central Enterprise Services Repository. In Section 3.1.2, Organizing Design Objects in the Enterprise Services

Transport and shipment

Repository, you learned that you can use the release transfer to transfer design objects in the Enterprise Services Repository to other software component versions. You can also exchange objects between different Enterprise Services Repositories, for the following reasons:

▸ Design objects are necessary to configure the collaborative process at the customer site. Customers must import the SAP NetWeaver PI content to their Enterprise Services Repository.

▸ For quality assurance reasons, we recommend importing the SAP NetWeaver PI content to an intermediate Enterprise Services Repository before the shipment. This step enables import problems to be identified and corrected at an early stage. In very large development landscapes, you may want to use additional Enterprise Services Repositories for consolidation purposes.

Because the configuration of design objects is customer-specific, the Integration Directory does not contain shipped content. Therefore, there are no software component versions in the Integration Directory. Nevertheless, transports between different Integration Directories are still necessary to test the configuration before using it in a production landscape. We discuss this in more detail in Section 6.6, Transports Between the Test and Production Landscape.

Original objects
Now, however, let's take a closer look at design objects. They always have one original repository; that is, the Enterprise Services Repository from which the object originates. Within an Enterprise Services Repository, you differentiate between the original objects and the copies by using an attribute of the corresponding software component version. This originality principle means that transport landscapes for Enterprise Services Repositories are star-shaped. Figure 3.3 shows an example.

Mechanisms for ensuring consistency
You must only make changes to an object in the Enterprise Services Repository from which the object originates. This ensures that during import to the target repository, the new versions of this object are created in such a way that the object has the same version in both repositories. The object versions in the different repositories are always consistent. The following mechanisms ensure this:

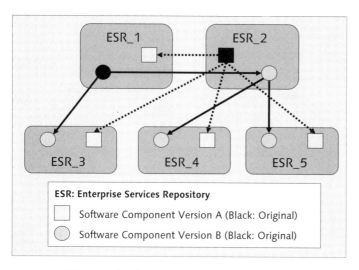

Figure 3.3 Transport Landscape

- Content managers lock objects in the target repository against changes. They can, however, allow changes if they are necessary for an immediate correction. As long as development makes the same changes to the original, this does not cause a problem. If they don't, this results in a conflict, which the user can resolve during import in the Enterprise Services Builder.

- When older object versions are imported to a target repository, any existing newer object versions aren't overwritten. The imported older version is visible in the object history of the Enterprise Services Builder after import, but the new version remains the current valid version.

The latter mechanism ensures that multiple imports to an Enterprise Services Repository always have the same result, irrespective of their sequence. There are three variants for the transport itself:

Transport variants

- You export the design objects to an export directory as a file. You copy these export files to an import directory of the target repository and follow the menu path TOOLS • IMPORT DESIGN OBJECTS in the Enterprise Services Builder to import them.

- Using the *Change Management Service* (CMS), you can transport design and configuration objects between multiple systems via predefined transport landscapes. Here, you can only transport objects from the SAP NetWeaver PI tools. You use the same function in the Enterprise Services Builder as previously mentioned, but you don't need to copy the export files manually.

▶ If you want to transport all ABAP and Java objects — such as design and configuration objects, proxy classes, programs, and additional ABAP and Java development objects, which you created and configured in your scenarios — using a transport technology, you use the transport via the *Change and Transport System* (CTS).

The next section looks at integration scenarios in the Enterprise Services Builder, which enable you to model the message exchange of the collaborative process using the products that you learned about in Section 3.1.1, Describing Products in the Software Catalog.

3.2 Modeling the Collaborative Process

A collaborative process, whether existing or new, consists of a sequence of steps that must be performed to execute the process. Before you can implement the process, you must determine and document the required steps and their sequence. As you've already seen in Section 1.2, Levels of Process Modeling, in Chapter 1, there are different process views in SAP systems, each with a different focus and level of detail in the steps. Regarding the level of abstraction, integration scenarios and process components in SAP NetWeaver PI are primarily at the same level as business processes in SAP Solution Manager. However, they are used very differently:

▶ **Business processes in SAP Solution Manager**
In SAP Solution Manager, you work with business scenarios[2] to derive business processes that model the process flow across applications. Customers use the business processes to configure applications that are required in a scenario within the involved systems (for example, to customize these applications).

---

2 SAP documents the business scenarios of its own solutions on SAP Service Marketplace in the portal for Integrated Business Content (*http://service.sap.com/ibc*).

▶ **Integration scenarios in the Enterprise Services Builder of SAP NetWeaver PI**
These scenarios document the message exchange between application components (see Section 3.3, Modeling Using Integration Scenarios, for more information).

▶ **Process components architecture models in the Enterprise Services Builder of SAP NetWeaver PI**
These describe business workflows in the application systems, their interactions, and the underlying data model (see Section 3.4, Modeling Using the Process Components Architecture Model).

Because the focus of this book is SAP NetWeaver PI, you will now learn about the modeling with integration scenarios and process components in the Enterprise Services Builder.

3.3   Modeling Using Integration Scenarios

Process integration scenarios (or *integration scenarios,* for short) in the Enterprise Services Builder of SAP NetWeaver PI focus on the following:

▶ Documenting the message exchange between application components. You can reference involved design objects of the Enterprise Services Repository directly from integration scenarios; for example, point from a connection to a necessary mapping. Integration scenarios therefore offer a central point of access. You can also derive and create all necessary design objects from an integration scenario or bundle existing design objects in an integration scenario.

▶ Providing a configuration template to use as a basis to generate and refine configuration content in the Integration Directory. Chapter 6, Section 6.2.1, Configuration Using Integration Scenarios, discusses this topic.

The following section examines how you can use integration scenarios in the Enterprise Services Repository. Technically, they aren't necessary to implement the collaborative process. However, it would be shortsighted not to use integration scenarios, because they provide an integrated overview of the design objects — thereby making them easier to maintain — and save time during configuration.

3.3.1 Mapping Application Components to Systems

As you saw in Section 3.1.1, Describing Products in the Software Catalog, a product is a piece of software that you can install and execute in a system. An installed product can also send and receive messages. To create a graphical model of these processes, integration scenarios use *application components*, which the integration scenario editor depicts by using colored lanes.

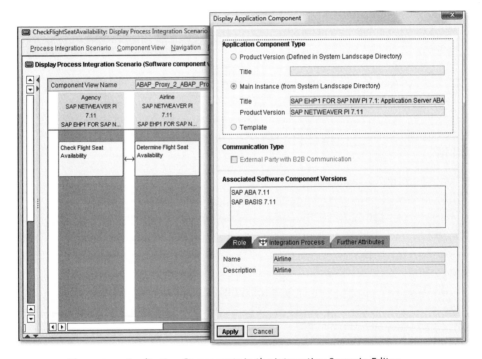

Figure 3.4 Application Components in the Integration Scenario Editor

Application component

Figure 3.4 shows a simple integration scenario that models a flight availability check. The left lane is an application component for the travel agency (Agency role); the right lane is an application component for the airline (Airline role). The same software unit is assigned to both application components (product version: SAP enhancement package 1 for SAP NetWeaver PI 7.1). You would normally expect there to be different product versions, such as SAP CRM and SAP APO. In real life, this is the case. However, the example presented is part of the demo examples that SAP ships with SAP NetWeaver PI. To ensure that the example is available in all systems based on SAP enhancement package 1 for SAP NetWeaver PI 7.1, it is part of the same product version. The demo example is described in more detail in Section 2.2, Simple Use Cases and Demo Examples, in Chapter 2.

Application components of integration scenarios can reference product versions from the SLD. You may ask yourself why you don't simply insert product versions in the integration scenario. The reason is that this does not cover the application cases where the product version isn't known. For example, only the product versions of a system landscape are saved in the SLD. In cross-company communication, you can't access this information. In other cases, the product version may not be known at the time of modeling. Therefore, integration scenarios use application components as the logical abstraction of all of these cases. The common feature is that applications (and not systems) are integrated. Which systems the applications are installed in isn't relevant in modeling.

The dialog window on the right in Figure 3.4 shows the properties of the application component with the Airline role with information about the associated software component versions for the product version. The upper part of the window displays the different types of application components:

Types of application components

▶ **Product version**
The application component references a product version in the SLD. This does not have to be an SAP product. Partners and customers can enter their own products and software components in the software catalog of the SLD.

▶ **Software unit**
The application component references a software unit in the SLD. Software units are different variants of a product that are installed on different servers. In such cases, a reference to a product version isn't sufficient, because there can be several software units for a product

version, and these have different roles in the scenario. Because modeling with software units is otherwise no different from modeling with product versions, we don't discuss this particular case in detail now.

▶ **Template**
The application component isn't dependent on information from the SLD. You use templates if the implementation of the application component isn't known (see above).

In addition to the type of the application component, you can also specify whether it is an external B2B communication party. Section 6.3, Configuring Cross-Company Processes, in Chapter 6, describes the configuration of such integration scenarios.

It's important to remember that application components aren't systems, but units that provide an executable function. Determining in which systems (or how many) this function is to be installed isn't relevant for modeling. Let's take another look at the flight availability check example in Figure 3.5.

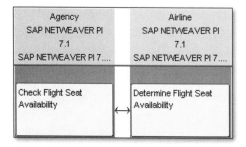

Figure 3.5 Check Flight Seat Availability Integration Scenario

The integration scenario is the same, whether or not the status is to be queried at several airlines: There is one communication party with the role of a travel agency and several communication parties with the role of an airline, all using the same product version. Therefore, you don't need additional application components for modeling. The final number of airlines to be checked is determined at configuration time. You can assign services of different systems to an application component in the

Integration Directory. This abstraction simplifies the modeling of collaborative processes considerably.

Figure 3.6 illustrates this principle for the flight availability check. At configuration time, the application component with the Airline role is assigned two business systems — Airline_LH and Airline_AA — for Lufthansa and American Airlines, respectively. Additional airlines are possible. Section 3.3.2, Modeling the Message Exchange, covers other examples of this type of abstraction and examines more closely how to describe the message exchange between the application components.

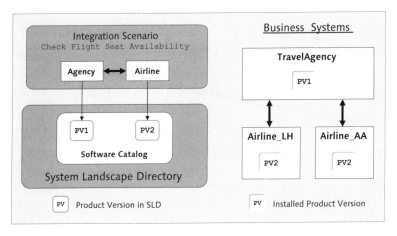

Figure 3.6 Modeling at the Application Component Level

The common feature of the application components that you've looked at so far is that you assign application systems to them at configuration time. Integration processes are an exception, because they are executed on the Business Process Engine on the Integration Server; that is, during message processing between different systems. In the integration scenario, you reference these processes from the Integration Process tab of an application component. Which integration processes you can reference depends on the type of application component. The next section takes a closer look at references.

Integration processes in the integration scenario

So far, you haven't learned what the *role* of an application component entails. It's a business description of the application component that aids the understanding of the integration scenario. A product can be used in

Roles

different application components in different roles. The role consists of a technical name and a description, which is visible in the integration scenario editor in the header of the application component. Table 3.1 shows examples of good role descriptions.

Type of Application Component in Integration Scenario	Role Description (Examples)
Business partner	Customer vendor
Different application components of a business partner	Vendor — customer management Vendor — production
Only application components of a business partner in the integration scenario	Customer management production

Table 3.1 Role Descriptions of Application Components

Component views

In the input field above all of the application components, you can also assign a name for the corresponding *component view*. To start with, there is only one component view of the integration scenario, in which you model the message exchange for a particular combination of product versions. In some cases, the only difference between integration scenarios is that they support different combinations of product versions. If this is the case, you can use the component view to define different views of the same integration scenario. In this example, it would not make sense to create a second integration scenario in the Enterprise Services Builder, because this would mean having two descriptions of scenarios that are essentially the same. Instead, you should proceed as follows:

1. Enter a role for each application component in the first component view. This role must be identical in all component views.

2. Enter a name for the first component view.

3. In the menu bar of the integration scenario editor, select COMPONENT VIEW • COPY.

4. To reference other product versions in a new component view, replace the application components with new components that use the same role name.

5. To the left of the graphical editor, the Enterprise Services Builder shows a screen area that displays a preview of all component views. To switch between component views, click the respective preview.

The component views are copies within an integration scenario. Technically, they are independent of one another. Now that you've examined application components in integration scenarios in detail, the following describes how you can model the message exchange between application components.

3.3.2 Modeling the Message Exchange

In the previous section, you looked at application components as a modeling abstraction and examined how they are mapped to systems. You saw that application components reference product versions or templates. Moreover, a product version consists of software component versions. Every object that you ship with your product is part of such a software component version, even the integration scenario itself.

In this section, you learn about actions and how to use them to describe the message exchange. *Actions* are separate reusable objects in the Enterprise Services Repository that are assigned to a software component version. At first glance, you might think that this appears to be somewhat complicated. Therefore, let's go back to the start of modeling and ask where you create which objects, where you can use them, and why. Then, let's look at the modeling of the message exchange in detail.

Actions

Initial Modeling Considerations

Let's start with the integration scenario itself. Because the integration scenario describes the message exchange between application components, it's at a higher level than the components and encompasses all of them. There are two ways to define to which software component version the integration scenario should belong:

▶ Define a "leading" application component of the collaborative process, which is responsible for higher-level design objects. These objects can also be mapping objects, which are located between the application components (see Section 5.2, Preconfiguration and Testing of Mapping Programs, in Chapter 5). In this case, you create the integration scenario in a software component version for the product version of the application component.

▸ Define a separate software component version for the integration scenario, which is not assigned to a product of the application component. The result of this is that the integration scenario is not automatically shipped with one of the products that exchange messages with each other.

Granularity of the integration scenarios

We recommend the first option because the integration scenario, in this case, is shipped along with a product. Once you've decided which option to use, you need to consider how many integration scenarios you need to describe the different subprocesses of the collaborative process. The subprocess should be an appropriate and self-contained unit of manageable scope. Sometimes it's possible to disconnect subprocesses at the start or end. (The use of component views for differentiating between different product versions was covered in the previous section.) You must also consider which parts of the process to configure together. You should group these parts into an integration scenario and transfer them collectively to the Integration Directory (see Section 6.2.1, Configuration Using Integration Scenarios, in Chapter 6).

Identifying application components

Let's look again at the application components. Section 3.3.1 described in detail the mapping of application components to systems. The important factor in modeling is that an application component offers a range of functions and can later be installed in multiple systems. If the following prerequisites are met, you can use an application component to model several communication parties of a collaborative process that is to be modeled in the integration scenario.

▸ The communication parties must have the same business role.

▸ The communication parties must offer the same functions.

▸ The communication parties must use the same product version.

Once you've identified the necessary application components, you must clarify one more technical detail, namely, whether the application component relates to a product version or whether you're using a template:

▶ Ideally, a product version is known and entered in the SLD that provides the functions of the application component. In this case, you reference the product version from the application component.

▶ If the product version is not (yet) known, use a template. In this case, you may be dealing with non-SAP products that aren't entered in the SLD. Therefore, the principal use of templates is to model cross-company processes.

You may ask yourself why it isn't simpler to always use a template. Aren't templates sufficient to produce a graphical description of the integration scenarios? Why not simply enter the missing information (the product version) in the templates by hand? Indeed, this is how you proceed with products outside your own system landscape. However, using this method within your system landscape would mean forfeiting numerous advantages:

Product version or template?

▶ Because templates are separate from the SLD, all attributes of the template simply serve as documentation. Consistency checks aren't possible.

▶ A reference to a product version in the SLD bridges the gap to configuration in the Integration Directory: The Integration Builder can call the product versions installed in systems in the SLD. This enables you to identify the services of a system. In this way, application components of the product version type simplify the subsequent development and are more than mere documentation.

Therefore, you should use application components of the product version type for all products in the SLD that are part of a collaborative process.

To describe the message exchange between application components, you use actions. You've already seen actions in the flight availability check in Figure 3.4 of Section 3.3.1, Mapping Application Components to Systems (CheckFlight-SeatAvailability is an action), although they were not identified as such. Before looking at the modeling of actions in more detail, let's examine the different types of actions that exist and where you can use them. These restrictions are necessary to ensure that actions are shipped together with the integration scenario in which they are used:

Internal and external actions

▸ Actions relating to a function of a product version should be shipped using a software component version of that product version (or, alternatively, using an underlying software component version). These actions can be used only within the corresponding product version and are therefore referred to as *internal actions*.

▸ In templates, the product version is not known, so you cannot assign an action to it. Such actions are defined outside a product version and are therefore referred to as *external actions*. To guarantee that the actions are shipped together with the integration scenario, you can use only external actions in integration scenarios of the same or an underlying software component version.

In addition to referencing actions, you can also reference integration processes from application components. The Enterprise Services Builder allows references in a similar way. Table 3.2 provides a summary of the software component versions for which you must create actions and integration processes to be able to use them in application components. In principle, either the product version of the application component or the software component version of the integration scenario determines which objects you can use. To simplify the table, the following two terms are used:

▸ **Product-version-based**
The object to be inserted is determined by the product version of the application component. Therefore, you create the object in a software component version (or underlying software component version) of the product version.

▸ **Integration-scenario-based**
The object to be inserted is determined by the software component version of the integration scenario. Therefore, you create the object in the same software component version or an underlying software component version of the integration scenario.

To summarize, the following can be said of actions: You can use external actions in all application components of the corresponding integration scenario, whereas you can use internal actions in only the respective product version.

Object To Be Inserted	Application Component	Type
	Product Version	Template
Internal action	Product-version-based	Not applicable
External action	Integration-scenario-based	Integration-scenario-based
Integration process	Product-version-based	Integration-scenario-based

Table 3.2 Possible Uses by Application Component Type

Modeling with Actions and Connections

How do you model the actual message exchange of a collaborative process in the integration scenario? Integration scenarios focus exactly on this point, the modeling of the message exchange, and nothing else. Therefore, the only steps that you model as an action in the integration scenario are those required to exchange messages with other application components. Local processes within an application component are irrelevant, and you should insert them only as actions if they are required for the understanding of the integration scenario.

The communication between actions of different application components is indicated by an arrow and is referred to as a *connection*. Figure 3.7 shows an example of each connection type:

Connection types

- ▶ **Synchronous communication**
  A double-headed arrow represents *synchronous communication*. To graphically represent that the execution of the process can only be continued after receiver processing, the two relevant actions are shown at the same level.

- ▶ **Asynchronous communication**
  In *asynchronous communication*, the sender and receiver are separated by a time difference, and only a request message is sent. Therefore, the actions aren't shown at the same level.

- ▶ **Sequence**
  A sequence is not a type of communication, but a sequence of actions within an application component that is important for the understanding of the integration scenario. In the example shown, there are

two follow-up actions, and thus branching takes place. Because you don't define routing until configuration time, you can't assign conditions to this or to other connection types.

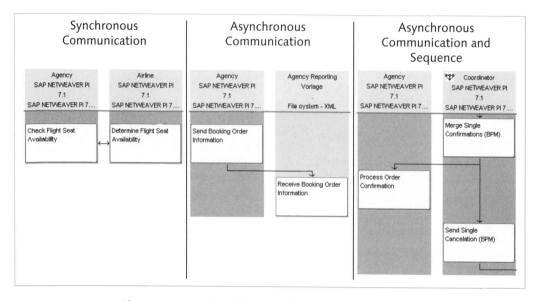

Figure 3.7 Examples of Connection Types

Of course, at the start of modeling, no actions have been inserted. You insert application components and actions in the integration scenario editor by using the context menu. All you must remember is that the connection type is determined automatically from the position of the actions. For example, if two actions are at the same level, you can insert only synchronous connections by using the context menu. Therefore, you must arrange your actions according to the connection type you want to use and comply with the rules described above. To select the actions that you want to connect, hold down the shift key ⟨⇧⟩ and then click both actions, one after the other. Alternatively, select them by using the mouse to drag a box around the actions (rubberband function).

Modeling at the type level   Figure 3.8 shows the attributes of the DetermineFlightSeatAvailability action. In addition to the type of use, you also specify the relevant outbound and inbound interfaces for the step that you are modeling with the action. Multiple outbound or inbound interfaces may be necessary to

The DetermineFlightSeatAvailability action is implemented on the receiver side using a server proxy. For older systems, there is an alternative implementation using RFC. In a connection, you assign an outbound interface to each inbound interface. In the synchronous connection in Figure 3.9, two service interfaces are selected for communication. If a mapping is necessary, specify it in the Assign Mapping tab. The Integration Builder can evaluate this information automatically at configuration time. The information that you specify also documents the integration scenario and enables you to navigate directly to the interfaces and mappings. You can reference existing objects (bottom-up development) or create these objects from the integration scenario (top-down development).

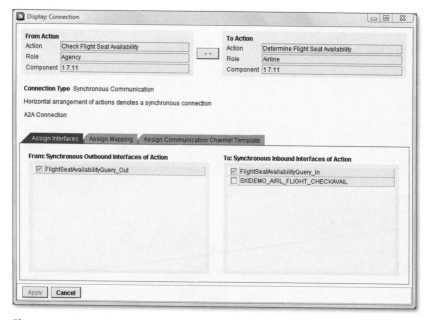

Figure 3.9 Connection for Synchronous Communication

Alternative connections In individual cases, it may be necessary to define multiple connections between two actions; for example, if a connection has different mappings, depending on customer requirements. If this is the case, you simply create additional connections between the actions. The integration scenario editor displays alternative connections in the same way as a single connection, and you can display or edit them using the context menu. If alternative connections exist, you must first select the connection you want to use in the corresponding dialog box. There can be only one valid connection at configuration time and at runtime.

Advanced Functions

Your new knowledge regarding software logistics and modeling integration scenarios now enables you to work intuitively with the graphical integration scenario editor. Therefore, all that remains is to point out the following useful commands:

▸ You can print integration scenarios by using the COMPONENT VIEW • PRINT menu path or export them as a graphic via COMPONENT VIEW • EXPORT AS JPEG. The latter, in particular, saves you time if you want to insert the component view of an integration scenario into Word documentation.

▸ You can use the same editor menu to export integration scenarios as BPEL4WS files. BPEL (*Business Process Execution Language*) is a cross-tool standard that enables you to import integration scenarios and processes to other tools and edited, for example, in ARIS for SAP NetWeaver.

BPEL file

In closing, you should note that integration scenarios in the Enterprise Services Repository contribute significantly to a better understanding of the whole collaborative process and the need to reduce configuration effort. The effort that you expend at the start will save you time later on. In this way, SAP also simplifies the configuration of RosettaNet standards, as we will see in Chapter 6, Section 6.5, Adapters for Industry Standards.

3.4   Modeling Using the Process Components Architecture Model

In contrast to the message-based view of integration scenarios, the process components architecture model provides a generic description of the *business* workflows. This approach is based on the assumption that the basic workflows of an enterprise hardly differ from one another.

Therefore an abstraction level is implemented for the modeling; this level disregards the details of the implementation. For the same — self-contained — part of the value chain, you always use the same modeling object: the *process component*. The process components architecture model consists of three model types:

▶ **Process components model**
Process components models describe the inner structure of the process components. This includes the underlying data of the process component and the service interfaces and operations that you can use to access this data. Moreover, the model illustrates via which operations the provider process component accesses the data of other process components.

▶ **Integration scenario model**
Integration scenario models describe dependencies between process components.[3]

▶ **Process components interaction model**
Process components interaction models describe the communication between two process components.

The following sections describe these model types and their components in detail.

3.4.1 Process Components Models

Elements Process components models describe the logical structure of one or more service providers. They represent the data objects (business objects) and the accesses to data (service interfaces and operations). Table 3.3 shows the icons that are available for modeling.

Because the elements service interface and operation are indispensable for the system integration, you will learn more about them in the course of this book. Chapter 4, Service Interfaces, Messages, and Proxy Generation, provides a detailed description of these objects.

---

3 Note that the integration scenario models and integration scenarios presented in Section 3.3, Modeling Using Integration Scenarios, are different approaches.

Icon	Meaning
Process component	The process component describes the internal structure of a business process. It represents the elementary and closed section of the value chain. The following characteristics are available: process component, partner process component, and third-party process component.
Business object	Business objects represent the data of a process component. They are uniquely assigned to a process component. It is a good modeling procedure to design business objects without overlaps and redundancies.
Operation	The operation describes the possible accesses to data of a process component. It is uniquely assigned to a business object.
Operation 1 / Service interface / Operation 2	Via service interfaces you can logically group operations.

Table 3.3 Objects of the Process Component Model

The process component model is used to describe the internal structure of a service provider and the data exchange with neighboring process components. Indicate that synchronous data accesses are drawn horizontally and asynchronous accesses are drawn vertically, to increase the readability of models. SAP recommends interface patterns to access the business objects.

Modeling procedure

85

Figure 3.10 shows a highly simplified version of a hypothetic process component of an order process. The Purchase Order Processing process component allows for access to the Purchase Order business object only via the operations Find Purchase Order by ID, Find Purchase Order by Customer, and Create Purchase Order.

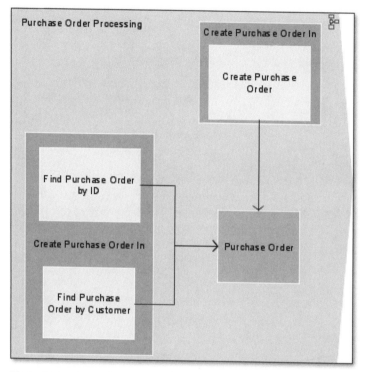

Figure 3.10 Process Components Model

3.4.2 Integration Scenario Models

To describe the full scope of a business process, you use the integration scenario models. They determine how you structure an executable process chain using various process components. You use *process components*, their *interactions*, and *deployment units* as modeling objects.

In the integration scenario model, process components exist as *process components*, *partner components*, and *third-party components*. Because you use integration scenario models to provide an overview of integral business processes, the internal structure of the process component is omitted here. This is referred to as a *black box* approach.

Process components

The interaction describes how two process components exchange data. Whereas in the process component model, the corresponding interfaces are indicated through the respective operations, the focus is on the communication technique in the integration scenario model. The following interaction types are available in modeling:

Interactions

▶ **Enterprise service interaction**
For interactions that have been implemented based on service interface definitions in the Enterprise Services Repository.

▶ **Web service interaction**
For general Web service communication.

▶ **Direct interaction**
For interactions between process components that are implemented within a deployment unit. This type of interaction can involve the access to a shared database table or a local RFC call.

▶ **Other interaction**
For interactions between process components of various deployment units that aren't based on enterprise service or Web service technology.

A deployment unit is an executable unit of a group of process components. If you require a specific process component for the implementation of your process flow, you must install the entire deployment unit.

Deployment unit

Figure 3.11 describes a simple integration scenario model. The third-party process component of E-Commerce Portal uses a Web service interaction to call the process component, Purchase Order Processing, which calls the Billing process component via a direct interaction. Purchase Order Processing and Billing are part of the Purchase Application deployment unit.

Example

With process components interaction models, you describe the message exchange between two process components via asynchronous and synchronous operations. In real life, the following communication patterns have become established:

Modeling procedure

▶ **Asynchronous patterns**

  ▶ *Request confirmation*: Loosely coupled message pair consisting of query and confirmation

  ▶ *Notification*: One-level notification of a receiver

  ▶ *Information*: Subscription events to be expected later

▶ **Synchronous patterns**

  ▶ *Query business object*: Search of a business object

  ▶ *Read business object*: Reading data of a business object using a known ID

Figure 3.12 shows a simple process components interaction model to describe the message exchange between the E-Commerce Portal and Purchase Order Processing process components. The communication is based on the notification pattern and uses the PO_Msg message type. It is assumed that the data structure of the sending and the receiving operations is identical; therefore no mapping is required. The generic communication channel template, Portal Component, is assigned to the Create Purchase Order In service interface.

Example

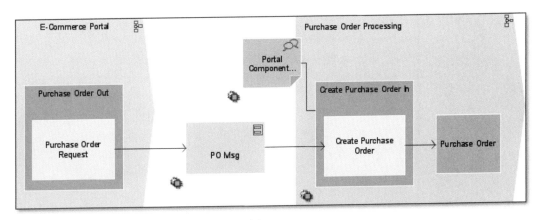

Figure 3.12 Process Components Interaction Models

Service interfaces are at the heart of message exchange with SAP NetWeaver PI. This chapter looks at the different programming models from the point of view of service interface development and how you communicate with parties that aren't interface-based.

4   Service Interfaces, Messages, and Proxy Generation

In all types of communication, you're faced with the question of how the sender is to transfer the data and how the receiver is to collect it. Software developers are used to using function calls to transfer data within a program, and it's hardly noteworthy to use this established form of data exchange to transfer data between systems; remote function calls (RFCs) follow this principle, for example. Therefore, it isn't surprising that in SAP NetWeaver PI, every message is assigned to a service interface to simplify the sending and receiving of messages and the configuration steps that you're required to make.

The most straightforward scenario is if all of the systems you want to connect use the same interface technology. However, in reality, this is rarely the case. At the same time, the demand for cross-company applications (for example, business-to-business applications [B2B] and marketplaces) is increasing. The challenge is therefore to bring together the various approaches while at the same time not lose sight of the current requirements for cross-company communication. SAP NetWeaver PI supports the following programming models:

Inclusion of different interface technologies

▶ You can create interface descriptions directly in the Enterprise Services Builder and generate executable proxies in application systems that are based on SAP NetWeaver.[1] Systems such as these can exchange messages directly with the Integration Server.

---

1   This applies to SAP NetWeaver PI 7.1 only. The relationship between SAP NetWeaver XI 3.0, SAP NetWeaver 7.0, and SAP NetWeaver PI 7.1 is explained in greater detail later.

▶ You can use established SAP interfaces from SAP systems (RFCs, BAPIs, IDocs) or other interfaces from third-party systems. In this case, the interfaces exchange messages with the Integration Server by using adapters. Later in the book (mostly in Chapters 6 and 7), you'll see that it's also possible to use these adapters to connect third-party systems that don't use interfaces to exchange messages.

This chapter discusses both models with regard to the development of service interfaces and their use in the design process. You should be familiar with the terms *outbound interface, inbound interface, synchronous,* and *asynchronous* before continuing (see Section 1.3.1, Communication Using the Integration Server, in Chapter 1).

4.1   Developing Using the Proxy Model

You can significantly improve the maintainability of cross-system applications if you can access all relevant objects centrally. Service interfaces play an important role here, because the signature of a service interface determines the structure of the message. If you don't know the structure of a message, you cannot define a mapping or model an integration process.

Outside-in   When you develop using the proxy model, you create service interfaces in WSDL (Web Services Description Language) directly in the Enterprise Services Builder. A service interface is actually a description that cannot be executed. In fact, you don't need to be able to execute it during the remainder of the design process, because just knowing the structure of the message will suffice. You use this description to generate proxies in ABAP or Java in your application system. Because you develop the interfaces outside the application system, this approach is known as *outside-in*.

Why proxies?   At first glance, it may seem odd that SAP has created yet another kind of interface technology. But there are a few reasons for this:

▶ The interface technology isn't really new, because the target languages already exist (ABAP Objects, Java).

▸ Using WSDL enables you to develop interfaces according to recognized standards. This is particularly important for minimizing the amount of effort required to coordinate cross-company scenarios.

▸ You can use a service interface in both ABAP and Java scenarios. The range of target languages could be increased, although none are planned at present.

After this brief introduction to the proxy model, the following section details the objects of the Enterprise Services Builder that are required for the proxy development.

4.1.1 Service Interface Development in the Enterprise Services Builder

Before you can start exchanging messages by using proxies, you must create the relevant service interfaces in the Enterprise Services Builder. Service interfaces can reference the following objects: | Referenced objects

▸ Message types, which you create in the Enterprise Services Builder

▸ IDoc or RFC messages, which you import to the Enterprise Services Builder

▸ External messages from imported WSDL, XSD, or DTD documents

▸ External messages from imported table structures

Let's begin by concentrating on the first case, in which you create the interface description directly by using the Enterprise Services Builder. This primarily concerns new developments in which no interfaces in SAP or third-party systems need to be accessed. Other scenarios are addressed in Section 4.2, Supporting Adapter-Based Communication.

Structure of Service Interfaces

Service interfaces from the Enterprise Services Builder are based on WSDL. Therefore, their structure is similar to that of a WSDL document. You don't need to be a WSDL expert to develop service interfaces in the Enterprise Services Builder; however, it's useful to know the basics. Figure 4.1 shows which objects you use to construct service interfaces

93

in the Enterprise Services Builder and to which WSDL elements these objects correspond.

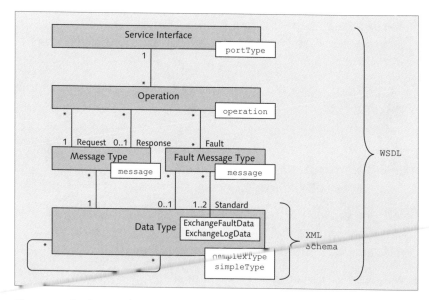

Figure 4.1 Service Interfaces and WSDL

WSDL export The range of WSDL commands has been restricted to simply cover the scenarios that are most important for message exchange. The cardinalities shown in Figure 4.1 and the range of XML Schema commands used in data types are therefore just a subset of WSDL. For those readers interested in using Web services, note that the Enterprise Services Builder does not contain any information about the technical receiver of a message. Whereas it's possible to use the Enterprise Services Builder to export service interfaces as WSDL,[2] the exported WSDL document does not contain any receiver information for an executable Web service. You don't use the export function to publish Web services, but you do need it to use interface objects created in the Enterprise Services Builder externally (for example, to archive them or to use a message type for an XSLT mapping that you've developed using external tools). However, you'll see later that the world of SAP NetWeaver PI service interfaces and the

---

2   By selecting TOOLS • EXPORT WSDL in the editor menu. There is also an export function for (fault) message types and data types.

world of Web services complement each other (see Section 7.3.2, ABAP
Proxies and Web Services, in Chapter 7).

You use the various object types in the Enterprise Services Builder as
follows:

Object types

▸ **Service interfaces**
This is the *outer shell* for all messages. You define the interface pattern
(TU&C/C, stateful, stateless, or stateless [SAP NetWeaver XI 3.0 com-
patible]), the security profile (no, low, medium, high), and the type of
communication (outbound or inbound, from the application system
perspective, abstract), also referred to as category, as attributes of a
service interface.

A service interface can contain one or more *operations* that as such
don't represent an object type in the navigation tree. The example in
Figure 4.2 shows the result of the FlightSeatAvailabilityQueryIn
service interface with the FlightSeatAvailabilityQueryEconomyOut
and FlightSeatAvailabilityQueryEconomyOut operations. Operations are the various functions provided by the interface. They represent the level that is used for the configuration of the message
exchange later on. The attributes *mode* (synchronous or asynchronous) and *release status* (Not Defined, Not Released, Released With
Restrictions, Released, Deprecated, Revoked) are set separately for
each operation of the interface. The different attributes of the service
interfaces are discussed in more detail later in this chapter.

▸ **Message types**
Message types describe the structure of the message by referencing a
data type. A message type does not specify a particular direction and
can be used for describing both inbound and outbound messages.
This depends on whether the message type in the service interface is
used as a request or response message type.

▸ **Fault message types**
Fault message types enable developers to send information about
errors in the receiver application program to the sender or to monitoring by using a fault message. In most standard cases, the structure
specified by the ExchangeFaultData and ExchangeLogData data types
is sufficient. You can also reference other data types, if required.

Fault messages aren't available for asynchronous outbound service interfaces or asynchronous abstract service interfaces. For these service interfaces, you can query the status by using *acknowledgment messages* in the application program or in the integration process.

▶ **Data types**
The message type predefines the structure of a message. However, the message type determines only the name of the message instance. Although this intermediate layer seems superfluous at first, it corresponds to the WSDL standard and enables the message instance to be identified via an element. You use data types to describe which elements and attributes may be used to construct the message. Data types can reference other data types, but recursive definitions aren't permitted.

▶ **Data type enhancements**
You can use data type enhancements to add your own fields to the SAP data types in the Enterprise Services Builder. Section 4.3.2, Enhancing Partners' and Customers' Data Types, discusses this in more detail.

Attributes of service interfaces

To precisely define the properties of a service interface for use in communication scenarios, the aforementioned attributes are available, which can be set for the entire service interface or separately for individual operations of the interface. The following describes the individual attributes in more detail and highlights the mutual dependencies of some attributes. The example of the `FlightSeatAvailabilityQueryIn` service interface in Figure 4.2 shows some of attributes that are described in the following.

For the entire service interface, you define the attributes, which specify the direction and type of the communication and the security settings of the interface:

▶ **Category**
The direction of the interface is described in the *category* attribute; it's always specified from the application system's perspective. *Outbound* service interfaces therefore refer to service interfaces that are used for sending requests; they are also referred to as outbound interfaces. An *inbound* service interface, or inbound interface, is used to receive an incoming request, to process it, and to return a response.

Abstract service interfaces don't have a direction and aren't implemented in an application system. You use them in the *RosettaNet Implementation Framework* (RNIF) adapter and to define the process signature of an integration process.

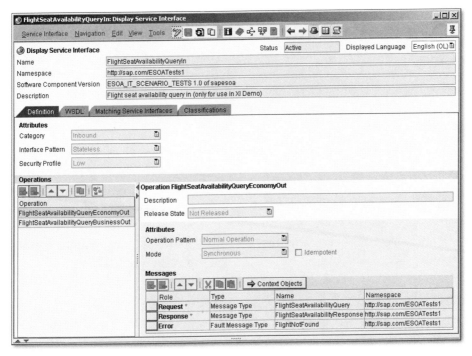

Figure 4.2 FlightSeatAvailabilityQueryIn Service Interface

▶ **Interface pattern**
The interface pattern determines the type of communication to be executed. The service interface can be defined as a *stateless* interface, in which no state is stored at the receiver, or as a *stateful* interface, in which the runtime enables the storing of a state. The state in the interface pattern always refers to the state of the receiver, also referred to as a provider in the Web service communication, and not to the state in the integration server. A specific feature of the stateful interfaces is that only the synchronous stateful communication is supported and that the stateful interfaces can only be used for communication via Web services, but not for communication via the Integration Server.

Tentative Update & Confirm/Compensate (TU&C/C) is an interface pattern that is based on the existing logs for synchronous and asynchronous communication and enables a cross-system rollback. The TU&C/C interface pattern is used if the data at the receiver must be updated consistently despite synchronous calls. After one or more synchronous tentative update messages, which lead to the marking of updates, either an asynchronous compensate message that declares all marked updates as invalid is transferred, or a confirm message that triggers the update of all tentative update operations marked for this transaction ID is transferred. TU&C/C supports both point-to-point communication via Web services and communication via the Integration Server.

Message interfaces from previous releases, such as SAP NetWeaver 7.0, that were imported or migrated, are automatically converted to service interfaces with the stateless interface pattern (SAP NetWeaver XI 3.0 compatible) because previous releases only supported stateless communication. You can release the SAP NetWeaver XI 3.0–compatible service interfaces explicitly for point-to-point communication via Web services by selecting the Point-to-Point enabled checkbox.

▶ **Security profile**
The security profile is required for the use of the service interface for Web service communication. Depending on the specified interface pattern, you can select different settings. For all service interfaces except the SAP NetWeaver XI 3.0–compatible service interfaces, you can set the security profile to No (no authentication and no transport security), Low (basic authentication with user ID and password without transport security), Medium (basic authentication with user ID and password with transport security), or High (authentication via SSL or SSO with transport security).

For SAP NetWeaver XI 3.0–compatible interfaces, the field for selecting the security profile is only available if you selected the Point-to-Point enabled checkbox, because the settings of the security profile are only relevant for Web service communication. For the SAP NetWeaver XI 3.0–compatible interfaces, you can only select Basic (authentication via user and password without transport security) or Strong (authentication via SSO or SSL with transport security) as the security profile, for compatibility reasons.

For interfaces that were imported or migrated from previous releases the Point-to-Point enabled checkbox isn't activated by default, and thus the field isn't available for selecting the security profile.

To describe the individual operations of a service interface in more detail, the following attributes are available:

▶ **Mode and operation pattern**

Depending on the interface pattern used, you can set various operation patterns and modes for individual operations. For stateless service interfaces you use the normal operation in either the synchronous or the asynchronous mode; for stateful service interfaces, however, the *commit operation*, *normal operation*, and *rollback operation* operation patterns are available for the synchronous mode. For service interfaces with the TU&C/C interface pattern, you can define both synchronous or asynchronous normal operations and synchronous *tentative update operations*, asynchronous *compensate operations*, and asynchronous *confirm operations*.

Because not every operation pattern is available for every interface pattern, in case of subsequent changes to the interface pattern information could get lost; moreover, a possibly already existing implementation would have to be changed. You should therefore decide on an interface pattern during definition.

▶ **Release state**

Using the *release state* attribute, SAP informs you about the development state of the object. Depending on the release state, the use of the interfaces is permitted for the customer, not permitted, or subject to restrictions. *Not released* interfaces must not be used by the customer, because SAP can change or delete them at any time. If an interface is *released with restrictions,* the customer may use it, but SAP can change the object without prior notice or revoke the release. For *released* interfaces, SAP guarantees that no incompatible changes will be made and that a revoke of the release is announced in subsequent releases by changing the release state to *deprecated* before SAP revokes the release. SAP provides replacement objects to be used for deprecated objects. If the release was revoked for an interface, it must not be used in the future. After import or migration, interfaces from previous releases have the *not defined release state* because this attribute did not exist until SAP NetWeaver PI 7.1.

> ▸ **Idempotent**
> The Idempotent checkbox is used for service interfaces that can ensure that the receiver can correctly handle a message if it's resent. For example, if a response was already sent and an error occurred then, a repeated request isn't not processed again, and the stored response message is resent. The Idempotent field is available for inbound, synchronous service interfaces. It can be set for all interface patterns except for TU&C/C. If an interface was imported or migrated from a previous release, the Idempotent field isn't not activated.

Compatibility with previous releases

If you want to communicate with older releases in certain scenarios, you must observe their downward compatibility in the definition of interfaces. Service interfaces, which are supposed to be used for communication with application systems of older releases, must be marked as Stateless (XI 3.0–compatible) and may contain only one operation. In this case, only the normal operation is available as an operation pattern.

When developing service interfaces, the largest amount of time is spent developing data types. Therefore, the next section discusses data types in more detail. You can find information about reusing message types and data types in Section 4.3, Enhanced Concepts.

Developing Data Types According to CCTS

Within WSDL, data types are described using XML Schema. A data type in the Enterprise Services Builder is therefore also an *XML Schema Definition* (XSD) that you can create and edit by using an XSD editor. You can either freely model the data types or develop them according to UN/CEFACT Core Components Technical Specification (CCTS). Here, the development according to CCTS ensures a high degree of reusability of data types. In the data type editor of the Enterprise Services Builder you can find CCTS-specific attributes and properties of this methodology.

Data types for development according to CCTS

If you decide on the development of data types according to CCTS, one step precedes the actual development work. You first ask the development department for information on design guidelines and boards that implement the unification and standardization process; only after consulting these boards can you start with the development of your data type. For the definition of your data types, you proceed according to the strictly defined guidelines. Two different data types are available:

▶ **Core data types**

The primary, basic data types are defined as core data types. When you create such a data type, you must define a *representation term* that describes the character of the data type. For example, the characterization of a data type with the `Amount` representation term determines that the value of such a type must additionally be specified in more detail via a currency. Therefore, some attributes of the data type are already specified with the representation term. If the representation term permits it, you can add additional attributes.

During the creation of a core data type, you must ensure that the name of the core data type according to CCTS depends on the representation term, which means that the representation term is also the last name component of the core data types. For a core data type with `Quantity` as the representation term, you must specify a name that ends with `Quantity`, for example, `ProductBundleFixedQuantity`.

For core data types with the `Code` representation term, you can define additional fixed values, which can be used later on in the UI development. Figure 4.3 shows an example of the use of different fixed values in the core data type `AcceptanceStatusCode`.

▶ **Aggregated data types**

You use the core data types and other, already existing aggregated data types to create more complex, aggregated data types. In this process, you accept the elements and attributes of the inserted data types and add further data types to describe the aggregated data type.

Don't create overly complex substructures; instead, build a large data type using various smaller data types. You can then reuse them multiple times. In Figure 4.4 you can view the aggregated data type `BusinessDocumentMessageHeader`, which consists of the core data types `BusinessDocumentMessageID`, `GLOBAL_DateTime`, `Indicator`, and `BusinessSystemID` and the aggregated data types `BusinessDocumentMessageHeaderParty` and `BusinessScope`, which, in turn, comprise multiple core and aggregated data types. In the Type column you can view the name of the referenced data type. Double-clicking on the data type takes you directly to its data editor.

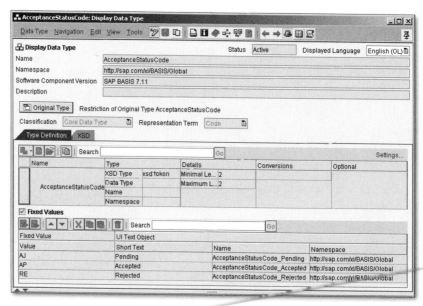

Figure 4.3 AcceptanceStatusCode Core Data Type

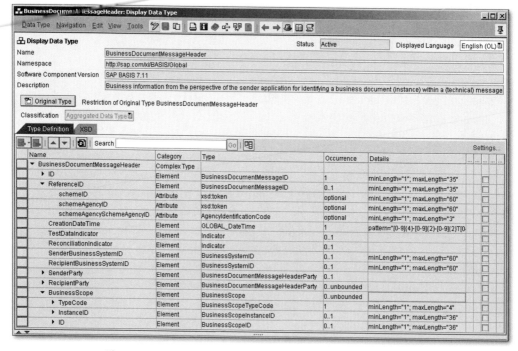

Figure 4.4 BusinessDocumentMessageHeader Aggregated Data Type

Importing Data Types As a Template

After you've decided whether you want to develop the data types freely or according to CCTS, you have two options to create the data types:

▶ You can create a new data type and use the XSD editor to describe its structure from scratch.

▶ You can use an existing XSD in the Enterprise Services Builder as an editable template.

The second option would obviously save you the most time. However, you must ensure that the XSD editor supports the range of commands in the XSD file that you want to import.[3]

If you want to specify multiple data types in an XSD definition, the XSD editor can import only one of the globally defined data types. So if the XSD data type references other data types, the XSD editor does not also import these data types. Once imported, the references become invalid. You can, however, import the data types into the Enterprise Services Builder one at a time. After the import, the Enterprise Services Builder automatically completes any references that were previously invalid. To import a data type, proceed as follows:

References between data types

1. To import a data type from an XSD file to the Enterprise Services Repository, first check whether the XSD file contains multiple global data type definitions. You can import only one definition with each import.

2. Using the Enterprise Services Builder, create a data type that has the same name as the data type that you want to import from the XSD file. If the XSD file has a `targetNamespace`, it must be identical to the namespace in which you want to create the data type.

3. In the XSD editor, select TOOLS • IMPORT XSD, and then select an XSD file from the subsequent dialog box.

4. If the file contains more than one global data type definition, the processing log shows that the remaining data type definitions have been ignored.

---

3   You can find an overview in the SAP Developer Network (SDN) under *https://www. sdn.sap.com/irj/sdn/nw-esr* via the menu path SUPPORTED XML SCHEMA AND WSDL (SAP NETWEAVER 7.1) • DESIGN TIME GOVERNANCE & LIFE CYCLE MANAGEMENT.

5. Any references to other data types that the imported data type contains — if there are any — are shown in a corresponding message. You import these data types by following the procedure described in steps 3 and 4.

You can now change and enhance the data types you've imported by using the XSD editor. The original file remains unchanged.

Editing Data Types Using the XSD Editor

Using XML Schema, you define elements and attributes that may be used in an XML document.[4] In other words, XML Schema Definition (XSD) describes a grammar for the message's payload. You don't need to know the exact XSD syntax when using the XSD editor. Once you've created and saved a data type with the XSD editor, it automatically becomes valid (the Enterprise Services Builder checks the objects before saving).

Root element   Figure 4.5 is a screenshot of a data type. A line in the XSD editor corresponds to the definition of either an element or an attribute, The root element (the first line in the editor) specifies the category of the data type:

▶ **Simple type**
Simple data types correspond to the `<simpleType>` tag in XML Schema. They are scalar data types for which you restrict the value range, for example, by using a string pattern or by specifying a maximum permitted value in the Details column. The data in this column corresponds to the facets in XML Schema.

▶ **Complex type**
Complex types correspond to the `<complexType>` tag in XML Schema. You use complex types to define structures by adding subelements to the root element or to other existing elements.

You assign a data type to an element or an attribute in the Type column. This can either be a scalar data type that is built-in using XML Schema (for example, `xsd:string`) or a data type that is already in the Enterprise

---

4   The term *XML instance* is more generally used when the way that the XML document is saved is not important (as a file, in the main memory, and so on).

Services Builder. References such as these enable you to construct complex data types from other data types and to reuse data types.

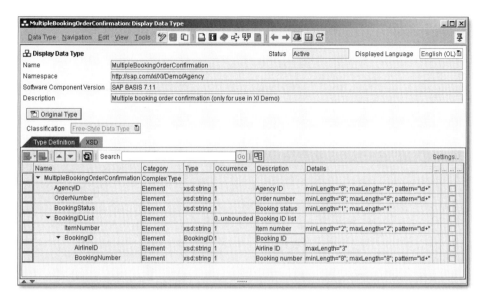

Figure 4.5 XSD Editor

There are no tables in XML Schema. Instead, you specify how often the individual elements can occur in the XML instance in the Occurrence column. In this example, the `BookingIDList` element has the occurrence value `0..unbounded`, which means it can occur any number of times.

Occurrence

Once you've described the structure of your message by using a data type, you can use the definition for further processing in the Enterprise Services Builder. Now let's look at how service interfaces are converted to executable interfaces in the application systems.

4.1.2 Proxy Generation

Proxies are classes and interfaces that developers use to implement the exchange of messages. Figure 4.6 shows an example in which two service interfaces are used as the basis for generating proxies for communication via the Integration Server: a *client proxy* for the outbound service interface and a *provider proxy* for the inbound service interface. You can, of course, also use service interfaces to generate provider proxies for Java and consumer proxies for ABAP.

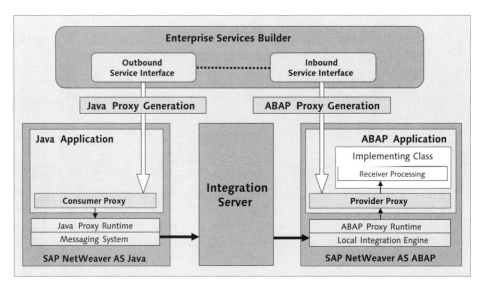

Figure 4.6 Example of Proxy-to-Proxy Communication

Regeneration   When you generate proxies, the executable parts (classes and interfaces) are created in the application system. Proxy generation saves attributes of the interface and the operations, which were specified for this interface (for example, the type of communication and the security settings) and the name of the original service interface in metadata, because the data in the Enterprise Services Builder must be consistent with the data in the application system. If any changes need to be made to an interface, simply regenerate the proxies after the changes have been made to make them visible in the application system as well. The relationship between the Enterprise Services Builder and the various application systems begs the question of what happens if you need to migrate SAP NetWeaver PI or perform a system upgrade. Note the following:

▶ Proxy generation is already available in application systems based on SAP Web AS 6.20, SAP NetWeaver 2004, or SAP NetWeaver 7.0. This has the following result when you upgrade the application system or SAP NetWeaver PI:

▶ When you upgrade an application system from SAP Web AS 6.20 to a higher release, and if you use SAP NetWeaver XI 3.0 or an SAP NetWeaver PI release, you must regenerate the proxies that were generated for SAP NetWeaver XI 2.0 (Java and ABAP) in this system. The reason for this is that the proxy protocol has changed with the transition from SAP NetWeaver XI 2.0 to 3.0.

▶ After an upgrade of an application system from SAP NetWeaver 2004 or SAP NetWeaver 7.0 to a higher release, you do *not* have to regenerate the generated proxies (Java and ABAP) in this system, because the proxy protocol has not changed since SAP NetWeaver XI 3.0.

▶ You do *not* need to regenerate the proxies when you migrate the SAP NetWeaver XI 3.0 or SAP NetWeaver PI 7.0 Integration Repository to the SAP NetWeaver PI 7.1 Enterprise Services Repository.

▶ In SAP NetWeaver 2004 and SAP NetWeaver 7.0 application systems, you can use ABAP proxy generation to create ABAP proxies for service interfaces of the SAP NetWeaver PI 7.1 Enterprise Services Builder. However, as already described in Section 4.1.1, Service Interface Development in the Enterprise Services Builder, you can only use the service interfaces, message types, and data types to the extent that it was possible for SAP NetWeaver XI 3.0 or SAP NetWeaver PI 7.0.[5]

For the sake of simplicity, the following section on proxy generation covers only application systems as of SAP NetWeaver 7.1 and based on SAP NetWeaver PI 7.1. (Figure 4.6 also shows the runtime components that are involved in the transfer of the message; this aspect is discussed in more detail in Chapter 7, Runtime.)

ABAP Proxy Generation

To generate ABAP proxies, you must log on to the application system in which you want to use proxies for exchanging messages. You can access ABAP proxy generation as follows:

▶ If your user is assigned the relevant SAP NetWeaver XI role, you can call ABAP proxy generation from the role menu. This entry calls

---

5 For more details, see the SAP NetWeaver PI 7.1 online documentation.

Transaction SPROXY, which, similar to the Enterprise Services Builder, provides you with an overview of the software component versions that exist in this application system.

► ABAP proxy generation is integrated in the Object Navigator (Transaction SE80). You access proxy objects from the navigation tree in the Object Navigator. You can use the Enterprise Services Browser entry in the navigation tree to start the display of the component versions.

You can use both starting points for generating proxies. In Transaction SPROXY or the Enterprise Services Browser, the software component versions in the Enterprise Services Builder are the starting point for creating or locating proxies. In the Object Navigator, you create a new proxy or locate an existing one by starting with the packages in the ABAP Repository. This way of working is more straightforward, because application developers can better concentrate on the objects in their packages.

Proxies are part of the Web Service Library in the ABAP Repository. In Figure 4.7, proxy generation displays the properties of the II_SDEMO_PD_BY_ID_QR provider proxy in the Object Navigator:

► The data in the External View tab provides the reference to the original object in the Enterprise Services Builder. In this example, it's an inbound service interface. The individual operations indicate whether they are synchronous or asynchronous interfaces.

► The ABAP Key frame in the External View tab displays the name of the generated ABAP Objects interface for the inbound service interface. Proxy generation creates an ABAP Objects class as a consumer proxy for outbound service interfaces.

► To provide a service in the application system, the application developer implements the generated proxy interface. If there is no separate class name of an existing class with an appropriate signature in the Interface frame in the Properties tab prior to generation, ABAP proxy generation creates a proxy class for provider proxies in addition to the proxy interface.

► For inbound service interfaces, in addition to the proxy class and the ABAP Objects interface, you generate the service definition that is displayed in the Interface frame in the Properties tab. This is required to create the runtime configuration for the Web service runtime.

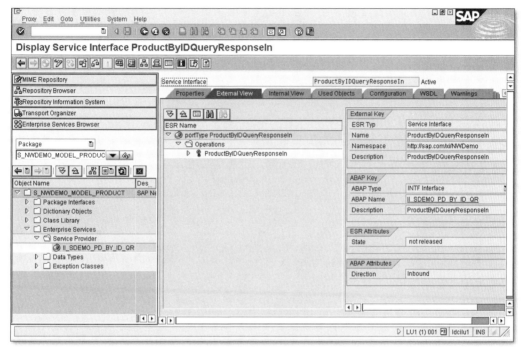

Figure 4.7 ABAP Proxy Generation in the Object Navigator

To generate a proxy in the Object Navigator, proceed as follows:

ABAP proxy generation in the Object Navigator

1. Call the Object Navigator (Transaction SE80) in the system in which you want to generate a provider proxy or a consumer proxy. Select a package and then select CREATE • ENTERPRISE SERVICE in the context menu.

2. In the next dialog box, choose whether you want generate a Service Provider or a Service Consumer. At this point, you can also generate proxies for individual objects, such as data type or data type enhancements.

3. If you decide on the Enterprise Services Repository as the source of the WSDL document, you can use the generated proxies both for

communication via SAP NetWeaver PI and for communication via the Web service runtime.[6]

4. The system now displays the hierarchy of software component versions of the Enterprise Services Builder. Select an interface object for which no proxy has been generated and confirm by selecting Continue.

5. In the next dialog box, enter the name of the package in which the proxy objects are to be created. You can also specify a prefix for the names of all objects to be created to avoid naming conflicts with any existing objects in the system.

Note the following important information:

Notes
▸ To enable access of the ABAP proxies and the ABAP proxy runtime from the application program, there must be a use access for the SAI_ PROXY_PUBLIC_PIF package interface. Note that if there is a parent package, you must also create a use access to the SAI_TOOLS_PIF parent package interface.

▸ The creation of dictionary objects and classes and interfaces during proxy generation can result in numerous objects that require translation. Because it isn't necessary to translate proxy objects because they aren't on the user interface, you must ensure that they're separated at the package level. Create a separate package for the proxy objects, and set it as not relevant for translation.

Converting names in ABAP
To create the proxies, ABAP proxy generation uses HTTP to read the WSDL description of the service interface and then converts it into proxy objects. However, this does not happen immediately because there may be objects in the application system that have the same name. Furthermore, technical names in XML can be as long as required, whereas in ABAP they are restricted to a certain number of characters. Technical names are also not case-sensitive in ABAP. To make the names easier to

---

6 As mentioned earlier, the range of commands in the WSDL from the Enterprise Services Builder has been restricted. Therefore, you cannot specify any other source (URL/HTTP destination, local file, for example) for the generation of proxies that you want to use in proxy communication with the Integration Server.

read, ABAP proxy generation inserts underscores, shortens any names that are too long, and adds a counter in the event of naming conflicts. Because this doesn't always result in appropriate names, the system displays a warning in the last two examples indicating that a log exists in which problems that occurred during generation are recorded. You can view the log by selecting GOTO • SHOW LOG. You can check and modify the changes to the technical names in the Name Problems tab.

You can also change the other ABAP names to fit your requirements by calling the context menu in the Internal View tab. No objects will be created in the ABAP Repository until you activate the proxy. Only the proxy object metadata is saved when you save but don't activate the proxy. The name mappings to the object in the Enterprise Services Builder, which are also required at runtime, are saved in the metadata. Messages sent using proxies don't contain any ABAP names — just the original names of the WSDL definition. Therefore, transport requests for ABAP transports include both the generated proxy objects and the corresponding metadata.

Finally, let's take a brief look at converting WSDL to ABAP proxy objects. Figure 4.8 shows the structure of the `II_SDEMO_PD_BY_ID_QR` provider proxy.

Converting from WSDL to ABAP

The input message type was converted to an `INPUT` importing parameter, which references a structure that is determined by the `ProductByIDQuery` data type. To go into detail about conversions would exceed the scope of this book. Instead, note the following:

▶ Proxy generation converts elements in the XSD that can occur an unlimited number of times (`0..unbounded`) into a table type and a structure for the line type. Although it's common practice in ABAP, in XSD you should not define isolated data types for tables, because unnecessary types will be created.

Converting data types in ABAP

▶ XML Schema defines an exact value range for built-in data types; this value range doesn't always match the value range in ABAP. ABAP proxy generation lists any data types that cannot be mapped exactly in the Warnings tab.

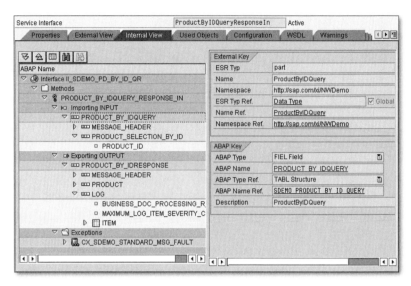

Figure 4.8 Structure of a Generated ABAP Provider Proxy

After this extensive overview of the ABAP proxy generation, the following details the specific features in the generation of Java proxies.

Java Proxy Generation

SAP NetWeaver PI 7.11 provides you with two technologies for generating Java proxies. The new development of Java proxies is implemented using the SAP NetWeaver Developer Studio (NWDS). The programming model is based on the development of Java Web services in the SAP Java EE environment. You can regenerate already existing Java proxies using the Enterprise Services Builder, a function restricted to service interfaces that use the Stateless (SAP NetWeaver XI 3.0–compatible) interface pattern. This is used to make minor modifications to the service interfaces that were originally developed in an SAP NetWeaver XI 3.0 or SAP NetWeaver PI 7.0 system and then migrated.

Generating in the SAP NetWeaver Developer Studio The Java proxy generation is analogous to the development of Web services and Web service clients in the NWDS, and is based on the Enterprise JavaBeans (EJB) 3.0 standard.[7] Java Web services and Java Web

---

7 Java Web service clients can also be created as a Java SE application. The procedure is a simplified form of the procedure for the Java EE implementation.

service clients can be generated independently of the type of communication (outbound or inbound). The following prerequisites must be met before you can start with the proxy development:

▸ You've created an EJB 3.0 project in the NWDS.

▸ You've created an enterprise application project and added the EJB 3.0 project.

▸ You've configured an SAP NetWeaver AS Java in the NWDS and selected the runtime environment of your Web services.

For the actual generation of the Java Web services and the Java Web service clients, proceed as follows:

1. Import the WSDL description of the interface to your NWDS. You can use the Enterprise Services Repository, the Services Registry, or an access via a URL or the local file directory as the source.

2. If you right-click the imported WSDL, you can use the Web Services context menu to select whether you want to create a Web service implementation (Generate JavaBean Skeleton) or a Web service client (Generate Client). Then the Web Service Wizard is displayed. You can use the wizard to generate a corresponding Web service client in parallel to the Web service implementation.

3. Use the wizard's controller to define the development depth of your proxies. The following categories are available for selection: Develop Service, Assemble Service, Deploy Service, Install Service, Start Service, and Test Service. Follow the wizard's instructions and supplement the specifications according to your requirements.

4. You can embed the generated classes and interfaces in your client program, or they are available as the framework for your Java Web service implementation.

Just as for the ABAP proxies, this section only briefly covers the most important conversions during generation:

▸ In the generation of client proxies, for service interfaces the system creates a *service endpoint interface* (SEI) of the same name and a corresponding service implementation by default. The methods provided by the SEI correspond to the operations of the service interface. The application developer can integrate these methods with his client program to call the Web service.

▶ Within the scope of the Web service generation, the system also creates a bean implementation that maps the service interface operations as methods in addition to the service endpoint interface (SEI). These methods are programmed during the Web service development. The runtime behavior of the generated Web services can be controlled using the SAP-specific annotations.

▶ A class is generated for each complex data type that contains set/get methods for accessing the respective fields.

▶ Classes aren't required for simple data types. For example, if you use a simple data type such as xsd:string, Java proxy generation doesn't generate a separate global class for the data type; instead, it uses the corresponding Java data type, java.lang.String.

▶ You can access elements that occur an unlimited number of times by using either list methods or an array.

As in XML, technical names aren't case-sensitive in Java; in addition, they aren't restricted in length, which also holds true in ABAP. To solve potential naming conflicts, automatic and semiautomatic methods that are based on the JAXB 2.0 standard are provided. Moreover, you can use your own JAX WS-based files to solve conflicts or renounce solving naming conflicts and overwrite existing objects of the same name.

Regeneration of existing Java proxies
The regeneration of existing Java proxies is part of the Enterprise Services Builder, which you can find in the main menu under TOOLS. You can generate Java proxies for J2EE applications on SAP NetWeaver AS; proxy generation creates J2EE beans and proxy classes for this purpose. The generated beans comply with the EJB 2.0 standard.

Converting names in Java
To avoid as many naming conflicts as possible in this procedure, the corresponding WSDL tags are appended to the names as a suffix (see Figure 4.1 in Section 4.1.1). This conversion is based on the Java API for XML-Based RPC (JAX RPC) specification[8]:

▶ Namespaces are mapped to packages.

---

8   http://java.sun.com/xml/downloads/jaxrpc.html

▶ Classes for interfaces have the `_PortType` suffix.

▶ Classes for data types have the `_Type` suffix.

If naming conflicts do nevertheless occur (for example, because a data type has the same name as a Java keyword), Java proxy generation resolves the conflict by simply changing the name (by adding an underscore or appending a counter).

Due to these prerequisites, the developer does not need to make any changes to the technical names. Therefore, to generate a proxy, all you need to do is select the service interfaces that you want to convert and specify the already existing archive in which the classes to be generated are to be saved. The service interfaces it contains are displayed and can be included when you regenerate.

Using Java archives

The generated Java package is part of the J2EE application and must be compiled together with it. To gain a better overview of what has been generated, we recommend that you use the Java standard tool, `javadoc`, to create HTML documentation for the generated classes. Just as for the ABAP proxies, this section only briefly covers the most important conversions during generation:

Generation

▶ A Java interface is generated for inbound service interfaces; the application developer uses this Java interface to provide a service. If `JavaInterface` is the name of the generated Java interface, then the implementing class must be `JavaInterfaceImpl`, and it must be in the same package as the generated Java interface.

▶ A class is generated for each complex data type that contains `set`/`get` methods for accessing the respective fields.

Converting data types in Java

▶ Classes aren't required for simple data types. For example, if you use a simple data type such as `xsd:string`, Java proxy generation doesn't generate a separate global class for the data type; instead, it uses the corresponding Java data type, `java.lang.String`.

▶ You can access elements that occur an unlimited number of times by using either list methods or an array.

▶ To access fields that have an enumeration specified as their value range, Java proxy generation generates a Java class for type-safe access to the enumeration's value set by creating constants for each value and restricting access to only methods.

Once the proxies have been generated, developers can then implement the message exchange for an application in the application system. For more details about programming with consumer and provider proxies, see Section 7.3, Proxy Runtime, in Chapter 7.

4.2   Supporting Adapter-Based Communication

So far, we have looked at development using only the proxy model. As a prerequisite for this, the application system must be based on a release as of SAP Web AS 6.20 or later (see Section 4.1.2, Proxy Generation). To connect SAP legacy systems or non-SAP systems to the Integration Server, you use adapters. In principle, an adapter works similarly to the proxy runtime: It converts XML and HTTP-based messages from the Integration Server to the specific protocols and formats of the application, and vice versa. The programming model is quite different, however. When you use the proxy model, development occurs in the Enterprise Services Builder; when you use adapters, development either takes place or has already taken place in the application system.

Communication parties without interfaces

The first question you should ask is what information must be available in the Enterprise Services Builder for further development to take place. At configuration time, you require an interface name and a corresponding namespace to configure how messages should be exchanged. This also applies to those adapters for which the interfaces aren't important; for example, the file adapter or the JDBC adapter.[9] In such cases, you must define a corresponding interface name and namespace when configuring the adapter. You cannot, of course, import interfaces that aren't available. Therefore, you can enter interface names manually in the Integration Builder, because this enables you to also connect application systems to the Integration Server, from which you cannot import interfaces or descriptions of the message structure. You need these user-defined interface names, for example, for operation mappings, which

---

9 This only applies to inbound processing in the Integration Server. This is addressed in more detail in Section 6.4, Adapter Configuration, in Chapter 6.

are required later for executing mapping programs. (Section 5.2, Pre-configuration and Testing of Mapping Programs, in Chapter 5 discusses mappings in more detail.)

Ideally, however, you can import the interfaces' signature or required message structure descriptions to the Enterprise Services Builder. Because the information you're accessing is already available in the application system, this is known as the *inside-out approach*. Just like the service interfaces or message types discussed in Section 4.1, Developing Using the Proxy Model, this information is then available centrally so you can use it during the remainder of the design process. The following section explains which Enterprise Services Builder mechanisms are available to you specifically for this purpose.

Inside-out

4.2.1 Importing Interfaces and Message Schemas

You can import SAP interfaces and various message schemas using the Enterprise Services Builder. Both cases are discussed below.

Importing SAP Interfaces

Until the introduction of SAP NetWeaver XI, the established SAP interfaces used for exchanging messages between systems were BAPIs, RFCs, and IDocs. One way of including these interfaces in the SAP NetWeaver PI design process would be for the Enterprise Services Builder to contain one interface description for all existing BAPIs, RFCs, and IDocs. However, applications use only a few of these interfaces for SAP NetWeaver PI scenarios. Therefore, you can import interfaces using the Enterprise Services Builder import mechanism. This enables each application to import to the Enterprise Services Builder those interfaces that they actually require in a scenario.

BAPI, RFC, and IDoc

You can import interface descriptions of BAPIs, RFCs, and IDocs from SAP Release 4.0 and higher to the Enterprise Services Builder.[10] You enter an SAP system from which the interface descriptions are imported for each software component version in the Enterprise Services Builder.

---

10 This is because the relevant function modules with which you can call this information don't exist in older systems. However, the RFC and IDoc adapters support SAP Release 3.1I and higher.

To do so, open the relevant software component version by double-clicking it in the Enterprise Services Builder navigation tree.

Determining the connection data for the import

Figure 4.9 shows an example in which the connection data for importing from an SAP system is specified. To determine this information for the SAP system, proceed as follows:

1. Call the logon dialog for SAP systems (SAP Logon), and select Variable Logon....

2. In the Search For field, enter the system ID of the SAP system from which you want to import the interfaces. After you've selected the system, you can view all of the available groups with which you can log on to the system; for example, PUBLIC.

3. The Message Server field displays the address of the message server.

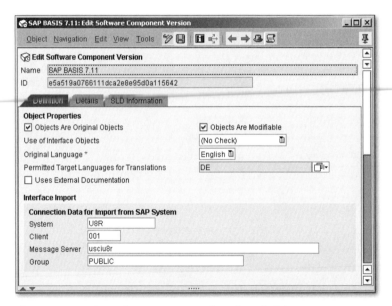

Figure 4.9 Attributes for Importing Interfaces from SAP Systems

Once you begin the import, the Imported Objects node is added as a subnode to the software component version node in the Enterprise Services Builder navigation tree. To import the interfaces, call the context menu for this node. You can also temporarily overwrite the connection data given in the software component version. Once the import is complete, you can reference the imported interfaces from other objects in the Enterprise Services Builder. This is covered in more detail in Section 4.2.2, Developing with Imported Interface Objects.

Importing Service Interfaces from WSDL Files

If the description for an externally defined service is available as a WSDL file, you can import it to the Enterprise Services Builder and use it as a service interface. For this purpose, SAP provides a wizard that is available via the menu path TOOLS • IMPORT SERVICE INTERFACE menu. You can use the wizard to create one or more service interfaces for a specific namespace in the Enterprise Services Builder.

In the WSDL definition, each `portType` represents a service interface, and the `messageType` represents the external messages. The wizard maps all messages in a service interface to the externally defined messages. The generated service interfaces have the same number of operations and request, response, and fault messages as defined in the WSDL file. The interface pattern of the generated service interface is set to Stateless during the import; if required, you can change the state later in the object editor.

When you select the Import All References option for the import, the wizard recognizes references of WSDL files to XSD files. The wizard then determines the referenced file via the `schemaLocation` attributes and adds it to the import list. Note that the wizard can only determine the referenced file if the reference to a file in the local file system is relative.

Resolving references

When the system creates the import list, the wizard checks whether a service interface can be created in the selected namespace for a file. If the check indicates warnings or errors, you can view the corresponding messages in the preview. The following causes exist for errors or warnings:

▶ The file cannot be imported if the *file format cannot be interpreted*. For example, this can be the case if the schema of the WSDL file to be imported is invalid or not supported, or if the WSDL file does not contain any `portType` definition.

Problems during import

▶ If a *service interface of the same name* already exists in the selected repository namespace of the Enterprise Services Builder, the import overwrites the interface. You must therefore check whether the two service interfaces are identical. If not, you must import the file with a different name.

▶ If there are multiple *files with the same file name* from different directories in the import list, the system displays a warning. To exclude naming conflicts, the wizard adds a number to the name of the service interface during the import. This occurs because the WSDL files to be imported are usually stored in a directory hierarchy, which gets lost when importing to the Enterprise Services Builder, because all service interfaces are created in a repository namespace.

After the import, you must activate the service interfaces and external definitions in the change list.

Importing External Definitions

You can use many standard schemas to describe the message structure at runtime; for example, WSDL, XSD, or Document Type Definitions (DTDs). If the description of a message structure is already in one of these formats, you can reuse it in the Enterprise Services Builder by importing it as an external definition instead of having to enter it manually in the data type editor. You can import individual external definitions or use a mass import to import all referencing external definitions to the namespace at the same time.

Converting to WSDL

As described in Section 4.1.1, Service Interface Development in the Enterprise Services Builder, service interfaces in the Enterprise Services Builder are based on WSDL. In addition, other Enterprise Services Builder editors expect this WSDL description, or, rather, the XSD description that it contains. Therefore, the Enterprise Services Builder converts all external definitions to WSDL during the import. However, you can define which parts of the external definition are to be interpreted as message schema beforehand. For example, when you import an XSD document, you can decide whether all global elements or just those that aren't referenced are to be included in the definition of a message. The result of the conversion is a WSDL document that contains the identified message definitions. If external definitions reference each other, simply import them one at a time and enter the source for each definition. An example of a source is a URL that other documents use to reference this definition.

As you've already seen, the Enterprise Services Builder specifies restrictions for WSDL descriptions. Therefore, even if the import has been successful, this does not ensure that you can use the imported external definitions everywhere in the Enterprise Services Builder. It would be too restrictive to prevent an external definition from being imported merely because it's not supported by the mapping editor, for example, because you may not even want to use the definition for a mapping. Table 4.1 shows the possible applications of external definitions.

(Part of) External Definition	Use
Entire definition	Archiving in the Enterprise Services Repository
Message	An external message in the graphical mapping editor, XSLT, or Java mappings
Message	An external message in service interfaces
Complex type	In mapping templates to map data types to one another

Table 4.1 Applications of External Definitions

Unfortunately, there is currently no check available during the import to determine in which areas you can use a specific external definition. You can find an overview of supported tags in the SAP Developer Network (SDN) at *https://www.sdn.sap.com/irj/sdn/nw-esr* via the Supported XML Schema and WSDL (SAP NetWeaver 7.1) in the Design Time Governance & Life Cycle Management area.

Importing Table Structures from a Database

If you want to use table structures as external messages in operations, the Enterprise Services Builder provides the option to import these structures. To be able to use this import option, however, you must meet the following prerequisites:

▶ The table must be defined in the database.

▶ A JDBC adapter with access to the database must be available.

▶ A JDBC receiver channel must be configured and activated in the Integration Directory to access the tables.

Prerequisites for importing table structures

121

If these prerequisites are met, you can start the import in the created external definition. Select the dbtab category and the From Table Definitions mode and start the import wizard by clicking the button on the right side of the communication channel field. In the subsequent steps, the system prompts you to select the configured JDBC receiver channel and the table whose structure you want to import. Figure 4.10 shows how the imported table structure is mapped in the message.

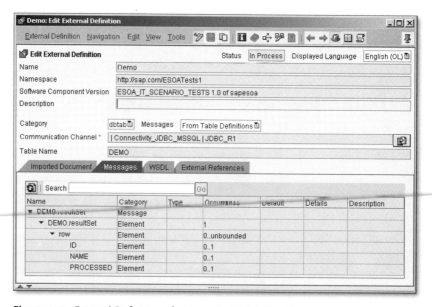

Figure 4.10 External Definition of an Imported Table Structure

You can now use the imported table definition as an external message in the operation of a service interface or for defining a graphical JDBC lookup in a message mapping. Section 5.4.3, Advanced Message Mapping Techniques, in Chapter 5 discusses the definition and use of JDBC lookups in more detail.

4.2.2 Developing with Imported Interface Objects

Section 4.1, Developing Using the Proxy Model, discussed which steps you need to take in the Enterprise Services Builder to develop objects using the proxy model approach. In this case, it was assumed that both communication parties exchange messages with the Integration Server by using proxies. But how does it work when adapters are used to exchange messages? In the following examples, it's assumed that one of the parties (either the sender or the receiver) uses an adapter to communicate. Note the following different cases:

▶ **The application system at the other communication party does not support development using the proxy model approach.**
Create a service interface that references the imported message schema for this party; this can be an RFC message, an IDoc message, or an external message. The imported messages are then used in the same way as message types. You don't need to define a mapping, because the service interface references the same message schema that the adapter uses. Proxy generation can process both RFC and IDoc messages. External messages can also contain language constructs that aren't supported by proxy generation; this can result in proxy generation being aborted.

Proxy model support

▶ **The application system at the other communication party does not support development using the proxy model approach.**
If RFCs or IDocs are involved, use them on the same level as service interfaces in the Enterprise Services Builder. For third-party systems, enter the interface names and namespaces manually and reference imported messages. The adapters use the message protocol of the Enterprise Services Builder, but the payload schema is adapter-specific. Therefore, a mapping is required if both communication parties are using different adapters.

No proxy model support

The adapter configuration is described in Chapter 6, Section 6.4. You can use the imported message schemas during the rest of the design phase; for example, in the mapping editor (see Section 5.4.1, Introduction to the Mapping Editor, in Chapter 5). The Enterprise Services Builder also has a series of other export and import options to enable you to develop using external tools. Note again that you don't have to import message schemas to the Enterprise Services Builder to exchange messages with the Integration Server via adapters. However, if you do import the message schemas to the Enterprise Services Builder, you have the advantage of being able to access them centrally and use them for further design purposes in the Enterprise Services Builder.

4.3 Enhanced Concepts

So far we've only covered the fundamental concepts behind development using the proxy model approach and adapter-based communication. This section looks at the concepts for some general topics. Sections 4.3.1 and 4.3.2 cover only development using the proxy model, whereas Section 4.3.3 covers both development models.

4.3.1 Using Message Types Across Components

Message instances generally need to be assigned to a namespace. Enter this namespace for (fault) message types in the Enterprise Services Builder in the XML Namespace field (see Figure 4.11). In the default setting, the Integration Builder uses the repository namespace[11] in which the (fault) message type was created.

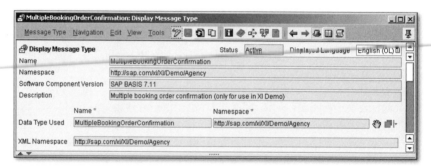

Figure 4.11 Message Type with Default XML Namespace

Use case for XML namespaces

In the following instance, we advise using a different XML namespace to the repository namespace: Two applications communicating with each other by using SAP NetWeaver PI are normally located in different software component versions that aren't necessarily shipped together to customers. To ensure that the customer does not receive incomplete service interface definitions, the Enterprise Services Builder permits only references from service interfaces to (fault) message types in the same software component version or a sub–software component version.

---

11 These are the namespaces that the Enterprise Services Builder displays in the navigation tree. See also Chapter 2, Section 2.1.

However, both applications want to regularly use the same message types for communication. Because it isn't possible to use a reference, the only solution is for one of the applications to copy a message type from the other application to its repository namespace (see also Section 2.1, Introduction to the SAP NetWeaver PI Design and Configuration Tools, in Chapter 2). If the copy, in turn, has the new repository namespace as its XML namespace, this would be the only difference from the original. Even though the message structure is otherwise identical, a mapping would be required, because the message instance belonging to the message types has a different namespace.

The XML namespace therefore enables two applications to agree on a namespace for a message. The XML namespace is applied by proxy generation and used by proxy runtime in the message instance: An XML namespace for a message type or a fault message type qualifies the element tag for the message. In certain cases, you may not need to or want to use an XML namespace for the message instance. In this case, leave the XML Namespace field empty.

The following example refers to an SAP development project. However, it could easily also be a new customer or partner development project: A message is to be used to send a customer sales order from an SAP Advanced Planner and Optimizer (APO) system to an SAP Customer Relationship Management (CRM) system. Within an SAP CRM software component version, the SAP CRM developer has created the `SalesOrder` message type in the Enterprise Services Builder, which references a data type that in turn describes the structure of the message. The APO application on the outbound side requires the same message type (and the corresponding data types that are referenced from there). The SAP APO developer then copies the message type to a repository namespace in the SAP APO software component version and uses the With All Dependent Objects option in the copy function. With this option selected, the message type and all data types that describe the structure of the message are copied to the SAP APO software component version.

Example

The SAP APO developer agrees with the SAP CRM developer to use the SAP CRM namespace for the `SalesOrder` message type. The developer then enters the namespace "*http://sap.com/CRM*" in the XML Namespace field of the copy. The Enterprise Services Builder automatically sets this

XML namespace in the original message type, because it corresponds to the repository namespace for `SalesOrder` in the SAP CRM application. Listing 4.1 shows how the proxy runtime sets the XML namespace in the message instance.

```
<ns1:SalesOrder xmlns:ns1="http://sap.com/CRM">
    <OrderHeader>
    . . .
    </OrderHeader>
    <OrderItems>
    . . .
    </OrderItems>
</SalesOrder>
```

Listing 4.1 XML Namespaces in the SalesOrder Message Instance

Because SAP CRM and SAP APO have specified the same XML namespace, the message instances are identical. If the SAP APO developer had not changed the namespace in the copy, the namespaces would have been different, and a mapping would have been required.

4.3.2 Enhancing Partners' and Customers' Data Types

SAP applications enable customers to enhance application programs without the need for modifications[12] to satisfy customer-specific demands that go beyond what is provided in the standard shipment. The applications can use BAdIs (*Business Add-ins*) for this purpose, for example.

Cross-system modifications

If the SAP application uses proxies to exchange messages, such enhancements must be seen as cross-system enhancements: The customer may want not only to access data that is available locally in the system, but also to exchange data between the applications in the communication scenario. Because you cannot modify proxy objects in the application system, this kind of enhancement applies to the data type definition in the Enterprise Services Builder. The following section investigates how customers or partners can enhance data types in the Enterprise Services Builder without the need for modifications. The proxy runtime does not provide a generic solution for enhancements in the application program.

---

[12] "Without the need for modifications" means that customers' enhancements aren't lost when the SAP application is upgraded.

The application developers must decide which methods they want to use for customer enhancements.

To explain how customers and partners can use data type enhancements, you need to look at some different aspects. We'll use the SAP APO and SAP CRM example from Section 4.3.1, Using Message Types Across Components, for this purpose.

Using Top-Node Software Component Versions

SAP CRM and SAP APO ship the `SalesOrder` message type as part of their application by using the software component versions SAP_APO 2.0 and SAP_CRM 2.0. Figure 4.12 shows which interface objects `Sales Order` references — in other words, where this message type is used — for the SAP_APO 2.0 software component version.

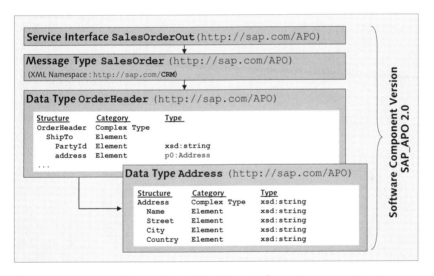

Figure 4.12 Interface Objects of the SAP_APO 2.0 Software Component Version

If customers want to enhance the `Address` data type, they cannot do so directly in the SAP_APO 2.0 software component version. Such an enhancement would be a modification, which would mean that if SAP were to change the data type again — such as, for example, in a support package — the customer enhancement would be lost.

Basis objects

The first step when making a data type enhancement is to create a customer-specific software component version in the System Landscape Directory; for example, CUST_APO 2.0. To be able to use objects of SAP software component version SAP_APO 2.0, declare it a subsoftware component version of CUST_APO 2.0 (CUST_APO 2.0 uses SAP_APO 2.0). Once you've imported CUST_APO 2.0 to the Enterprise Services Builder, all objects of SAP_APO 2.0 are available in the navigation tree under the basis objects of CUST_APO 2.0. You can now create your own objects in CUST_APO 2.0 and reference objects from SAP_APO 2.0.

Enhancing the data type

To enhance the `Address` data type in software component version CUST_APO 2.0, create a data type enhancement that references the data type from SAP_APO 2.0; for example, `AddressE`. You can add elements, structures, and attributes at the uppermost hierarchy level in the data type enhancement. The relationship to interface objects that previously referenced `Address` remains unchanged. If you display objects starting from the Basis Objects branch of the software component version CUST_APO 2.0, it appears that these objects also exist in CUST_APO 2.0. You then reference `AddressE` automatically. Figure 4.13 illustrates this. It helps if you imagine that all other objects "shine through" to the software component version that is based on SAP APO.

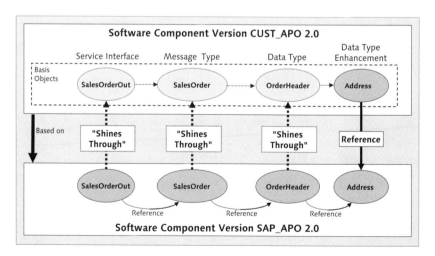

Figure 4.13 Objects in the SAP_APO 2.0 and CUST_APO 2.0 Software Component Versions

If you enhance the `Address` data type in CUST_APO 2.0, you must do the same for the `Address` data type of the SAP CRM system so that the additional data that is transferred can also be processed at the receiver. Therefore, you must also create a customer-specific software component version SAP_CRM 2.0 for software component version SAP_CRM 2.0 and perform the same steps as for CUST_APO 2.0.

Proxy Generation and Data Type Enhancements

Once you have released the data type enhancements, you can regenerate the proxies in your application systems:

▸ For ABAP proxies, select the `AddressE` data type enhancement in the customer-specific software component version CUST_CRM 2.0 or CUST_APO 2.0. ABAP proxy generation maps data type enhancements to `APPEND` structures in the ABAP Dictionary.

ABAP

▸ For Java proxies, select the service interface of the customer-specific software component version CUST_CRM 2.0, which references the data type enhancement. The service interface is located under Basis Objects. The elements and attributes of the enhancement are recognized by proxy generation, but they aren't handled in a special way. You cannot determine which classes or attributes originate from the data type enhancement from the generated objects. There are no separate Java objects for enhancements.

Java

After the creation and generation of data type enhancements, the parties involved in the communication must agree on the namespace to be used for enhancements. The following section provides a more detailed description that is based on an example.

XML Namespaces for Data Type Enhancements

Section 4.3.1, Using Message Types Across Components, explained that SAP CRM and SAP APO had to be in agreement on a common XML namespace for the shared message type. The same applies to the data type enhancements in CUST_APO 2.0 and CUST_CRM 2.0. In the message instance, an XML namespace is used to distinguish the enhancements from the original SAP elements and attributes. Thus, if SAP uses the same field name as a customer in an enhancement in a later release,

Avoiding naming conflicts

you can avoid a naming conflict. Data type enhancements also have an XML namespace that must be identical at the sender and receiver; otherwise, the XML namespaces would have to be mapped to each other via a mapping.

Let's assume that the customer decides to use the XML namespace `http://customer.com/CRM/AddrExtension` in both CUST_APO 2.0 and CUST_CRM 2.0. Listing 4.2 shows that the fields added by the customer have an additional qualifier added to the `http://customer.com/CRM/AddrExtension` namespace. The fields that have been added to the `Address` data type in Figure 4.12 are shown in bold.

```
<ns1:SalesOrder
xmlns:ns1="http://sap.com/CRM"
xmlns:ns2="http://customer.com/CRM/AddrExtension">
   <OrderHeader>
      <ShipTo>
         <PartyId>1234</PartyId>
         <Address ns2:Airport="SFAirport" >
            <Name>Johnson</Name>
            <Street>Lombard Street 10</Street>
            <City>SanFrancisco</City>
            <Country>US</Country>
            <ns2:State>California</ns2:State>
         </Address>
      </ShipTo>
   </OrderHeader>
   <OrderItems> ... </OrderItems>
</ns1:SalesOrder>
```

Listing 4.2 Enhanced Address Data Type

4.3.3 Accessing Message Fields by Using Context Objects

To process messages on the Integration Server, you must be able to access the content of a message. For example, the Integration Server reads fields from the message header to use this information, and it reads fields from the configuration in the Integration Directory to forward the message to the correct receiver. In addition, applications can define conditions for logical routing or an integration process, which reference fields in the payload.

Because the payload is an XML document, you can access the different parts of it by using XPath. XPath is a syntax that enables you to identify parts of an XML document in the same way that you access the directory structure of a file system. For example, look at the message instance from Listing 4.3.

Context objects instead of XPath

```
<InvoiceOut>
   <customerData>
      <address>
         <name> ... </name>
         <postalCode> ...</postalCode>
         ...
      </address>
      ...
   </customerData>
</InvoiceOut>
```

Listing 4.3 Sample Structure of a Message Instance

To access the content of the <postalCode> field, you would use the following expression in XPath:

`/InvoiceOut/customerData/address/postalCode`

If you require this expression in multiple conditions, you have to type it out each time or copy it. Instead, you can assign a context object to the <postalCode> field. Give this context object the name postalCode, for example. Now, when you require the value of the <postalCode> field for a condition, you only need to use the postalCode context object, which makes your conditions easier to read:

▶ Comparison using XPath
  `/InvoiceOut/customerData/address/postalCode > "69120"`

▶ Comparison using a context object
  `postalCode > "69120"`

In the Enterprise Services Builder, you create context objects as interface objects; they only consist of a name and a reference type. The type determines what kind of comparisons are in the conditions in which you want to use the context object (lexicographical, numerical, date comparison, time comparison). To use this reference type in conditions, you must have already assigned it to a field. As you can see in Figure 4.14, you

Reference types for context objects

must click the Context Objects button in the service interfaces editor for this purpose.[13]

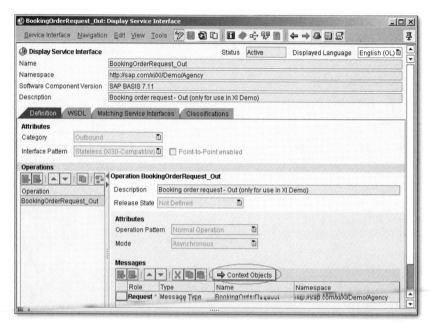

Figure 4.14 Assigning a Context Object

Technical context objects There are also technical context objects, which you can use to access assigned fields of the message header. Therefore, you don't need an assignment for these context objects.

---

13 You can also assign context objects for RFCs and IDocs.

In the previous chapter, you learned how to describe the structure of messages and assign them to an interface. This chapter looks at how message structures and value representations differ at the sender and receiver sides and explains how they can be mapped to one another.

5 Mappings

Data exchange within a single system is relatively unproblematic. Even in a complex development project where developers may be working in different components using different programming languages, they are nevertheless working in a relatively homogeneous environment. In a heterogeneous system landscape, the components that exchange data with each other are distributed across different systems. When you implement a cross-system process, development takes place in more than one system, and you must consider the following additional factors:

▶ The involved systems can originate from different vendors with different technologies.

▶ Even if all systems are from one vendor, the systems that need to communicate with one another may be different release versions, and you might not be able to change the interface signatures of the older systems.

▶ Even if the semantics of objects in components from different systems are identical, this does not mean they are identified using the same values. For example, the passenger class of a flight can be coded as a number or a string.

▶ In an existing cross-system process, a participating system is supposed to be replaced.

The emergence of XML (Extended Markup Language) raised hopes of a uniform XML-based data exchange format, which would improve the implementation of cross-system processes. Unfortunately, there are

Mapping XML documents

now countless examples of such data exchange formats. However, using the XML standard enables you to map different XML languages to one another relatively easily.

Figure 5.1 shows a mapping in which the whole structure of the source document and the value of the <HH:CLASS> element are mapped to a target document. The following sections explore the options for structure and value mappings in SAP NetWeaver PI.

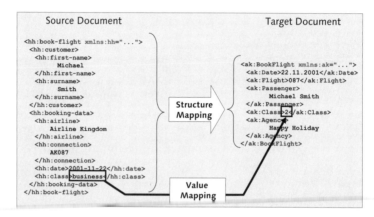

Figure 5.1 Structure and Value Mapping

5.1 Mapping Programs in SAP NetWeaver PI

To execute a mapping, you need a mapping program. Generally, the mapping program must be available on the Integration Server at runtime. Table 5.1 shows which mapping programs are supported by SAP NetWeaver PI and where they are executed.

Mapping Program	Runtime
Message mapping	Java EE Engine of the SAP NetWeaver AS system on which the Integration Server is running
Java program	
XSLT program	
ABAP program	ABAP Engine of the SAP NetWeaver AS system on which the Integration Server is running
XSLT program	

Table 5.1 Runtime Environment for Mapping Programs

Note the following:

▶ Mapping programs that are executed at runtime on the Java EE Engine of SAP NetWeaver AS must exist in the Enterprise Services Repository. You create message mappings directly in the Enterprise Services Repository, and you can import Java and XSLT programs to the Enterprise Services Repository. For message mappings, developers use a graphical editor in the Enterprise Services Builder to create a mapping. The Enterprise Services Builder uses this graphical description to generate an executable Java program.

▶ There is no delivery mechanism for mapping programs that are executed at runtime on the ABAP Engine of SAP NetWeaver AS. Customers can develop mapping programs on the same SAP NetWeaver AS system on which the Integration Server is running via the ABAP Workbench. Therefore, the option for this mapping program type is deactivated in the Enterprise Services Builder default settings.

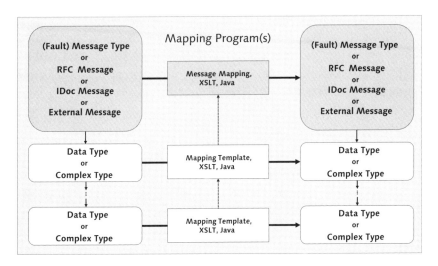

Figure 5.2 Hierarchy of Mapping Programs

Due to the restrictions on mapping programs on the ABAP Engine, the following sections concentrate solely on the mapping programs that are executed on the Java EE Engine. Figure 5.2 shows the (sub)objects in the Enterprise Services Repository for which you can develop these mapping programs. You can structure them hierarchically in the same way as messages:

Mappings for data types and messages

135

- You can create mapping programs for data types or complex types from RFCs, IDocs, or external definitions. You can use the same hierarchical structure of these types for mapping programs as well.

- To map a source message to a target message, you need a mapping program that maps the message schemas to each other. You can use mapping programs for data type mappings in this mapping program.

Hierarchy concepts There are different concepts for using one mapping program in another, depending on the mapping program type. You can use either a reference (to call a lower-level mapping program, in the same way as a subroutine) or a copy. In some cases, the various mapping program types (message mapping, XSLT, or Java program) can use each other.

5.1.1   Value Mappings

If a sender and receiver identify the same object in different ways, the corresponding values must be converted during message transfer. At first glance, the solution seems simple: Identify all source values using conditions in the mapping program and transfer them to target values. However, this solution isn't practical if there are countless values. Furthermore, this solution hides the mapping in the program. A preferable alternative is to save the values to be mapped in a value-mapping table and read them during the mapping.

Value-mapping table SAP NetWeaver PI uses a value-mapping table for all mapping programs. At design time, developers can specify the fields in the message schema for which a value mapping is to be executed, either in a Java program or within a message mapping. However, the actual values are often not known until configuration time, because they're dependent on customer-specific data. Therefore, you save the entries for the value-mapping table in the Enterprise Services Repository. The values can be populated either manually in the Integration Directory (see Section 6.2.3, Integrated Configuration, in Chapter 6) or automatically via the Integration Directory programming interface.

Value-mapping context The entries in the value-mapping table must be assigned to a value-mapping context. The values that you enter using the Integration Builder interface automatically belong to the context *http://sap.com/xi/XI/System*. You use the context to separate value mappings from different areas.

5.1.2 Mappings in Integration Processes

Chapter 8, Integration Processes, looks at how to process multiple messages in a process model in integration processes. Messages that are transferred from the Integration Engine on the Integration Server to an integration process are processed according to this model. Among other things, the model can stipulate that a certain number of messages must arrive and be processed before the integration process sends a result message to a receiver. This way of processing multiple messages enables you to bundle purchase order items from several messages into one message for a collective purchase order, for example. For integration process application cases such as these, the one-to-one mapping of messages would not suffice.

To map multiple messages to each other, the mapping runtime has a special feature: If a mapping has multiple source messages, the mapping runtime puts all involved source messages into one structure. The structure is always the same: The `<Messages>` root element has `<MessageN>` elements as subelements for each source message with a different message schema. For example, if an integration process expects two messages from a proxy, and these messages both use the `<Order>` message type in the Enterprise Services Repository, then an instance of the dynamic source structure would look like Listing 5.1 (without namespaces):

Multi-mappings

```
<Messages>
    <Message1>
        <Order>
            . . .
        </Order>
    </Message1>
    <Message1>
        <Order>
            . . .
        </Order>
    </Message1>
<Messages>
```

Listing 5.1 Message Structure for the Use of Multi-Mappings

The second occurrence of the `<Message1>` tag refers to the same message type. If the message types are different, the dynamic structure contains a corresponding number of additional tags with a higher counter.

As soon as more than one message is involved in the mapping, on either the source or target side, the mapping runtime uses this dynamic structure for the source and the target messages. In this way, mappings of multiple message instances are reduced to a mapping of one XML instance. Developers can develop these multi-mappings in the Enterprise Services Builder or by using external tools:

▶ The mapping editor for graphical message mappings in the Enterprise Services Builder allows you to specify multiple source or target messages. In the mapping editor, you define the message mapping with the message schema for the structure described above in the normal way.

▶ For multi-mappings in XSLT or Java, you can export the message schema from an *operation mapping* (see Section 5.3, Java and XSLT Mappings; operation mappings are explained in the next section). If your message schema does not exist in the Enterprise Services Repository, you can construct the schema for the dynamic structure yourself, as described above.

So far, our explanation of mapping programs has focused entirely on the messages that are to be mapped to each other. The next section examines the implications for the higher-level interfaces, when a mapping is required for message exchange.

5.2 Preconfiguration and Testing of Mapping Programs

In Chapter 4, Service Interfaces, Messages, and Proxy Generation, you saw that you specify service interfaces for message exchange in SAP NetWeaver PI. You specify these interfaces explicitly in the Integration Directory during the configuration of an interface determination (see Section 6.2.2, Overview of Configuration Object Types, Chapter 6). In the simplest case, you assign an inbound service interface to an outbound service interface. Once the Integration Server has read the outbound service interface of an inbound message from the message header, it can use the interface determination to identify the inbound service interface to which the message is to be forwarded. Depending on the type of the two interfaces, you use the interface determination to configure the exchange of not just one message, but of several. For example, you use synchronous service interfaces to exchange a message for a request first, and then a message for the response. Therefore, each interface pair may require several mapping programs.

In principle, users could reference the respective mapping programs for the request, response, and fault message from the interface determination for each operation. However, to do this, the consultants involved in the configuration process would have to know which mapping programs to use for which operation pairs. Moreover, it's more efficient to execute several mapping programs one at a time. This enables you to map multiple message formats to a central message format. This reduces the number of mapping programs, because the communication parties involved need only one mapping to the central message format, instead of numerous mappings for each communication party. This is a configuration task for the developer designing the entire mapping. For this reason, and to minimize the later configuration effort, developers create operation mappings in the Enterprise Services Repository, which act as an outer shell for mapping programs:

Operation mappings

▶ Before making the actual configuration settings in the Integration Directory, you define which mapping programs are to be executed for an operation pair during the processing of the request, response, or fault message. With the exception of multi-mappings, you can specify several mapping programs to be executed, one at a time, for each direction.

▶ You can also create multiple operation mappings for an operation pair; for example, if there are different customer requirements for mappings between an interface pair.

▶ Operation mappings have an integrated test environment for mapping programs of the Enterprise Services Repository. We'll look at this in more detail in the next section.

▶ You can export the message schema for external XSLT and Java programs. You can also export the message structure for multi-mappings in the same way. Because these mappings are intended just for integration processes, this is only possible for asynchronous abstract service interfaces.

If the messages that are exchanged between an interface pair don't require a mapping, you also don't need an operation mapping. In all other cases, operation mappings are mandatory.

Mapping programs and software component versions

Figure 5.3 shows an example of an operation mapping. It references a source and a target operation and mapping programs for the request, response, and fault message. Operation mappings can reference mapping programs from the same or an underlying software component version. There are no restrictions on references from operation mappings to service interfaces. In this example, the mapping objects are assigned to the same software component version S1 as the source service interface. This is, however, not necessary from a technical point of view. From a logical perspective, mappings are located between two application components. Therefore, the issue of which application component, and thus which software component version, a mapping should belong to is purely organizational. The communication parties involved could just have easily agreed to save the mapping objects in software component version S2.

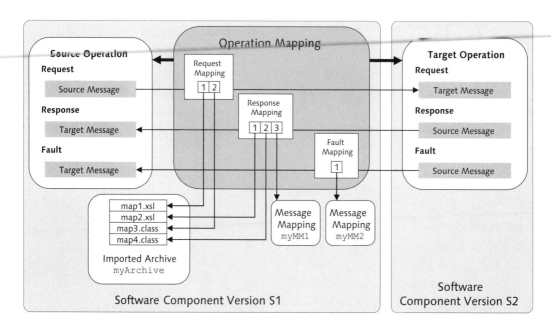

Figure 5.3 Example of an Operation Mapping

Because you've already configured the mapping program, all you need to do at configuration time is specify the operation mapping for an operation pair. The configuration in the Integration Directory enables the Integration Builder to recognize which mapping programs must be executed on the Integration Server at runtime. To ensure that these programs are available at runtime, the Integration Builder automatically copies all mapping programs to a system directory on the Integration Server.

Saving mapping programs at runtime

Mapping Test Environments in the Enterprise Services Builder

Let's now look at how to test mapping programs in the Enterprise Services Builder at design time. To do this, the mapping programs must be available in the Enterprise Services Repository. You can test message mappings — or Java or XSLT programs that have been imported into the Repository — in the Enterprise Services Builder.

The test environment is integrated into the editor for operation mappings. To test an operation mapping, simply select the corresponding tab. Figure 5.4 shows an example of a test instance, which is shown on the left side. In the default setting, the test environment generates an XML instance for the source message and displays it in a tabular tree representation:

Test instances

▶ The first column displays the hierarchical structure of the XML instance. To edit this hierarchy, use the options in the context menu.

▶ The second column is where you enter the values for the various fields.

The test environment functions also enable you to load other XML instances into the test environment and select other views for display or editing purposes; for example, a text editor.

The figure shows an operation mapping for asynchronous communication. In synchronous communication, you test the mapping programs for the request, response, and fault directions separately. In this case, the test environment has an additional list box so that you can switch between directions. You can also set the trace level for the testing of all mapping programs in a particular direction. The trace level relates to the messages that you write to the mapping trace within mapping programs. The

Trace level

mapping runtime has methods that enable you to differentiate between status information, warnings, and debugging information. The debug trace level also displays messages of the mapping runtime itself. The Enterprise Services Builder displays the trace outputs and information about the test execution status in the lower area of the test environment. The result of the transformation is displayed on the right.

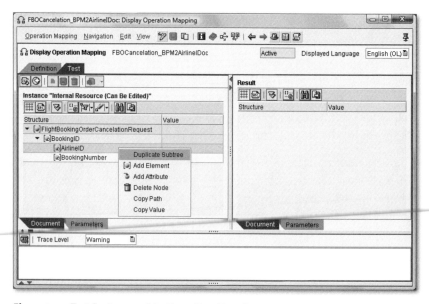

Figure 5.4 Test Environment in Operation Mapping

Of course, you can test individual Java and XSLT programs outside the Enterprise Services Builder by exporting the required message schemas from the operation mapping. Message mappings have the same test environment as the one integrated into the editor for operation mappings. In the operation mappings and the message mappings, you can manage the test instances that are shipped.

The following sections look at the different mapping program types in more detail. Section 5.3 deals with mapping programs in Java and XSLT. In Section 5.4, Developing Mappings in the Enterprise Services Builder, you'll learn that you can call Java programs as subroutines in graphical message mappings.

5.3   Java and XSLT Mappings

Let's start by looking at two established mapping program types: Java and XSLT. Because there is a range of development environments for these program types, the Enterprise Services Builder does not have its own tools to support this assortment. However, this does not mean you cannot use Java and XSLT programs. To develop Java or XSLT programs for mappings in SAP NetWeaver PI, proceed as follows:

1. Export the schemas for which you need a mapping from the Enterprise Services Repository. For example, you can use the export function under Tools in the editor menu to export message types. However, the simplest method is to first create an operation mapping for the relevant operations.   Development

   Once you've imported the interfaces in the operation mapping editor, you export the XSD schema of the respective request or response message as a Zip file. The Zip file can contain several schema files that reference each other, in a multi-mapping, for example. In such a case, the schema with the global element that is the root element of the message has the name MainSchema.

2. Use the exported schemas to develop your mapping program with a third-party tool. You may be using a schema that cannot be imported to the Enterprise Services Repository.

3. Save your mapping programs in one or more archives. These can be Zip or JAR files.

4. For each external Zip or JAR file, create a mapping object of the imported archive type in the Enterprise Services Builder. Objects of this type enable the external archives to be imported to the Enterprise Services Repository.

5. After the import, use the mapping programs in operation mappings by accessing the archive. You can make minor changes to XSLT mappings in a simple editor in the Enterprise Services Builder. You can change Java programs only externally, and you must reimport them.

The development of Java and XSLT programs is explained in depth in the technical literature. A W3Schools tutorial (*http://www.w3schools.com*) is available for free and provides a good introduction to XSLT; in addition, there are a number of books that offer a comprehensive and practice-oriented introduction to XSLT and Java. Therefore, Sections 5.3.1 and 5.3.2 cover only those features that pertain to the development of mapping programs for SAP NetWeaver PI.

5.3.1 Java Mappings

There are various technologies for parsing and transforming XML in Java. For example, the *document object model* (DOM) allows access to the entire XML tree via methods. Although this approach is straightforward and easy to understand, it isn't suitable for large XML documents, because loading such large documents is too memory-intensive. The best approach to use depends on the application.

Working with streams
Therefore, SAP NetWeaver PI does not provide fixed access methods to fields of the XML document. Instead, the mapping runtime transfers messages to Java programs as a TransformationInput object and similarly expects the result to be a TransformationOutput object. The two objects contain the XML payload as a *stream*. Developers have the freedom to choose which transformation method is best-suited to meet their needs. For example, you can use Java API for XML Processing (JAXP), which supports DOM, and Simple API for XML (SAX).

The following example uses the API[1] to access the stream. Listing 5.2 shows an example of how to use the API of the mapping runtime.

```
import java.io.InputStream;
import java.io.OutputStream;
import java.util.Map;
import java.util.HashMap;
import com.sap.aii.mapping.api.AbstractTransformation;
import com.sap.aii.mapping.api.AbstractTrace;
import com.sap.aii.mapping.api.TransformationInput;
import com.sap.aii.mapping.api.TransformationOutput;
import com.sap.aii.mapping.api.StreamTransformationException;
```

---

1 Note that the Java mapping API has been revised for SAP NetWeaver 7.1. The following examples are based on this new version. Correlations to the versions of SAP NetWeaver 2004 and SAP NetWeaver 7.0 are indicated explicitly.

```java
public class JavaMapping extends AbstractTransformation {
    private Map param = null;
    private AbstractTrace trace = null;
    private String receiverInterface = null;

    public void setParameter(Map param) {
        this.param = param;
        if (param == null) {
                this.param = new HashMap();
        }
    }
    public void transform(TransformationInput tInput,
            TransformationOutput tOutput) throws
StreamTransformationException {
        receiverInterface = (String) tInput.getInputHeader().
getReceiverInterface();
        trace = getTrace();
        this.execute(tInput.getInputPayload().
getInputStream(), tOutput
                .getOutputPayload().getOutputStream());
    }

        public void execute(InputStream in, OutputStream out) {
        try {
            // example for working with header parameters
            // and traces
            trace.addInfo("..."+receiverInterface);
            System.out.println(receiverInterface);
            // insert your coding here
    } finally {
    }
    }
}
```

Listing 5.2 Framework of a Java Mapping Program

To implement a Java mapping, a developer must enhance the Abstract-Transformation Java class and implement the following methods:

Stream transformation interface

▶ **setParameter()**
The Integration Engine calls this method to transfer runtime constants to the mapping program before it's executed. The implementation of this method is always the same. Simply use the method in Listing 5.2.

The method makes the constants within the implementing class accessible using a map, which has the name PARAM in this example.

▸ **transform()**
The Integration Engine calls this method at runtime to execute a mapping. This method receives a TransformationInput for the outbound messages and a TransformationOutput for the target message as parameters.

▸ **execute()**
This method is used as an encapsulation for converting the payload, and it's called in the transform() method. You can parse the substructures to be converted from the input stream and output the converted target document in the output stream. The encapsulation isn't mandatory and was introduced here to illustrate the relation to Java mappings that are based on the Java mapping API (SAP NetWeaver 2004 and 7.0).

Runtime constants and trace in Java programs

As the listing shows, you can access runtime constants via the getInput-Header() method of the TransformationInput class within the transform() method. You can use them to take into account sender and receiver information in the Java program, for instance. The getTrace() method, on the other hand, provides an object for trace outputs at runtime. Such trace outputs are visible in tests and in monitoring.

Value mapping in Java programs

The mapping runtime provides an API for executing value mappings. The values are saved in a Java database table. A lookup API enables you to enrich data using a synchronous JDBC, RFC, or SOAP connection. (For more information about APIs, see the online documentation.)

Important

To conclude, here are a few important notes about programming mapping programs for SAP NetWeaver PI in Java:

▸ Java mapping programs must always be stateless. Don't write data to a database table during a Java mapping, for instance. The Integration Server cannot track such side effects. Therefore, if an attempt is made to resend a message that has not been received by the receiver, the data may inadvertently be written to the database twice in a Java mapping.

► When using static variables in Java mappings, note the following points:

  ► Mappings can be executed in parallel. Therefore, several instances of a mapping may access a static field at the same time for read or write purposes.

  ► If mapping programs are executed more than once, the content of a static field may be lost, for example, because the Java class in question is reloaded. Moreover, during cluster operation of the mapping runtime, the classes of the mapping programs are loaded separately to each node of the cluster, so that each node has its own static fields.

Therefore, static fields can be used only for constants and as a buffer, taking into account, of course, the aforementioned points.

After this introduction to the Java mapping techniques, the following section discusses the basic principles of the XSLT mapping.

5.3.2 XSLT Mappings

The eXtensible Stylesheet Language Transformations (XSLT) standard belongs to the XSL language family. It was developed by the World Wide Web Consortium (W3C) for XML, to transform one XML structure into another. XSLT includes XPath, a syntax for selecting substructures in an XML document. In XSLT, you define mappings by using templates to define bindings for the selected substructures.

As of Version 7.1, SAP NetWeaver PI provides the option to execute XSLT mapping programs both with the SAP XML toolkit and with Java Development Kit (JDK) 5. Because JDK 5 includes some improvements with regard to processing XSLT, the SAP XML toolkit will no longer be supported in future releases. Therefore, SAP recommends using JDK 5 for new XSLT mapping programs, and testing and possibly adapting existing XSLT programs using JDK 5. The following example is based on the execution of XSLT mapping programs with JDK 5.

Replacing the SAP XML toolkit with JDK 5

We won't elaborate further on the extensive options provided by XSLT; rather, we'll examine just a few aspects. As is typical with Java programs, you can access mapping runtime constants in XSLT programs as well. For

Runtime constants in XSLT programs

example, the $ReceiverName constant provides the name of the receiver interface at runtime. To use the constant in an XSLT program, you must declare it using the param statement:

```
<xsl:param name="ReceiverName">
```

Java enhancements
The working draft of the specification for XSL Transformations (XSLT), Version 2.0 (*http://www.w3.org/TR/xslt20/*), does not define the functional scope of the enhancement mechanism of the XSL transformation. Nevertheless, some XSLT processors support the call of Java methods; the specific procedure strongly depends on the XSLT processor used. The SAP NetWeaver PI online documentation includes an example of a Java enhancement, which is supported by the SAP XML toolkit. There you can also find a list of the runtime constants for XSLT programs.

5.4   Developing Mappings in the Enterprise Services Builder

The Enterprise Services Builder has an integrated mapping editor that you can use to describe mappings graphically. Because these mappings are between messages, this description is referred to simply as a *message mapping*. The Enterprise Services Builder uses the message mappings to generate Java programs, which are compiled for runtime and packed in JAR files. The user does not need to concern himself with this; he works with just the message mapping in the Enterprise Services Builder at design time and at configuration time. Section 5.4.1 provides an introduction to the basic concepts of the mapping editor.

The challenge for all graphical mapping tools is to reconcile the need for clarity with the wide range of functions that can be integrated graphically. Section 5.4.2 specifies which standard functions exist in the mapping editor for describing mappings without developing program code. If the requirements are complex, the graphical description can become more complicated than the equivalent program code. If this is the case, you can enhance the pool of standard functions by adding your own user-defined functions in Java. Section 5.4.3 presents advanced mapping techniques. Section 5.4.4 explains how to create and reuse mappings for data types.

5.4.1   Introduction to the Mapping Editor

In all mappings, source fields of a source structure are assigned to target fields of a target structure. A field can be an element or an attribute of the respective XML document, and can be displayed in a graphical mapping tool by using lines to connect the corresponding fields of the source and target structure. If the XML document is large and many fields have to be mapped to each other, this representation can become very complicated. In addition to field mappings, calculations and format conversions are also required, which means that there are even more graphical elements for the mapping tool to represent.

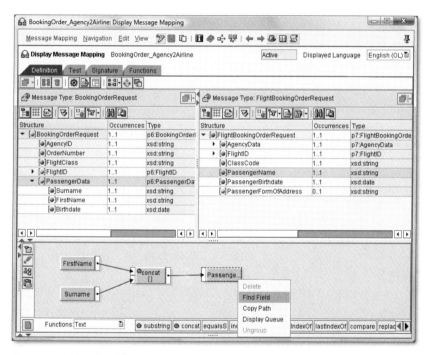

Figure 5.5   Mapping Editor

The mapping editor in the Enterprise Services Builder divides mappings into submappings. In Figure 5.5, the mapping editor shows such a submapping in the lower area. It refers to the target field, PassengerName, whose value is obtained by linking the FirstName and Surname source

Target-field mappings in the data-flow editor

fields. Because the representation in the lower area describes a data flow from the source to the target fields, this part of the mapping editor is called the data-flow *editor*. It always shows a mapping to a target field. Therefore, the whole message mapping in the mapping editor consists of target-field mappings. Moreover, the mapping editor provides the option to graphically map the entire mapping, or sections of the mapping, using lines. For the reasons mentioned, this tool is only used for representing already created target-field mappings, not for their new development.

Structure overview

The structure overview in the middle area is closely linked to the data-flow editor:

▶ To create a target-field mapping, double-click a target field or drag it to the data-flow editor using drag-and-drop. If a target-field mapping already exists, use the same actions to navigate between the different target-field mappings that you want to display in the data-flow editor.

▶ To transfer source structure fields to the data-flow editor for a currently displayed target-field mapping, double-click the source field or drag it to the data-flow editor using drag-and-drop.

Similarly, you can drag fields from the source structure to target structure fields (and the other way round) to assign them to one another.

Separating the structure overview and the target-field mappings in the data-flow editor may seem unusual at first, but it reduces the complexity of the display. The mapping editor also offers several functions for easier orientation. These include a where-used list for source fields, quick infos for target fields showing existing target-field mappings, and a general field search in functions of the data-flow editor and the structure overview. By using the Text Preview ( ) function in the editor toolbar, you can also display an overview of all target-field mappings in place of the data-flow editor. In the example in Figure 5.6, the header area and the structure overview are hidden as well. In addition to the text preview, the Dependencies function ( ) from the editor toolbar also provides a graphical overview function, which you can use to display the dependencies between source and target fields directly in the structure overview.

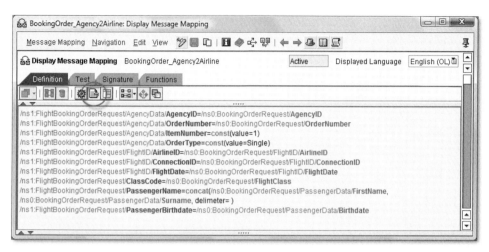

Figure 5.6 Text Preview

We'll now look at the procedure for designing a message mapping in the mapping editor. Once you've created a message mapping, you first load a source structure and a target structure into the structure overview. You can load a schema from the Enterprise Services Repository (fault) message types; IDocs; the request, response, or fault part of an RFC; and message schemas from external definitions or an XSD or XML document from a local file. The latter enables you to define message mappings for message schemas or message instances that cannot be imported to the Enterprise Services Repository.

Loading messages into the structure overview

The mapping editor displays the loaded message schema in a simplified XML representation in the structure overview in a tabular tree view. Table 5.2 provides an overview of the node symbols.

If a field can appear more than once in the target structure, the tree view displays only one node in the mapping editor, just as there is only one tag for the field definition in the XSD. In this representation, it isn't graphically possible to assign the value of a source field to a particular position in the target field. In such cases, you can use the Duplicate Subtree function in the context menu of the target structure to display multiple positions and specify them as the target. Section 5.4.2, Mapping Functions in Message Mappings, looks at additional functions for accessing positions and structures of XML instances. The context menu contains

Positions and restrictions of target fields

151

several other functions; for example, for deactivating or activating fields, using mapping templates, or creating variables. These functions are covered in Section 5.4.3, Advanced Message Mapping Techniques.

Node Symbol	Meaning
	Attribute
	Element
	Element with maxOccurs = unbounded
	Deactivated element
	Recursive element
	Variable

Table 5.2 Node Symbols in the Structure Overview

When designing and analyzing mappings, it helps to imagine that the fields and values of the target structure must first be generated. The target structure in the mapping editor specifies which conditions must be fulfilled for the generated structure to be valid. The mapping editor displays these conditions in the columns of the tabular tree view and uses colors to differentiate them:

▶ White fields have not yet been assigned and, according to the target structure specifications, don't necessarily have to be generated.

▶ Red fields must be included in the target instance, according to the target structure specifications. At runtime, a rule for the generation of these fields is required.

▶ Yellow fields have already been assigned to some extent, but the target-field mapping in the data-flow editor isn't yet complete.

▶ Green fields represent a complete target-field mapping.

Only when there are no more yellow or red fields in the target structure is the message mapping complete from a technical point of view. In the Enterprise Services Builder, you can test and release only complete message mappings.

If you want to develop a multi-mapping for an integration process or a message split, the procedure is the same as described above. The only extra step is to specify all source and target messages and their occurrence in the Messages tab. The mapping editor then displays the structure of the multi-mapping in the structure overview, as described in Section 5.1, Mapping Programs in SAP NetWeaver PI.

Multi-mappings

Work Method of Message Mappings

When a message mapping is complete, this simply means that it can be compiled, as when a Java program has the correct syntax. To help you understand runtime exceptions and undesired mapping results, let's take a brief look at the behavior of message mappings at runtime:

1. Message mappings import the values of the source XML instances into queues. Using queues improves performance and enables very large messages to be processed.

Queues

2. Queues are processed by the functions of the target-field mapping. The functions themselves have result queues that can be assigned further functions.

3. Finally, the result queues are read for the target fields and compared against their occurrence attributes. For example, if an upper limit has been specified for the occurrence of a target field, then any further result values of the result queue are ignored. The source XML instance probably had too many values. If it has too few values, this triggers an exception.

If you've already loaded a test instance in the Test tab, you can track each step of a target-field mapping in the Design tab by calling the Display Queue function for the objects in the data-flow editor. The target field queue is the result queue that compares the message mapping against the target structure restrictions at runtime. Figure 5.7 shows an example.

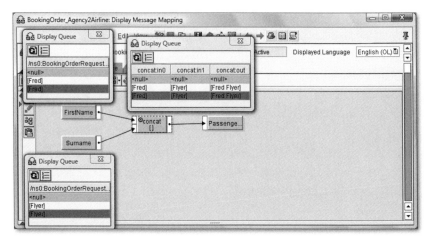

Figure 5.7 Queues in the Data-Flow Editor

5.4.2 Mapping Functions in Message Mappings

Before we look at the different types of mapping functions, we'll examine the hierarchical arrangement of XML structures. In the XML tree, the field of an XML instance is always in a *context* of the higher-level field. For example, in the XML instance in Listing 5.3, the `<person>` element is in the `<street>` context, and the `<city>` element is in the `<root>` context.

```
<root>
   <city>
      <street>
         <person> Fix </person>
      </street>
      <street>
         <person> Foxy </person>
      </street>
   </city>
</root>
```

Listing 5.3 Contexts Within a Sample XML Instance

Contexts The closing tag of the higher-level element marks the end of the context (the context is also referred to as closed). For example, Fix is in the first street context and Foxy is on the second street context (the two obviously live on different streets). Let's assume that you want to map this XML structure to a list of all inhabitants of the town, that is:

```
<AllCitizens>
   <citizen> Fix  </citizen>
   <citizen> Foxy </citizen>
</AllCitizens>
```

In this mapping, you must delete all contexts between ⟨person⟩ and ⟨root⟩ in the source structure. In other words, assigning all ⟨person⟩ elements to the ⟨root⟩ context simplifies the mapping. You would then have to assign only the ⟨person⟩ source field to the ⟨citizen⟩ target field. In the Context menu of the data-flow editor, you can set the context of each field of the source structure individually. In our example, you set the context of the ⟨person⟩ source field to ⟨root⟩. The data-flow editor displays the names of the fields where the standard context has been changed in italics. You can use the Display Queue function to track the steps of the target-field mapping. The context changes of the corresponding queue are indicated as gray bars that separate the values of the queue.

Generally, you need a range of additional mapping functions in a mapping. You access these functions in the mapping editor, in the lower area of the data-flow editor. Figure 5.8 shows the standard functions of the Boolean function category. Standard functions for text mappings, arithmetical calculations, (runtime) constants, conversions (for example, for accessing the value-mapping table), date conversions, statistical functions for all fields of a context, and functions for specific structure mappings are also available.

Standard functions

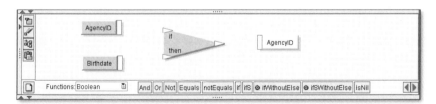

Figure 5.8 Standard Functions of the Boolean Function Category

In addition to variables that represent the value of XML fields, some standard functions use additional specifications, which are also referred

Parameters

to as parameters. These functions are indicated with an asterisk (). The parameters can either be set at design time during mapping development or be populated using import parameters at runtime.

Values of elements and attributes of the source message are a string. Therefore, all standard functions expect string-type arguments and return a string-type value. Nevertheless, the transferred value can have a different semantic data type; namely, the one that you specified when you defined the schema for the payload for the field. Standard functions exhibit the following standard behavior:

► Depending on the standard function, data type conversions are used to ensure that the values are transferred in a format suitable for the function (using a cast). If the value cannot be interpreted, the mapping runtime triggers a Java exception.

► If clauses evaluate conditions that deliver Boolean values. Standard functions that return Boolean values return the string true or false. Standard functions that expect Boolean values interpret the values "1" and "true" (not case-sensitive) as true, and all other values as false.

The following section presents options of advanced message mapping techniques.

5.4.3 Advanced Message Mapping Techniques

Advanced message mapping techniques enhance the functional scope of message mapping by user-defined functions, allow for the use of mapping parameters, and support the data enrichment through lookups.

User-Defined Functions

If the standard functions for a target-field mapping aren't sufficient, or if the graphical display is unclear because of the complexity of the mapping, you can create a user-defined function, and then use it to create Java source code. The Enterprise Services Builder includes the function as a Java method in the Java program that is generated for the message mapping. You can use the following execution types for the user-defined functions:

▶ **Single values**

These functions process individual input values of assigned fields for each function call. Therefore, simple functions expect strings as input values and return a string.

▶ **All values of a context**

Such functions process multiple values for each function call. Before you call the function, you can import all field values of a context for the field in an array. At runtime, the function is called once for each context. If the function has various input parameters, you must ensure that they have the same number of contexts at runtime. The result is returned to the mapping runtime in the form of one or multiple objects of the ResultList type.

▶ **All values of a queue**

Such functions process multiple values for each function call. Before you call the function, you can import all field values of a queue for the field in an array. At runtime, the function is called once for each mapping. The result is returned to the mapping runtime in the form of one or multiple objects of the ResultList type.

In addition to the execution type, you must specify the following properties when you create the user-defined function:

▶ A technical name

▶ A title for the display in the data-flow editor

▶ A description for the tooltip text of the function in the data-flow editor

▶ A category in which the function is displayed in the data-flow editor (a standard function category or a user-defined function category)

Ultimately, you must specify the signature (input and return fields) of the function. The use of variables and the result list has already been described in the context of execution types of functions. As for the standard functions, you can use parameters for the user-defined functions. These are added to the function's signature like variables and can be used in the Java code.

Objects in user-defined functions Using Java methods from imported archives in user-defined functions is an obvious approach. You can access the following objects in user-defined functions:

▶ Java programs from imported archives that are in the same software component version as the message mapping or an underlying software component version

▶ Mapping runtime objects for trace output and for transferring values between user-defined functions

▶ Standard packages of the Java Development Kit and the Java EE environment

The comments on the implementation of mappings in Java at the end of Section 5.3.1, Java Mappings, also apply to user-defined functions.

Function Libraries

When you create user-defined functions while developing a message mapping, you can use them only within the corresponding message mapping. They are automatically part of the *local function library*, and they can be displayed and processed via the Functions tab in the mapping editor. If you want to use functions in different message mappings or mapping templates, you create them in function libraries. Function libraries are created as independent object types in the Enterprise Services Repository. A function library corresponds to a Java class. When you create a function library, the Enterprise Services Builder automatically assigns the name of the function library to the class name and derives the package name from the repository namespace. The user-defined functions created within the library are mapped as methods of the Java class. In addition to the implementation of these methods, you also have the option to add Java code to the following generic areas:

▶ The *attributes and methods* area is used for defining global variables and global methods.

▶ The init method is used for initialization and is called at the start of the message mapping.

▶ The cleanUp method is carried out at the end of the message mapping.

The Enterprise Services Builder provides an editor for processing the function libraries and user-defined functions. Figure 5.9 shows an overview of the editor's basic functions. In the Functions area, you can add your own user-defined functions to the generic methods. The implementation of the functions is done in the right area of the editor and is based on the programming model of the local user-defined functions with regard to properties and signature. You can reference imported archives that are in the same software component version as the message mapping, or in an underlying software component version, and add import instructions.

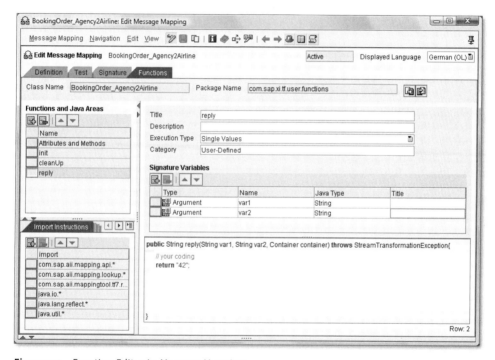

Figure 5.9 Function Editor in Message Mapping

You can edit the Java source code of a function library using an external development tool as well. For this purpose, an export and import function is available.

Within the framework of message mapping development, you can use function libraries that are in the same software component version as

Using function libraries

the message mapping or an underlying software component version. Via the Show Used Function Libraries function (▣), you can add function libraries to a message mapping or remove them from the message mapping. The functions of the function library entered in the mapping editor are displayed in the data-flow editor below the corresponding function category. The title of the function follows the schema: *<instance name>.<title of the function>*.

Parameterized Mapping Programs

Using mapping parameters, you can transfer information from the Integration Directory to the mapping programs.[2] This way, you can transfer information to mappings that aren't available until configuration time.

You define the parameters in the Signature tab of the corresponding message mapping. Parameters of the *adapter* type (values: SOAP, JDBC, RFC) transport a reference to a concrete adapter configuration to a mapping program. This reference can be used within a lookup. Parameters of the *simple* type (xsd:string and xsd:integer) can be used in standard functions marked with (▣) and in appropriately configured user-defined functions.

In addition to the type of the parameter, you must also define the transport direction. *Import parameters* provide information from the interface determination or the transformation step of an integration process to a mapping program. Using *export parameters*, you can provide information from the mapping program to the transformation step within the integration process.

In the operation mapping, you then need to click the Parameter button to establish a binding for the parameters so that the mapping parameters from the interface determination or the transformation step in the integration process can be passed to the mapping program.

---

2 You can use mapping parameters within the scope of message mappings, Java mappings, and XSLT mappings. The description of the use in message mappings is an example for all mapping program types.

Enhancing Mapping Programs and Lookups

In addition to the option to map value mappings using the integrated function (see Section 5.1, Mapping Programs in SAP NetWeaver PI), you can also use lookups for read access to application systems to enrich mappings. The access to application systems can be done via a SOAP, JDBC, or RFC adapter.

Lookups are supported in Java, XSLT[3], and message mappings using Java APIs. To facilitate the development of lookups, message mapping provides the option to define JDBC and RFC lookups graphically. To do so, proceed as follows:

1. In the Integration Directory, create a communication channel of the JDBC or RFC type.

2. Import the table structure as External Definition or the signature of the RFCs as Imported Object into your Enterprise Services Repository.

3. Use the standard function, JDBC Lookup or RFC Lookup, of the Conversions function category in the data-flow editor.

4. Double-click on the function to determine the input and output variables as properties of the lookup function.

5. Use the function in your target-field mapping.

So far, you've explored how to develop mappings for messages in the Enterprise Services Builder. To enable you to reuse parts of message mappings, the Enterprise Services Builder supports *mapping templates*, which provide mapping procedures of data types.

5.4.4 Developing Data Type Mappings in the Enterprise Services Builder

You edit mapping templates with the same mapping editor as the message mappings. There are two ways to create a mapping template:

▶ You can use a message mapping or mapping template by selecting an element in the source and target structure that references a data type in the Enterprise Services Repository. Using the context menu of the

Creating templates

---

3 Note that not all XSLT processors support the call of Java methods (see Section 5.3.2, XSLT Mappings).

target structure or using the editor menu, you can save the mapping for the two selected data types as a mapping template.

► You can create a data type template — directly in the Enterprise Services Builder — and load a data type into both the source and the target structure.

You can use saved mapping templates in other message mappings or other mapping templates. This means that the Enterprise Services Builder copies mapping templates into other mappings; it does not reference them. You can then adapt the target-field mapping of the copied template to meet your requirements. These changes don't modify the original mapping template. In the mapping editor, you can display the mapping templates that have been copied to the editor. Alternatively, you can develop mapping templates in the same way as message mappings, as described in the previous section.

The design of the collaborative process is independent of the technical details resulting from the customer's system landscape. This chapter describes how to configure this information centrally to control message processing at runtime.

6   Configuration

At design time, we look at collaborative processes at the logical level. In this view, messages are exchanged between application components and not between systems. In this chapter, we make the link between this abstraction and the settings that are required at runtime to actually implement message exchange. These settings concern the following areas:

▶ Information about the actual system landscape and the products installed there. This is discussed at the beginning of Section 6.1, Describing Systems and Communication Components.

System landscapes and communication objects

▶ Information regarding the communication components provided within a system landscape, and which technical communication channel other systems in the system landscape use to access a communication component, is discussed at the end of Section 6.1 after the basics are covered at the beginning of the section.

▶ Information about how the communication components are linked to one another by messages (logical routing) and whether a mapping is necessary is described in relation to internal company communication in Section 6.2, Configuring Internal Company Processes.

▶ Information about communication components that you want to make available to business partners outside your own system landscape is described in Section 6.3, Configuring Cross-Company Processes, which builds on the concepts introduced in Section 6.2.

With the exception of the area listed in the first bullet point, you configure all of the necessary information centrally in the Integration Directory. You have the following options:

- If there is an integration scenario for your collaborative process in the Enterprise Services Builder (see Section 3.2, Modeling the Collaborative Process, in Chapter 3), you should use this scenario for configuration. Section 6.2.1, Configuration Using Integration Scenarios, discusses this topic.

- If there is no integration scenario, a configuration wizard is available to guide you through the individual configuration steps.

- Alternatively, you can make the configuration settings manually. Unlike the first option — where the Integration Builder automatically recognizes from the integration scenario which configuration objects can be reused and which objects must be generated — manual configuration is very time-consuming.

Processes and scenarios

To avoid confusion, note that the term *collaborative process* means a process that exists in the real world and that you want to implement using your software technology. An *integration scenario* is a design object in the Enterprise Services Builder that you use to model the collaborative process. *Integration processes}* are also design objects that enable you to consider dependencies between messages in cross-system message exchange. Chapter 8, Integration Processes, discusses this topic in more detail.

Integration and configuration scenarios

During the configuration of a collaborative process, you can choose whether you want to work with an integration scenario from the Enterprise Services Builder. On the one hand, making the integration scenario an integral part of the Enterprise Services Builder would be too restrictive. On the other hand, the lack of an integration scenario means there is nothing to hold together the configuration objects of a scenario. By way of a compromise, the Integration Builder works with *configuration scenarios*, which are simply containers for all of the configuration objects that are required to configure a collaborative process. Figure 6.1 shows the XIDemo_SingleFlightBooking configuration scenario in the Integration Builder. The Objects tab shows all of the objects that are assigned to a configuration scenario. In this case, the objects were generated or suitable existing objects were automatically assigned using the Single-FlightBooking integration scenario. However, you don't have to use an integration scenario from the Enterprise Services Builder and can assign any configuration objects to a configuration scenario.

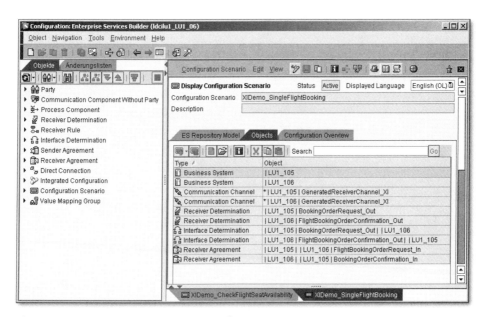

Figure 6.1 XIDemo_SingleFlightBooking Configuration Scenario

No matter which configuration option you choose, it's critical that you understand the various configuration objects. Next, we'll take a step-by-step look at how these objects are used.

Configuration in the Integration Directory is designed to support as many configuration scenarios as possible. Depending on the protocol, the configuration scenarios can have very different technical requirements. However, the procedure for configuring the configuration objects is valid for many configuration scenarios. Sections 6.1, 6.2, and 6.3 explain this procedure and highlight any exceptions. Sections 6.4, Adapter Configuration, and 6.5, Adapters for Industry Standards, address the special features of the various adapters. Finally, Section 6.6, Transports Between the Test and Production Landscapes, focuses on the transport of configuration objects.

Configuration scenarios

165

6.1   Describing Systems and Communication Components

To configure a collaborative process within your system landscape, you must first describe the system landscape in the System Landscape Directory (SLD). Section 6.1.1, Settings in the System Landscape Directory, discusses this topic. You have two options when it comes to dealing with the sequence of the configuration steps in the Integration Directory: You can work from the collaborative process (logical level) to the technical systems (technical level), or vice versa. The advantage of the latter option is that a system generally offers communication components for a wide range of collaborative processes and plays a role in different configuration scenarios. The technical options provided by the systems for message exchange are more constant, and you only need to enter them once for all configuration scenarios in a *collaboration* profile. For this reason, we advise that you focus on this profile first and then move on to configuration at the logical level. Therefore, we'll look at the settings in the SLD first and then examine the configuration of the collaboration profile in Section 6.1.2, First Steps in the Integration Directory.

6.1.1   Settings in the System Landscape Directory

Like the design and configuration tools, you call the System Landscape Directory (SLD) from the SAP NetWeaver Process Integration start page (see Chapter 2, First Steps). In addition to the software catalog, which you learned about in Section 3.1.1, Describing Products in the Software Catalog, in Chapter 3, you can also enter and call the following information about your system landscape:

▶ **Technical systems**
In this area, you can access information about the technical systems in your system landscape. Examples of technical systems are Application Server ABAP (AS ABAP) and Application Server Java (AS Java).

▶ **Landscapes**
Here you can create and configure groups of technical systems. For example, you can define landscapes for administration and transport.

▸ **Business systems**
In this area, you can access information about the business systems in your system landscape. This area is specific to SAP NetWeaver PI and enables you to identify those systems in your system landscape that use SAP NetWeaver PI to exchange messages.

The information about the technical systems of your system landscape isn't just of interest to SAP NetWeaver PI users. It can also be used by SAP support employees and customers to get an overview of the installed systems:

Technical systems

▸ **Technical SAP systems**
The SLD categorizes the technical SAP systems by the Basis, the SAP Web AS, or the SAP NetWeaver release on which they are based. The following systems register themselves automatically in the SLD when they're installed: SAP Basis 4.0B, SAP NetWeaver AS ABAP, and SAP NetWeaver AS Java. They also transfer data about their installed products. You must manually register all other technical SAP systems in the SLD by using a wizard and then assign them products from the software catalog.

▸ **Third-party systems**
You also manually register third-party systems in the SLD by using a wizard. You can assign these systems third-party products from the software catalog.

The technical attributes of a system are stored in the SLD. Examples of attributes for technical SAP systems are system name, system clients, message server, and installed products. Furthermore, you can use the Process Integration option to display all technical SAP systems on which SAP NetWeaver PI runtime components are installed; for example, the Integration Server. These components register themselves automatically in the SLD as soon as they're launched.

If a technical system is part of a cross-system process, you must also assign it to a business system. (In SAP systems, every client represents a business system.) During configuration, you then work with the name of the business system and not with the name of the technical system. First, this ensures that only those systems relevant to the process are displayed

Business systems

during configuration. Second, you can make changes to the technical system landscape without affecting an existing configuration.

Roles of the business system

Business systems are used exclusively for cross-system applications with SAP NetWeaver PI. Therefore, the attributes of a business system in the SLD relate directly to the particular application case. Figure 6.2 shows a section of a business system in the SLD. In addition to the header data (name, description, administration contact), you must specify the role of the business system:

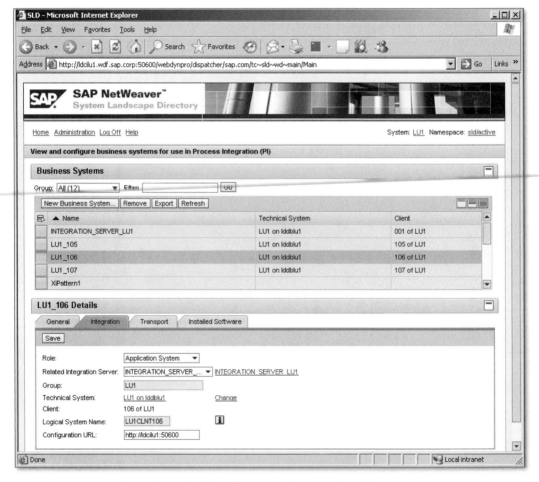

Figure 6.2 Attributes of a Business System in the SLD

▶ If it's an application system, you must assign it an Integration Server, with which the business system will exchange messages. Because you usually test the message exchange before using the process in a production environment, there can be multiple Integration Servers within a system landscape.

▶ Alternatively, you assign the business system the role of an Integration Server.

Just like the other data in the SLD, this information is merely descriptive. Therefore, defining a business system as an Integration Server in the SLD does not relieve you of the task of making the corresponding configuration settings for the respective clients in the technical system (see Section 7.1.1, Basics, in Chapter 7). Other SAP NetWeaver PI runtime components may also call data in the SLD. As we'll be discussed in Section 6.6, Transports Between the Test and Production Landscapes, the Group and Target Business System attributes are required for the transport of configuration objects between different Integration Directories.

We'll now focus on the uses of the data in the SLD for configuration in the Integration Directory. For a business system in the SLD, in the Installed Software tab you maintain the installed products in addition to the already mentioned data. The assigned technical system (in Figure 6.2, client 106 of SAP system LU1) uses the products listed here and the derived software component versions. Because business systems are used in the Integration Directory to configure internal company communication, the Integration Directory accesses information about business systems and associated technical systems from the SLD to derive further details. For example, the Integration Builder can use the software component versions of a system to determine all of the interfaces for a business system that have been saved in the Enterprise Services Builder for message exchange. Figure 6.3 illustrates this query. The Integration Builder also uses this mechanism for checks and input help.

Evaluating the SLD Data

The use of the software catalog in the Enterprise Services Builder, discussed in Section 3.1.1, Describing Products in the Software Catalog, in Chapter 3, completes the loop. The business system communication component shown in Figure 6.3 leads us to our next topic: the Integration Directory. The next section explains the configuration procedure in the Integration Directory.

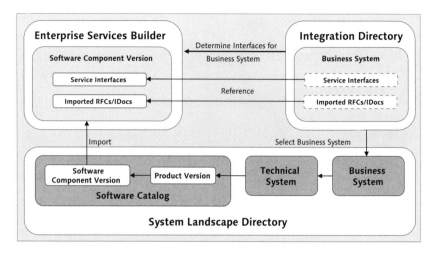

Figure 6.3 Referencing Content of the Enterprise Services Builder

6.1.2 First Steps in the Integration Directory

Objects in the Integration Directory

The Integration Builder provides a range of objects for configuring a collaborative process. Before discussing in detail how to use these configuration objects, let's first get a general overview. Because there are dependencies between the various objects, we advise that you adhere to the following sequence during configuration:

1. The configuration objects *communication party, communication component,* and *communication channel* reference each other and together form a *collaboration profile*. To exchange internal company messages, it's generally sufficient to use collaboration profiles, where the communication components and communication channels are specified. Therefore, Section 6.3, Configuring Cross-Company Processes, discusses communication parties in detail.

2. At this stage, the collaboration profile is still independent of a specific configuration scenario. You use the configuration objects *sender agreement* and *receiver agreement* to define the communication options that you want or have to use. These agreements are collectively referred to as a *collaboration agreement*.

3. Finally, you use *receiver determinations* and *interface determinations* to configure the logical routing, which defines where a message should be forwarded and whether a mapping is necessary beforehand.

The description of the collaboration profile is the basis for the following configuration steps. You can use the profile in different configuration scenarios. Therefore, let's take a closer look at this area before moving on to the configuration of internal company processes in Section 6.2, Configuring Internal Company Processes.

Figure 6.4 shows the object hierarchy of communication parties, communication components, and communication channels. As already mentioned, we'll discuss the communication parties in more detail later. At this point, you only need to know that an enterprise uses a communication party to enter the communication components provided by a business partner in the Integration Directory. Therefore, you don't actually need a communication party as a configuration object for internal company processes. (The exception to this is a configuration scenario with IDocs. Section 6.4.2, Special Features of the RFC and IDoc Adapters, discusses this topic.)

Collaboration profile

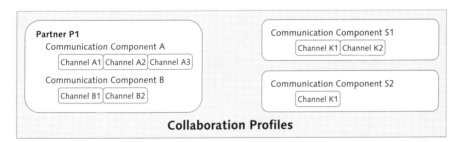

Figure 6.4 Object Hierarchy in Collaboration Profiles

The *communication component* is an additional level for business systems to enable other sender and receiver types to be modeled and addressed. There are three types of communication components:

Communication component

▶ **Business systems**

These communication components refer directly to a business system from the SLD. To create business systems, you call the context menu for the Communication Component Without Party or Business System node in the Integration Builder navigation tree and select Assign Business System.

▶ **Integration processes**
These communication components refer to integration processes from the Enterprise Services Builder. Chapter 8, Integration Processes, discusses the configuration of integration processes in more detail.

▶ **Business components**
These communication components enable business partners to address receivers of your system landscape without having to publish the receivers. Section 6.3, Configuring Cross-Company Processes, provides details on this topic.

Input helps for interfaces

A communication component offers a range of interfaces for communication using SAP NetWeaver PI. These interfaces are displayed in the Sender and Receiver tabs. In the previous section, Figure 6.3 showed that the Integration Builder automatically determines these interfaces for business systems from the Enterprise Services Builder. Consequently, they're displayed in the input help (that is, the help that users can call up to enter a value in an entry field) in subsequent configuration steps. If the interfaces of a business system aren't in the Enterprise Services Builder because they have not been created or imported, you must enter them manually in the subsequent configuration steps.

The business systems in the Integration Directory can also be used to communicate with one another via the Web service runtime based on the *Web Services Reliable Messaging* (WS-RM) standard. For business systems as of Release SAP Application Server ABAP 7.10, you can implement a central Web service configuration using the Integration Builder for these business systems. This configuration option is discussed in Section 6.2.5, Direct Communication.

Communication channel

When creating a business system, the Integration Builder automatically creates communication channels for the business system, which you must then adapt to your configuration scenario:

▶ For an SAP system, separate receiver communication channels are generated for RFC, IDoc, HTTP, and proxy communication (*adapter type XI*).

▸ For a non-SAP system, an HTTP receiver communication channel is generated.

Communication channels define the inbound and outbound processing in the Integration Server. To start, the channels of a business system simply reflect the options in the business system for receiving and sending messages. You define the channel to be used for a selected communication for the sender or receiver by using the collaboration agreement.

You may ask yourself which system a receiver communication channel refers to: the Integration Server or the application system. The communication channel for the sender configures the sender adapter, which converts the sender message for more processing in the Integration Server. Therefore, the channel for the sender determines the inbound processing in the Integration Server. Outbound processing works in a similar way. All configuration object names in the Integration Directory are based on the symmetry displayed in Figure 6.5. A configuration object for the receiver always refers to the receiver application system or the receiver business partner — *not* the Integration Server sending the message.

Receiver communication channel

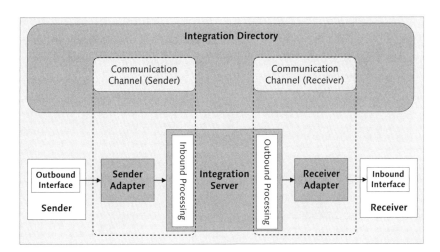

Figure 6.5 Sender and Receiver in Configuration

The representation of the adapters reflects the logical point of view. It does not show where the runtime components of the adapters are actually installed. The proxy runtime, in particular, is installed in the application

Sender and receiver configuration

173

system. Nevertheless, you configure the proxy runtime in the same way as the other adapters; that is, by using a communication channel and choosing the SAP XI adapter type. We'll look at adapter configuration in more detail in Section 6.4.

You should now understand the symmetry of the configuration objects with respect to the sender and receiver. In configuration, however, you don't always require both sides. Because the Integration Server must define a receiver for the message, the configuration objects for the receiver side are mandatory. On the sender side, however, whether you have to configure anything depends on the adapter type and the configuration scenario. For example, the proxy runtime in the sender application system uses information from the SLD to determine the address of the Integration Server. Therefore, in this case you make configuration settings in the Integration Directory on the sender side only if security settings are required for message transfer.

Let's take another look at the object hierarchy of the collaboration profile from Figure 6.4. In the Enterprise Services Builder, you saw that namespaces ensure that object names are unique. Objects in the Integration Directory don't have any namespaces; instead, the name of the higher-level object type serves as the namespace in collaboration profiles. It's normal for two communication channels of different communication components to have the same name, because the adapter type of the channel is often the same. For example, the names of the communication channels generated for business systems are always the same. The configuration of the channels, on the other hand, is specific to the business system.

Communication channel templates

For adapter types where no communication channels can be generated, it would be laborious to always have to manually edit the frequently used attributes. Certain attributes are often known at design time. For example, the RosettaNet industry standard stipulates security settings (encryption, signature) for the *Partner Interface Processes* (PIPs). To accelerate the configuration of such scenarios, the Enterprise Services Builder provides communication channel templates, which you create in the Enterprise Services Builder and reuse in the Integration Directory. Section 6.5, Adapters for Industry Standards, explains how SAP NetWeaver

PI supports industry standards. You can use communication channel templates for all adapter types.

6.2 Configuring Internal Company Processes

So far, you've learned about the basic settings that form the foundation for a range of configuration scenarios. This section focuses on internal company scenarios. Section 6.2.1 presents the configuration based on a demo example[1] using the corresponding integration scenario. In this case, the Integration Builder supports the automatic generation of configuration objects using information from the integration scenario. This example is used to explain the general concepts in the following sections.

6.2.1 Configuration Using Integration Scenarios

Section 3.2, Modeling the Collaborative Process, introduced you to the CheckFlightSeatAvailability integration scenario, which models a flight availability check in which a travel agency exchanges messages with one or more airlines. In the demo example, there are three airlines. For simplicity, let's say that these airlines are three clients of the same SAP system:

▶ Client 105 is the travel agency on the sender side.

▶ On the receiver side, client 106 is the airline Lufthansa, and client 107 is American Airlines and United.

The following steps are based on the assumption that the description of the technical systems and the business systems is already contained in the SLD. When writing this book, we worked with SAP system LU1 and created the business systems LU1_105, LU1_106, and LU1_107. We also created the corresponding business systems, as described in Section 6.1.2, First Steps in the Integration Directory, and generated and adapted the required communication channels.

---

1 The demo example is described in Section 2.2, Simple Use Cases and Demo Examples, in Chapter 2.

Transferring the
integration
scenario Now we'll explain how to configure this scenario in the Integration Builder. To do this, first select TOOLS • APPLY MODEL FROM FROM ES REPOSITORY in the main menu to access the integration scenario from the Enterprise Services Builder. This creates a configuration scenario that references the integration scenario. After the transfer, the Model Configurator dialog box appears, which displays the first Component View of the integration scenario (see Figure 6.6).

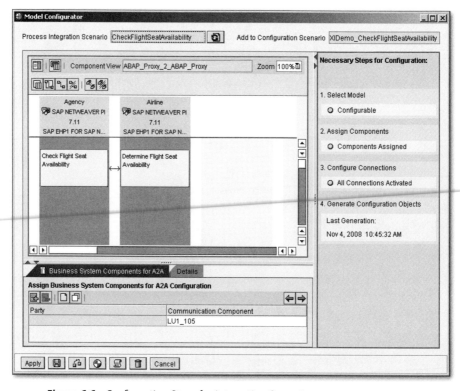

Figure 6.6 Configuration Steps for Integration Scenarios

To make the configuration settings, perform the configuration steps in the order displayed on the right side of the figure. To implement a step, either click the corresponding button above the graphic or select the corresponding configuration object. For example, for the component assignment, you can click the corresponding communication component and assign it. To configure the connections, you can click the connection in the figure and then assign it:

1. In the first configuration step, specify the component view (see Section 3.3.1, Mapping Application Components to Systems). In this case, keep the component view that is already selected, ABAP_Proxy_2_ABAP_Proxy.

2. In the second configuration step, assign a communication component to each application component. The system then displays the first application component, Agency. Assign the communication component LU1_105 to it. Use the blue navigation arrow to switch to another application component, Airline. Assign the communication components LU1_106 and LU1_107 to it.

3. The third configuration step deals with connections (see Figure 6.7). Each receiver communication component requires a communication channel to enable the Integration Server to forward the respective message to the technical system. On the sender side, on the other hand, it isn't necessary to configure a communication channel for the XI adapter (this is discussed in detail in Section 6.4, Adapter Configuration).

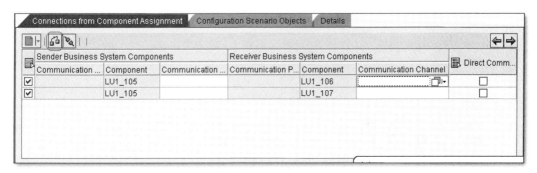

Figure 6.7 Configuring Connections

4. Let's concentrate for the moment on how to select a communication channel. In Section 6.1.2, First Steps in the Integration Directory, you learned that a collaboration agreement is required to select a particular communication channel at runtime. This example deals with a receiver agreement for the message to the receiver business system LU1_106 or LU1_107. There are two cases:

   Receiver agreement

   ▶ If no existing receiver agreement matches the receiver business system and the inbound interface, you must assign the required communication channel using the input help. An appropriate receiver agreement is generated later. The input help displays all communication channels that are available for the receiver communication component.

▸ If a receiver agreement already exists for your receiver, you can use the function circled in red in Figure 6.7 to automatically define the channel. As shown in Figure 6.8, in this case the dialog box displays only the communication channel defined by the receiver agreement in the communication channel selection. If the receiver agreement is for all inbound interfaces of the receiver system (referred to as a generic receiver determination), you can expand the communication channel selection by creating a more specific receiver determination; that is, one that is intended for a specific inbound interface. Section 6.2.2, Overview of Configuration Object Types, addresses generic and specific configuration objects.

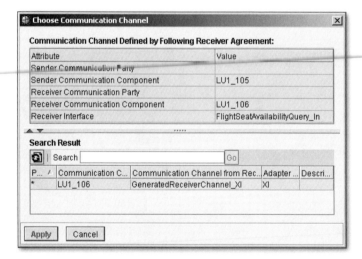

Figure 6.8 Selecting a Communication Channel

Generating the configuration objects

5. Finally, once you've made these preparations, you can have the integration scenario configurator generate all of the remaining configuration objects, and restrict this generation to particular object types. To check the generation without creating new configuration objects, you can also simulate the procedure. In both cases, the Integration Builder shows the results in a detailed generation log.

Figure 6.9 shows a screenshot of the log. The traffic lights in the log represent generation steps with errors (red traffic light), incomplete generation steps (yellow traffic light, as in Figure 6.9), and complete generation steps (green traffic light). If a generation step is incomplete, this means you may have to add information that cannot be generated automatically; for example, routing conditions.

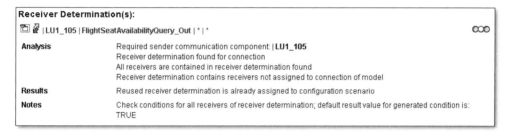

Figure 6.9 Generation Log

The Integration Builder automatically adds all generated and reused objects to the object list of your configuration scenario. You can also use the Configuration Scenario Objects tab in the component view to display the configuration objects belonging to each connection.

To finish the configuration, work through the generation log by navigating directly from the log to the corresponding objects and adding the missing information. The next section deals with the background knowledge necessary to complete the configuration.

Generation log

6.2.2   Overview of Configuration Object Types

We've looked at the configuration objects of the collaboration profile: party, communication component, and communication channel. Before examining other configuration objects, let's see how all of the objects are related to one another.

Key Fields

Unlike the objects in the Enterprise Services Builder, the configuration objects aren't organized using software component versions. Therefore, all configuration objects become globally visible in the Integration Directory as soon as they are released, and are simultaneously activated for the runtime environment. Consequently, it's worth taking a closer look at the key fields of the objects. To simplify this overview, the objects are separated into three tables according to their use.

Key fields of the collaboration profile

There is little more to say about the key fields of the objects of the collaboration profile, shown in Table 6.1. There are communication components without a party, but no parties without a communication component. In objects without a party, the key field accordingly remains initial. The communication channel consists of the key fields of the assigned communication component and its own name. As has already been determined, you choose the objects of the collaboration profile during the remaining configuration steps and determine the relationships between them. Therefore, the key fields of the communication component are always part of the key fields of the other configuration objects.

Key Field	Object Type		
	Party	Communication Component	Communication Channel
Communication component	(X)	X	
Communication channel	(X)	X	X

Table 6.1 Key Fields for Objects of the Collaboration Profile

Key fields for the collaboration agreements

Table 6.2 focuses on collaboration agreements. To ensure that the information in the table is complete, we added the following information to the table:

► The values from four fields of the receiver agreement can be mapped to other values using a header mapping. Section 6.3, Configuring Cross-Company Processes, examines the reasons for doing this in the cross-company scenarios.

► Key fields marked with an asterisk (*) can be filled *generically*. Don't confuse these fields with the input fields in the Integration Builder that are marked with a red asterisk. The latter are *required* fields.

► Key fields that are marked with an X in parentheses aren't mandatory; there are also communication components without parties and consequently communication agreements and objects for the logical routing that don't contain parties.

Key Field	Object Type	
	Sender Agreement	**Receiver Agreement**
Sender party	(X)	(X)* *(Header mapping)*
Sender communication component	X	X* *(Header mapping)*
Outbound interface	X	
Namespace of the outbound interface	X	
Receiver party	(X)*	(X) *(Header mapping)*
Receiver communication component	X*	X *(Header mapping)*
Inbound interface		X*
Namespace of the inbound interface		X*

Table 6.2 Key Fields for Sender and Receiver Agreements

You use generic fields to define the configuration for multiple cases by entering an asterisk in the field. For example, you can create a receiver agreement independently of a specific inbound interface. During message processing, the Integration Server checks for receiver determinations with matching key fields and selects the most specific. In some constellations, the Integration Builder cannot determine this due to overlapping. If this is the case, the Integration Builder checks this and notifies you during creation. You must also be aware that generic configurations are globally valid in the Integration Directory. If several configuration scenarios use the same generic object, any changes to this object will result in side effects for all of these scenarios.

Generic and specific fields

The remaining two configuration objects are for logical routing. The key fields are listed in Table 6.3. The virtual receiver is relevant only to cross-company communication, which we discuss in Section 6.3, Configuring

Cross-Company Processes. If you don't specify a virtual receiver when creating a receiver determination, the Integration Builder inserts an asterisk for both fields (in other words, the receiver determination is independent of a virtual receiver).

Key Field	Object Type	
	Receiver Determination	Interface Determination
Sender party	(X)*	(X)*
Sender communication component	X*	X*
Outbound interface	X	X
Namespace of the outbound interface	X	X
Receiver party	(X)* (Virtual receiver)	(X)*
Receiver communication component	X* (Virtual receiver)	X*

Table 6.3 Key Fields for Objects of Logical Routing

We'll now expand on this brief overview and look at the individual object types and their uses in more detail.

Collaboration Agreements

Sender and receiver

Senders and receivers of a message use a collaboration agreement to agree on the communication channel to be used to exchange messages. The obvious question here is what is meant by *sender* and *receiver*, because the Integration Server sends and receives messages, as do the application systems. Logically speaking, the Integration Server is situated between the application systems; therefore, we need not just one, but two communication channels: one between each application system and the Integration Server. Therefore, there are collaboration agreements that define the channel on the sender side and others that define the channel on the receiver side. Figure 6.10 illustrates this symmetry. Accordingly, there are sender and receiver agreements.

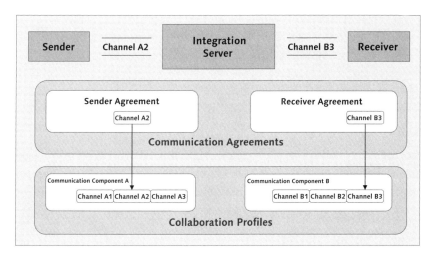

Figure 6.10 Sender and Receiver Agreement

You can see from the key fields of collaboration agreements in Table 6.2 that both the sender agreement and the receiver agreement have the sender communication component and the receiver communication component in their key. They are always intended for a communication pair, but each configures just one side of the communication with the Integration Server.

Receiver agreements are *obligatory*, because the Integration Server must know to which adapter to forward the message. The situation is different on the sender side, because the sender adapter can use information from the SLD to determine the address of the Integration Server. Section 6.4, Adapter Configuration, examines in more detail when sender agreements are necessary and why. The communication channel for the sender is also not absolutely necessary if the adapter can find the required configuration data itself.

Sender and receiver agreement

The RNIF, CIDX, XI, and marketplace adapters also support security settings (signatures, authentication). The corresponding attributes are part of the communication channel, where you define whether and which security settings are supported. You configure these settings for a specific connection in the collaboration agreement.

Security settings

Another setting that you maintain in the collaboration agreements concerns the implementation of an XML validation for receiving or sending

Settings for XML validation

183

a message. If this setting is activated, the system checks the message structure of the received messages (sender agreement) or the structure of a message to be sent to the receiver (receiver agreement).

Receiver and Interface Determination

The remaining task is to configure the logical routing. Logical routing has two steps. In the receiver determination, you define the receiver of the message, and in the interface determination you specify the inbound interfaces for the receiver. The following sections detail the various options for defining receiver and interface determinations.

Types of receiver determinations

You specify the receiver of a message in the receiver determination. You have two options:

- In a *standard receiver determination* you define one or more receiver communication components directly in the receiver determination. You can define a condition for each receiver communication component in XPath or with context objects (see Section 4.3.3, Accessing Message Fields by Using Context Objects, in Chapter 4). If you want to use a receiver more often with the same condition, we recommend that you don't maintain the condition in the receiver determination directly, but use reusable *receiver rules* (see Figure 6.11). You maintain the receiver rules as separate configuration objects in the Integration Directory, whereas you define the conditions using context objects only. In this example, the conditions are defined in the XIDemoAirlineID_all receiver rule via the AirlineID context object. Because you define the receiver rules independently of the outbound interfaces, the structure of the message isn't available. Therefore, they cannot include XPath expressions — unlike conditions in receiver determination.

- If you cannot or do not want to determine the receivers of the message in the configuration phase, you can use a *dynamic receiver determination*. For this purpose, you specify an operation mapping instead of the receiver in the receiver determination. This operation mapping is then executed at runtime, and the actual receiver is determined from a table or from the payload of the message. You define the operation mapping in advance in the Enterprise Services Builder, whereas you assign the abstract service interface, `ReceiverDetermination`, of the software component SAP BASIS (namespace *http://sap.com/xi/XI/ System*) to the operation mapping as the target interface.

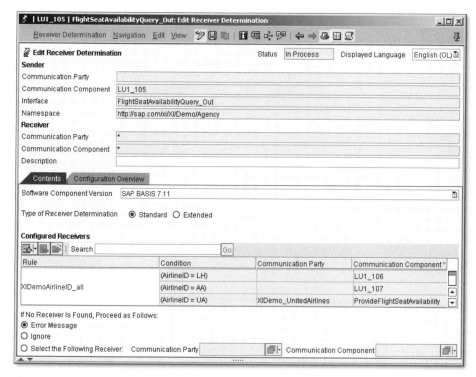

Figure 6.11 Receiver Determination with Receiver Rule

When you create a receiver determination, you must initially specify for interfaces that include multiple operations (see Section 4.1.1, Service Interface Development in the Enterprise Services Builder, in Chapter 4) whether you want to define the receiver determination operation specifically or for all operations of the interface. If you decide on an operation-specific receiver determination, you must specify one or multiple receivers or an operation mapping for receiver determination for each operation.

Operations in the receiver determinations

In a receiver determination, whether operation-specific or for all operations, you also determine what should happen to a message at runtime if no receiver can be found. For example, this can happen when you've defined conditions and the currently incoming message does not contain the application data that is required for meeting the condition. You can choose whether the message is aborted with an error, forwarded to a specific receiver, or simply canceled; in this last case, no further pipeline steps are performed, no error message is generated, and the message cannot be restarted.

There is no guaranteed receiver sequence for receiver communication components, and this is generally not important in stateless message processing. You encounter such requirements using integration processes, which are discussed in Chapter 8.

Types of interface determinations

After you've created the receiver determination, you define one or more inbound interfaces as receiver interfaces for the message in an interface determination. You have two options: a static determination where the interfaces are specified directly and a dynamic determination where the interfaces and the resulting messages are determined using multi-mappings:

▶ You use an *interface determination* to define one or more inbound interfaces as receiver interfaces for the message. You define a receiver sequence using the sequence in which you enter the inbound interfaces in the interface determination. You can change this default setting by deselecting the Maintain Order at Runtime checkbox. In this case, no order is guaranteed for the forwarding of the message. This setting makes sense if you want to avoid the case where an error in the sending of a single message impedes the sending of all subsequent messages, or if an adapter is used that does not support the processing according to the EOIO quality of service.

▶ Instead of an interface determination with predefined inbound interfaces, you can also define an *extended interface determination* by specifying a multi-mapping that is executed at runtime in the interface determination. The inbound interfaces result from the target interfaces of this multi-mapping. You use this configuration, which is also referred to as mapping-based message split, to dynamically generate multiple individual messages from one message at runtime. Chapter 5, Mappings, discussed the definition of multi-mappings.

The example in Figure 6.12 shows two receiver communication components, which are configured using a receiver determination for a sender communication component and an outbound interface. If conditions are specified in the receiver determination for the forwarding of the message, it isn't a problem if these overlap. The Integration Server copies the message for each true condition, generating a new message ID for each receiver communication component.

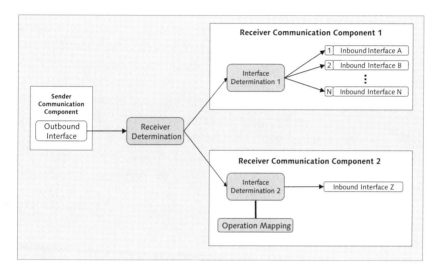

Figure 6.12 Example of Logical Routing

Whether an interface determination is required depends on the configuration scenario. If a mapping is necessary, you definitely need an interface determination to configure the selection of mapping programs. Section 5.2, Preconfiguration and Testing of Mapping Programs, in Chapter 5 showed that you can bundle mapping programs for an interface pair by using an operation mapping. If you need to use a mapping, specify the operation mapping in the interface determination. If you use an integration scenario to generate the configuration, the operation mapping is entered automatically.

Configuring mapping programs

A mapping isn't always necessary, because the sender and receiver both use the same interface technology; for example, IDoc-IDoc communication or RFC-RFC communication using the Integration Server. In these cases, the name and namespace of the interface remain the same throughout the entire message transfer, and it's therefore not necessary to determine an interface. Outbound and inbound service interfaces, however, are located in different namespaces or have different names,

187

which means an interface determination is always necessary (even if no mapping is needed).

Configuration Overview

In addition to the configuration scenarios, which bundle all of the configuration objects of a scenario together, the Integration Builder also provides a *configuration overview*. This overview focuses on all objects that are required to process and forward messages to the receiver once the inbound processing in the Integration Server is complete: the receiver determination, the interface determination, and the receiver agreement. The Integration Server first uses the sender information in the message header to determine the configured receiver or receivers (receiver determination), then uses the configured inbound interface or interfaces and a corresponding operation mapping (interface determination), and finally, uses the communication channel (receiver agreement). Figure 6.13 illustrates this relationship.

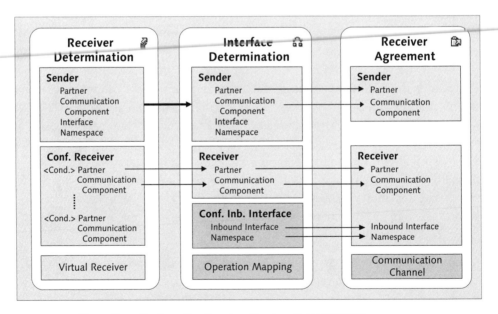

Figure 6.13   Configuration Based on Receiver Determinations

Because the processing steps proceed from the receiver determination, this is where the configuration overview is located. You can add configuration information to this table and navigate directly to the configuration objects listed there by double-clicking them.

After you've activated the configuration for a scenario, you can simulate the processing of a message based on the existing configuration data. Enter the header and the payload of the message as the input parameters. After you've implemented the *configuration test*, you can display and analyze the state after each individual step and at the end of the entire message processing.

Testing the configuration

You can start the configuration test via the TOOLS • TEST CONFIGURATION MAIN MENU. After you've entered the header data and the payload for a message transfer to be simulated, you can simulate message processing step by step or run it completely. To enter the payload of the message, you have the following options:

▶ If you have a sample payload available, you can enter it *directly* in the input field.

▶ If you have no payload available for this scenario, you can have the system generate a message from the *test tool of the mapping editor*. Section 5.2, Preconfiguration and Testing of Mapping Programs, discussed the test environment of the mapping editor.

▶ If you've already processed messages for this scenario at runtime, you can copy the payload from the *message monitoring*. Chapter 7, Section 7.4 discusses the monitoring in more detail.

After the test has been implemented, the system generates a log like the one shown in Figure 6.14. The system displays both the log of the individual pipeline steps and the payload of the message after the implementation of the corresponding pipeline step. From this log, you can double-click the corresponding configuration objects to navigate to the receiver determination, for example.

Test log

So far, we've only covered the configuration of the message exchange via the Integration Server, but there is also the option of message processing in the Advanced Adapter Engine only, which allows for better performance for specific scenarios. The following details the restrictions and the configuration.

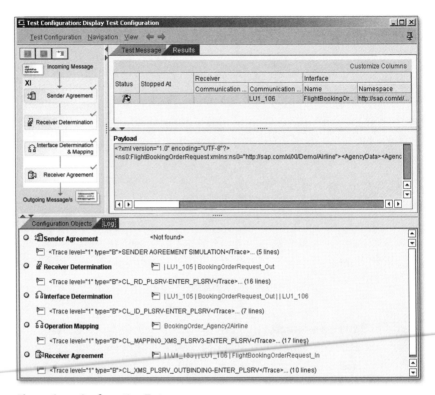

Figure 6.14 Configuration Test

6.2.3 Integrated Configuration

For example, if you require only adapters of the Advanced Adapter Engine in your communication scenario, and if the receiver is already specified at the time of configuration, you can improve the performance of the message exchange by configuring it in such a way that the message is processed only in the Advanced Adapter Engine. The configuration object for this type of configuration is called *integrated configuration*. The individual steps of message processing, for instance, the receiver and interface determination and the mapping, aren't implemented by the Integration Server, but by the Advanced Adapter Engine. Because the functionality of the Adapter Engine has been enhanced by these functions, as of SAP NetWeaver PI 7.1 it's no longer referred to as "Adapter Engine" but as "Advanced Adapter Engine."

However, because the Advanced Adapter Engine does not provide all functions of the Integration Server, there are some restrictions for this kind of communication:

▶ The Advanced Adapter Engine can process only simple 1:1 mappings; therefore, you cannot configure a dynamic receiver determination, in which the name of the receiver component isn't determined until runtime, or mapping-based message splits.

▶ Because the business process processing takes place in the Integration Server, you cannot use any integration processes as communication components.

▶ For processing in the Advanced Adapter Engine, you can only configure communication scenarios where the message is transferred only within an Adapter Engine from the sender to the receiver adapter. As a result, not all adapters are available for the integrated configuration. IDoc, XI, HTTP, RNIF, CIDX, and WS adapters aren't supported.

You can implement scenarios that require these functions or adapters only via the Integration Server.

As for configuration via the Integration Server, for the integrated configuration you first require the objects of the collaboration profile, such as parties, communication components and communication channels, the sender, and the receiver (see Section 6.1.2, First Steps in the Integration Directory). After you've defined these, you configure the message processing via the Integrated Configuration configuration object, which replaces all configuration objects that you need for the configuration of scenarios in which communication is provided with the Integration Server: sender agreement, receiver determination, interface determination, and receiver agreement.

To create the Integrated Configuration object, under Communication Agreement, select the Integrated Configuration ENTRY in the dialog and enter the communication component and the interface for the sender. After you've created the object, multiple tabs are available (as illustrated in Figure 6.15) to configure the individual processing steps in the Advanced Adapter Engine.

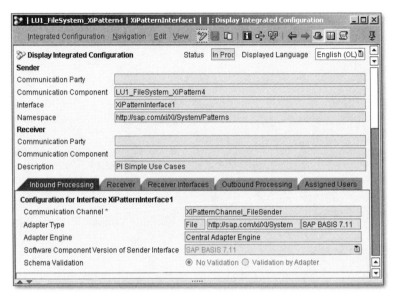

Figure 6.15 Integrated Configuration

▸ Select the communication channel of the sender in the Inbound Processing tab. Additionally, you can define whether a validation of the sent XML payload is supposed to be implemented or not. Section 7.2.2, Adapter Framework, in Chapter 7 outlines the XML validation of the Advanced Adapter Engine in more detail.

▸ Next, in the Receiver tab, you specify the possible receivers with the corresponding conditions. The conditions can be defined as XPath or using context objects. You also specify how a message is supposed to be handled at runtime when no receiver can be found (see Section 6.2.2, Overview of Configuration Object Types).

▸ In the Receiver Interfaces tab, you define the inbound interfaces and, if required, the appropriate operation mappings.

▸ In the Outbound Processing tab, you select the communication channel of the receiver. The communication channel, which you select here, must run on the same Adapter Engine as the one you used in the inbound processing, because otherwise the configuration cannot be activated.

Publishing in the Services Registry The Integrated Configuration is completely defined with these specifications and can be activated via the change list. You can publish the configuration in the Services Registry via the menu path INTEGRATED CONFIGURATION • PUBLISH IN SR to make the WSDL description available to other applications or business partners. Chapter 2, Section 2.1.2 discussed the Services Registry.

For the processing options discussed so far, however, even within an enterprise, the sender and receiver might identify the same object in different ways. If this is the case, the receiver would then incorrectly interpret the corresponding values in the message payload. The next section explains how to handle such ambiguity using SAP NetWeaver PI.

6.2.4   Value Mapping

If the same objects are identified differently at the sender and receiver sides, you need a value mapping. As you saw in Section 5.1, Mapping Programs in SAP NetWeaver PI, in Chapter 5 SAP NetWeaver PI has a value-mapping table for all value mappings. Before you learn how to enter the source and target values of an object in the table, let's take a closer look at a table entry in Figure 6.16. To illustrate this point, we've taken a fictitious table entry from the business-to-business (B2B) world. This example involves a long-serving SAP employee who orders from an online music store (Thomann) in his free time. At SAP, he is uniquely identified by his employee number (D000002). The online music store isn't aware of any employee numbers and instead identifies the same person with a customer number (05940). Though unlikely, if SAP were to offer a service whereby its employees could place orders with the online music store using a B2B application and have the payments deducted from their salaries, these values would have to be mapped to each other.

Agency	Identification Scheme	Value	Agency	Identification Scheme	Value
SAP	EmployeeId	D000002	Thomann	CustomerId	05940
...	...	...	...	...	...

| | Source Values | | | Target Values | |

Figure 6.16 Entries in the Value-Mapping Table

Identifying
representations A person is identified differently at SAP than at Thomann. This is referred to as different *representations* of the same object. The important thing is that the person in this example can be identified by the following trio:

- **Agency**
  An issuing agency, which defines how an object (in this example a person) is to be uniquely identified. In this example, the issuing agency is SAP or the online music store.

- **Identification scheme**
  The agency uses an identification scheme to identify the object. In this example, this is the employee number or the customer number.

- **Value**
  This is actual value for identification according to the conventions of the identification scheme.

You use this trio (agency, identification scheme, value) to identify the representation of an object. It's up to you which representations you use in the value-mapping table, and this depends on how the value of the representation is defined. The above example addresses cross-company communication. For internal company communication, the following cases are possible:

- The issuing agency of the representation can be determined by the application components that exchange messages with each other; for instance, SAP APO or SAP CRM.

- In a production landscape, you can identify objects by their technical unit. In this case, the agency is the name of the business system, and the identification scheme is determined by the object type (for example, the Customer object type for a business object).

Value-mapping
table If you want to execute value mappings within a Java mapping or a message mapping, you reference the values to be mapped by specifying the agency and the identification scheme in the mapping. Therefore, you need to consider how to identify values that are to be mapped at design time. You can enter the values in the value-mapping table in the following ways:

- Use the Integration Builder to enter all representations of an object in a *value-mapping group*. Create a value-mapping group and enter all representations of the same object. To display the resulting value mappings, select TOOLS • VALUE MAPPING… in the main menu.

▶ Use the ValueMappingReplication service interface that is defined in the software component version SAP Basis 7.11 in the *http://sap.com/xi/XI/System* namespace. SAP ships a Java server proxy for this inbound service interface, which executes the mass filling of the value-mapping table. For this filling, you implement the outbound side and configure the communication in exactly the same way as for any other configuration. Specify the Java proxy runtime as the communication channel that runs on the same SAP NetWeaver AS on which the Integration Server is running.

The advantage of the first method is that it has object versioning and a transport connection for value-mapping groups. In the latter method, you access the value-mapping table directly in the runtime cache of the Integration Server. Therefore, you cannot call and edit entries made in this way in the Integration Directory.

You should now understand how to configure communication via the Integration Server or the Advanced Adapter Engine, and how to integrate different types of mappings. If you require a direct connection between two systems via the Web service runtime for your scenario, you can also maintain this connection in the Integration Directory, and propagate the configuration to the sending and receiving systems. This configuration option is discussed in more detail in the next section.

6.2.5 Direct Communication

If you don't require any services of the Integration Server or the Advanced Adapter Engine — for instance, mapping — for the integration scenario to be configured, and if the systems are supposed to communicate via the Web service runtime, you can set up a *direct connection* between the communication components. You maintain the configuration centrally in the Integration Directory; the configuration settings are then distributed to the participating business systems via cache notifications when you activate the change list. AS ABAP 7.10 is the minimum requirement for the business systems to support the central configuration. If you want to directly connect older systems, you must carry out the Web service configuration locally in the systems to be connected.

To enable the distribution of the configuration to the business systems, you must first configure the connections between the system and the Integration Server:

Settings for the central configuration

▶ To be able to send the cache notification to the business system, you must define the business system in the Integration Directory. For this purpose, create the business system in the SLD and import it to the Integration Directory as described in Section 6.1.2, First Steps in the Integration Directory. As shown in Figure 6.17, in the Logon Data tab of the business system, you must then explicitly enable communication via the Web service channel, and define a service user with the password in the corresponding backend system. The SAP_XI_ID_SERV_USER_MAIN role must be assigned to this user in the backend system. Only then can the Integration Builder send a cache notification to this business system.

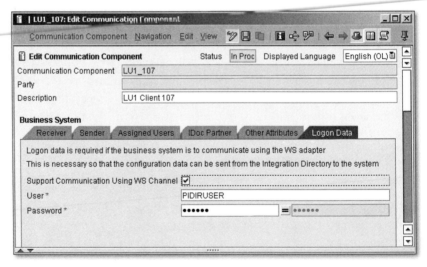

Figure 6.17 Configuration Settings for Business Systems that Communicate Via the Web Service Runtime

▶ After the notification has been sent, the business system retrieves the configuration data from the Integration Directory. This requires an

HTTP connection. You define this connection in Transaction SM59 in the business system. Create a connection with the name INTEGRA-TION_DIRECTORY_HMI of the type *HTTP connections to ABAP system*. Enter the server name and the port of the Integration Directory as the target host and the service. Use /dir/CacheRefresh as the path. Select Basic Authentication in the Logon & Security tab and enter a user who has the SAP_XI_IS_SERV_USER role in the Integration Server.

With these two settings, you have provided the basis for maintaining the configuration centrally in the Integration Directory and for distributing it to the participating systems. You only need to make the settings once for each business system that is supposed to be used in a direct connection.

After you've defined these default settings, you can concentrate on the configuration of the direct connection. To create a direct connection, you use the following configuration objects:

Configuration

▶ You've already defined the *business systems* required for the scenario with the default settings.

▶ You need a receiver communication channel of the WS type for the connection to the receiver business system. You may need to create it, or, because you can use a receiver channel for multiple direct connections, it may already be available in the Integration Directory.

▶ To define the direct connection, use the Direct Connection configuration object. Enter the sender and the receiver communication component and the sender interface as the key for the direct connection. Select the receiver interface and the receiver communication channel in the direct connection. You can also specify adapter-specific attributes, such as the proxy and the timeout settings.

After you've activated the change list, the system distributes the configuration data to the two business systems used in the direct connection, and the connection can be used.

So far, you've learned about the configuration of internal company processes; the following section discusses the specific features of cross-company processes in more detail.

6.3 Configuring Cross-Company Processes

When configuring cross-company processes, you must consider the following additional configuration requirements:

▸ The enterprises must be able to be addressed as the sender and receiver of messages.

▸ Each enterprise has an internal system landscape, which must not be revealed during communication with business partners.

▸ More importance is placed on standard protocols than in internal company communication.

B2B configuration using integration scenarios

As you saw in Section 6.2.1, Configuration Using Integration Scenarios, using an integration scenario from the Enterprise Services Builder simplifies configuration considerably. The same is true for cross-company configuration scenarios. The only prerequisite is that you must identify the application components of your business partner as B2B components in the integration scenario (see Section 6.3.1, From Internal to Cross-Company Communication). Like in internal company communication, the Integration Builder guides you through the configuration procedure and generates the missing objects automatically. Therefore, Section 6.3.1 just looks at the additional steps and differences in cross-company communication and does not cover the individual configuration steps. It's assumed that both business partners use SAP NetWeaver PI.

If your business partner does not have SAP NetWeaver PI, this does not make any difference to the configuration on your side of the communication. Your business partner has the following options:

▸ The business partner supports a standard protocol that SAP NetWeaver PI also supports; for example, RNIF 2.0. Section 6.5 looks at adapters for industry standards.

▸ The business partner uses the *Partner Connectivity Kit* (PCK), which provides a limited selection of SAP NetWeaver PI features and is a more cost-effective alternative for small business partners. Section 6.3.2 looks at the PCK in more detail.

XI log

In addition, the Integration Server in SAP NetWeaver PI 7.1 understands the message protocol of the Integration Server in legacy SAP NetWeaver

PI or SAP NetWeaver XI releases; Figure 6.18 provides an overview of the possible variants. To understand the figure, you must note that SAP NetWeaver XI 2.0 uses an older XI protocol, the XI 2.0 protocol; as of SAP NetWeaver XI 3.0, all SAP NetWeaver XI and SAP NetWeaver PI releases use the XI 3.0 protocol.

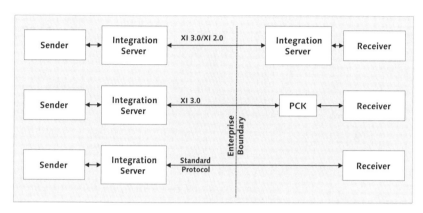

Figure 6.18 Variants of Cross-Company Communication

6.3.1 From Internal to Cross-Company Communication

In internal company communication, you work with communication components in the configuration that reference either business systems or integration processes. In cross-company communication, the company itself must also be addressed. To consider this in the configuration, we first have to clarify how to identify companies independently from SAP NetWeaver PI.

If two business partners want to exchange messages, they can simply agree on corresponding technical names (SAP, Bosch, ALDI). This is further simplified if all involved parties have a central agency issue an ID for their enterprise. To do this, they contact the agency to identify a company for the purposes of electronic message exchange. Unfortunately, this tried and tested method has one drawback: Several agencies issue such IDs on a worldwide scale, so the IDs alone aren't unique. The following are examples of issuing agencies:

▶ 016: D-U-N-S — Data Universal Numbering System
   (Dun & Bradstreet Corporation)

Identifiers for enterprises

▸ 009: EAN — International Article Numbering Association

▸ 166: NMFTA — National Motor Freight Traffic Association

As you can see from the list, issuing agencies are also numbered. Fortunately, there is only one agency that issues IDs for issuing agencies[2], so this does not cause an additional problem. Therefore, each enterprise has an issuing agency identify it via the identification scheme used by the agency and a value. (This is exactly the same as the trio that you encountered in value mapping in Section 6.2.3, Integrated Configuration.) This trio is referred to as an *identifier*.

Normalization to SAP NetWeaver PI Party

During configuration in the Integration Builder, you address companies by using the *communication party* object. The name of this object is required only within SAP NetWeaver PI, and must be unique there. Specify alternative identifiers for this communication party (for example, BOSCH), which can be used to identify the enterprise. This makes the following conversion possible:

▸ **Normalization**
If the Integration Server receives a message with an identifier for a company (for example, a D-U-N-S number), it can map it to the communication party in SAP NetWeaver PI.

▸ **Denormalization**
During configuration, you can stipulate which identifier the Integration Server writes in the message header before it forwards the message. In this way, the communication party in SAP NetWeaver PI is mapped to an identifier in the message header.

Identifiers in the communication channel Select which identifier to send in the communication channel for the receiver (Identifiers tab). This conversion means you have to reference the communication party object, or party for short, only when configuring a cross-company process, and all possible identifiers are automatically included. However, some protocols have exceptions or enhancements, and these are listed below:

---

2 All issuing agencies are listed in the code list DE3055, which is managed by UN/EDIFACT (*www.unece.org/trade/untdid/welcome.htm*).

- In IDoc communication, you can work with IDoc partners. These must, in turn, be mapped to the communication party (see Section 6.4.2, Special Features of the RFC and IDoc Adapters).

- The RFC adapter uses the SAP system ID and the client as alternative identifiers to map sending or receiving business systems to communication components in the Integration Directory. Section 6.4.2 includes a detailed explanation on this topic.

- Communication parties aren't common practice for communication with marketplaces. Instead, the marketplace adapter works with a *Document Destination ID* (DDID) to address the senders and receivers. You map the DDID to any communication component in the Integration Directory by entering it using the editor menu path SERVICE • ADAPTER-SPECIFIC IDENTIFIER.

We'll now return to the general procedure and examine how you can provide communication components to your business partner without revealing details about your internal system landscape.

Business Components for Business Partners

To address communication components independently of the system landscape, you work with business components. Like all communication components, you can define business components with or without a party. The important thing is that the business component assumes the role of an alias for the business system. If business partners exchange messages using SAP NetWeaver PI, you simply reference the business component. The names of the business components then appear in the message header instead of the names of the internal systems.

How do you configure this alias? As shown in Figure 6.19, each business partner has its own configuration area. Let's consider the configuration for the configuration area of Party A. Party B makes the configuration settings in the same way on the other side (when we refer to Party A and Party B, in regular font, in the following, we're referring to the person making the configuration settings, not the configuration object).

Party A uses business component A to mask its internal systems and exchanges messages with the business component B of Party B. Therefore, it must create both business components in its Integration Directory

Business components

(Party B configures business services *with the same name* in its configuration area). To set the alias to the internal systems, it assigns business component A to one or more business systems during configuration.[3] It must also configure the technical details of the message exchange by using communication channels:

▸ Because business service A has been assigned to the business system, you can use the communication channels of these communication components.

▸ Party B must let Party A know how to access business component B (address of the Integration Server or PCK). Party A uses this information to create a communication channel of adapter type XI. Party A can also enter all relevant interfaces in business component B.

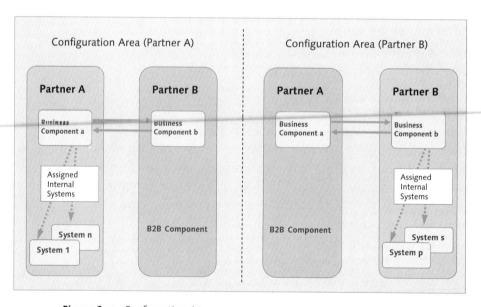

Figure 6.19 Configuration Areas

Virtual receiver and header mapping

Let's assume that Party A sends a message to Party B and receives a message from Party B. Table 6.4 shows the attributes that the Integration

---

3 This is only possible when using an integration scenario. If there is no integration scenario, Party A must make the settings described below manually.

Builder generates in the receiver agreement and the receiver determination for the B2B-specific configuration.

Step	Configuration Object: Attribute	Use
Send	Receiver agreement: Header mapping	Converts the sender business system to the business component A and the communication party Party A.
Receive	Receiver determination: Virtual receiver	Logical routing of business component B to the internal business systems (receiver-dependent routing)

Table 6.4 Converting Business Components and Business Systems

You may have looked at the overview of the key fields and wondered why you can enter receiver information in the key field of the receiver determination (see Table 6.3 in Section 6.2.2, Overview of Configuration Object Types). Specify a *virtual* receiver in the key field in the receiver determination to hide the *actual* receiver from outside parties. When sending, on the other hand, you must adapt the message header with a header mapping.

Moreover, if the payload contains the business component and the communication party, you can configure the header mapping in such a way that the values are read from the payload at runtime. This is just one way to enhance the static routing configuration dynamically. In Chapter 7, Section 7.3, you'll see that the proxy runtime provides other methods for this purpose.

Payload-based routing

Header mapping and denormalization both modify the message header in the following order: First, you can use the header mapping to modify sender and receiver information, which you can then denormalize to an alternative identifier. Whether you need to do both depends on the application case. In addition to the mapping of business systems to business components, you also use header mappings to delete or insert a communication party in the header, depending on whether the receiving adapter type requires this modification. If you don't use a header mapping or normalization, the Integration Server leaves the sender information as is when it receives the message.

Header mapping and denormalization

We've now covered the central concepts of configuration. Of course, you may still have questions relating to specific configuration scenarios, but the sections in this chapter thus far have provided you with an understanding of how to use the individual configuration objects. Before we turn our attention to the differences between the various adapter types in Section 6.4, Adapter Configuration, the following section discusses the Partner Connectivity Kit (PCK) as an addition to the central functions of SAP NetWeaver PI.

6.3.2 Partner Connectivity Kit

SAP NetWeaver PI is a comprehensive solution for exchanging messages. However, in some cases, the advantages of SAP NetWeaver PI don't justify the costs and effort required to install and run it; for example:

▸ A large enterprise has a head office and several smaller branch offices, which are separate organizational units in different geographical locations. At the head office, systems are integrated using SAP NetWeaver PI. The branch offices need to exchange messages only with the head office.

▸ A large enterprise that uses SAP NetWeaver PI wants to exchange messages with a smaller enterprise. To make this message exchange possible, the smaller enterprise needs only a selection of the SAP NetWeaver PI functions.

PCK areas of operation — SAP provides the PCK as a supplementary solution for such cases. SAP NetWeaver PI and the PCK are based on the same technology, although the features of the PCK are limited to smaller areas of operation:

▸ The PCK always forwards messages to an Integration Server and receives messages from an Integration Server. Therefore, you cannot use the PCK to exchange messages directly between two application systems.

▸ The PCK has the same interface as the Integration Builder, but the features are restricted to mappings (message, XSLT, and Java mappings) and the necessary configuration objects. No SLD is required.

▸ The PCK does not contain any routing logic. Each message can have only one receiver: either the Integration Server (send) or an application system that is connected using an adapter supported by the PCK. Mappings are supported in the PCK.

▸ The PCK offers the following adapters: file/FTP, JDBC, JMS, SOAP, RFC, BC, and mail adapter (see also Section 6.4.1). Customers can license additional SAP adapters or non-SAP adapters. The PCK uses the SAP NetWeaver XI adapter (SAP NetWeaver XI 3.0 protocol) to communicate with the Integration Server.

▸ If you have a development license, you can use the PCK to develop your own adapters for your system landscape.

Due to the limited features in the PCK, you work with fewer configuration objects than in SAP NetWeaver PI: communication party, business component, communication channel, mapping objects, and sender and receiver agreement. Additionally, you can specify the inbound interface and a mapping program in the receiver agreement in the PCK. Because the PCK does not support routing, the receiver agreement determines the receiver of the message directly. Therefore, the receiver determination and the interface determination that you know from the configuration of the Integration Server aren't required in the PCK. Let's take a brief look at configuration in the PCK with the help of the configuration objects in Figure 6.20.

Configuration objects in the PCK

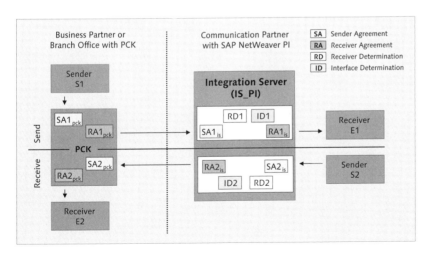

Figure 6.20 Configuration with the PCK

To understand the configuration procedure in the PCK, it helps to imagine the Integration Server as the receiver application system and the PCK as the Integration Server. You configure the sender and receiver agreement between sender S1 and the Integration Server IS_PI accordingly (in this and the following step, whether or not you need the sender agreements SA1pck, SA1is, SA2is, and SA2pck depends on the adapter type and on the encryption requirements). To understand the configuration in the Integration Server, on the other hand, it helps to imagine the PCK as an application system and to make the configuration settings for forwarding the message normally using the receiver and interface determination. If you do this, a message from sender S1 is forwarded to the receiver R1 using the PCK and the Integration Server. Because there are the two intermediate stations (PCK and Integration Server), the specification of senders and receivers in the collaboration agreement is a little more complex. Therefore, the specifications are summarized in Table 6.5 (to keep matters simple, the table is limited to the specification of S1, R1, S2, R2, and IS_XI instead of using the communication party and service). The direction is from the perspective of the PCK.

Direction	Collaboration Agreements	Sender	Receiver
Send	SA1pck, RA1pck	S1	**IS_PI**
	SA1is, RA1is	S1	R1
Receive	SA2is, RA2is	S2	R2
	SA2pck, RA2pck	S2	R2

Table 6.5 Sender and Receiver for Each Configuration Area

It's notable that the PCK specifies the Integration Server (in bold) as the communication party when sending to the Integration Server, but not in the receive direction. This is because the Integration Server sets the receiver in the message header but leaves the sender unchanged. In addition, the Integration Server and the PCK address each other using a corresponding communication channel.

PCK simple use cases
To get you started with the PCK configuration, SAP provides PCK simple use cases, and you use these examples to configure and execute basic communication scenarios. The content, mapping programs, and test files, which are required for the configuration and execution of the simple use

cases, are provided in addition to the configuration guideline in the SDN. The scenarios enable you to become familiar with the SAP Partner Connectivity Kit and to perform tests. They aren't intended for use in production. Detailed documentation is available on the configuration and execution of the individual scenarios.[4] Now that you an understanding of the PCK, let's examine the details of adapter configuration.

6.4 Adapter Configuration

Adapters convert a transport protocol and a message format to the XI protocol, and vice versa. This section does not cover every attribute of the individual adapters but instead focuses on a few common features that are relevant to the configuration in the Integration Builder.

6.4.1 Overview

Section 1.3.1, Communication Using the Integration Server, in Chapter 1 discussed the adapter architecture and strategy. The open architecture allows partners and customers to develop their own adapters and configure them centrally in the Integration Builder. This poses the question of how to describe the interface for configuring such adapters in the Integration Directory, because after the SAP NetWeaver PI installation, the Integration Builder does not yet know these adapters. You enter the relevant information in the Enterprise Services Builder, and it's evaluated in the Integration Directory. You use adapter metadata to define the attributes that the adapter can handle and what the corresponding configuration interface looks like. SAP provides adapter metadata for adapters that they ship.[5]

This section focuses on the adapter types that SAP ships with SAP NetWeaver PI. Table 6.6 gives an overview of the adapters shipped with SAP NetWeaver PI 7.1.

---

4 For further information, refer to the SDN at *https://www.sdn.sap.com/irj/sdn/soa-servicebus* via the menu path GETTING STARTED • GETTING STARTED DOCUMENTS.

5 With SAP NetWeaver PI 7.1 in software component versions SAP BASIS 7.10 and SAP BASIS 7.11 in the namespace http://sap.com/xi/XI/System.

Adapter Type	Transport Protocol	Message Protocol
XI	HTTP(S)	XI 2.0, XI 3.0
IDoc	Sender adapters: tRFC, file Receiver adapter: tRFC (no sender channel configuration)	IDoc-XML
RFC	RFC	RFC-XML
SOAP	Sender channel: HTTP Receiver channel: HTTP(S), SMTP(S)	SOAP 1.1
HTTP	HTTP(S) (no sender channel configuration)	XI payload in HTTP body
File	File system (NFS), FTP (via SSL/TLS)	File
JDBC	JDBC 2.0	XML insert format, XML SQL format, native SQL string
JMS	SonicMQ MS Provider, WebSphereMQ (MQ Series) JMS Provider, JNDI JMS Provider Lookup, JMS Provider Administrator Object via File, generic JMS Provider	JMS1.x
Marketplace	HTTP(S), JMS Sonic MQ35	MML
RNIF	HTTP(S)	RNIF 2.0
Mail	Sender channel: IMAP4, POP3 Receiver channel: SMTP, IMAP4	XIALL, XIPAYLOAD
BC (Business Connector)	HTTP(S)	RFC-XML with envelope, IDoc-XML

Table 6.6   Adapter Types

Let's now take a more detailed look at some of the configuration aspects that apply to several of the aforementioned adapter types.

Central and Non-Central Advanced Adapter Engine (All Adapter Types Except IDoc)

With the exception of the XI, HTTP, and IDoc adapters, all adapters in Table 6.6 run on the Advanced Adapter Engine, which you install centrally on the Integration Server or deploy non-centrally on a separate SAP

NetWeaver AS Java system. The latter case is recommended when you want or need the Advanced Adapter Engine to run in close proximity to the business system, whether for organizational or technical reasons (for example, operating system requirements for backend-specific drivers such as JDBC or JMS or performance or memory requirements). You select the Adapter Engine in the communication channel. The Adapter Engine will be responsible for inbound or outbound processing on the Integration Server.

Obligatory Sender Agreement (File/JMS/JDBC)

To process a message at the inbound channel of the Integration Server, the Integration Server retrieves the required information from the message header at runtime and evaluates the existing configuration data. To do this, the Integration Server needs information about the sender interface and the interface namespace, among other things. However, sender file, sender JMS, and sender JDBC adapters cannot provide this information, because the protocols don't require an interface. Therefore, the corresponding fields in the message header are empty. To enable messages to be exchanged, you must therefore configure the missing information in the Integration Directory:

▸ A sender channel that has exactly one sender agreement.

▸ A sender interface (name and namespace) and a sender communication component in the sender agreement. You are free to choose these values. The remaining fields in the sender agreement are optional.

The aforementioned entries are mandatory to configure the sender file, sender JMS, and sender JDBC adapters. All other adapter types in Table 6.6 provide the necessary information in the message header. An example of when the sender channel and sender agreement are necessary for these adapters is when you need to make message security settings on the sender side.

It isn't absolutely necessary to have an interface for outbound processing in the Integration Server. Therefore, you can enter an asterisk (*) as a generic interface in the receiver agreement instead, so that the receiver is determined only by the communication component. However, if you want to execute a mapping before outbound processing, this changes

Configuring outbound processing

209

matters. Because mapping programs are referenced using operation mappings, you need an interface on the receiver side (see Section 5.2, Preconfiguration and Testing of Mapping Programs, in Chapter 5) at design time. Because no such interface exists for the file, JMS, and JDBC adapters, you can use an abstract service interface to help you. This interface type is an option, because the interface is intended only for operation mapping, not for implementation in an application system with proxies, which don't exist for these adapter types.

Security Settings

There are various factors to consider in the configuration of security settings. Most adapters support authentication in the receiver system using logon data (XI, SOAP, RNIF, RFC, Marketplace, Mail, JDBC, HTTP, BC). Some adapters also support HTTPS and, in some cases, message security. The XI, SOAP, RFC, and Web service adapters also support the method known as *principal propagation* to forward user IDs.

HTTPS (XI, HTTP, Marketplace, RNIF, CIDX, BC, WS)

HTTPS is HTTP with the additional support of a *secure sockets layer* (SSL) and relates to security on the transport level. HTTPS is part of the transport protocol and is therefore configured in the communication channel. If you select HTTPS as the Transport Protocol in the receiver channel, you must specify a corresponding HTTPS port in the Service Number input field of the channel. You also have to configure this HTTPS port in AS ABAP (for the Integration Server) and in the receiver to be able to use the required certificates.

You enter an HTTP destination, which you specify in Transaction SM59 in the Integration Server, for receiving and sending messages in the HTTP adapter, and you must specify whether HTTP or HTTPS is to be used for this destination.

HTTPS in the sender channel

When you look at the configuration of other adapters, at first it may strike you as odd that the RNIF adapter and the CIDX adapter are the only adapters for which you can specify HTTPS as the transport protocol both for the sender channel and for the receiver channel. For all other adapters this is only possible in the receiver channel. Does this mean the other adapters can only send HTTPS and not receive it? The answer is no. To help you understand, let's compare the SAP XI adapter with the RNIF adapter:

▶ For the SAP XI adapter, it's always AS ABAP or Java that sends messages to the Integration Server. Because AS ABAP and AS Java support the HTTPS protocol (ICF framework), you configure the HTTPS protocol there as well.

▶ The standardized message exchange of RNIF requires the RNIF adapter to respond to an external partner with a signal as soon as a message arrives at the Integration Server. To send this signal using HTTPS, you choose HTTPS in the sender agreement in the RNIF adapter. The sender channel of the RNIF adapter therefore has an outbound semantic for sending this signal. The same applies to the CIDX adapter because it also uses the RNIF protocol.

With HTTPS, security can be guaranteed only at the transport level; that is, for the transfer path. The message content continues to be visible to the receiver (in a trace, for example).

Message Security (XI, HTTP, SOAP, RNIF, CIDX, WS)

The next level of security settings is at the message level. To configure message security, you specify whether it's required in the SAP XI or RNIF communication channel. Because the sender and receiver always agree on signatures and encryptions, you specify the actual certificates, views, and so on in the collaboration agreement. Therefore, the configuration settings in the communication channel represent a sort of declaration of intent, and the collaboration agreement references the algorithms to be used.

Principal Propagation (XI, SOAP, RFC, WS)

The forwarding of user IDs from the sender system via the Integration Server for the logon to the receiver system is referred to as principal propagation. For the XI, SOAP, and RFC adapters, you configure the forwarding via authentication assertion tickets; in a communication via the WS adapter, the configuration is based on *Security Assertion Markup Language* (SAML). In both methods, you first configure the backend systems involved in this communication and then activate the principal propagation in the sender and receiver agreement. It's also possible for the forwarding of user IDs to be based on SAML at the inbound channel of the Integration Server and on the authentication assertion ticket at the outbound channel, or vice versa. Note that the checkbox for activating the forwarding of user IDs is only displayed if you use a communication channel with the appropriate adapter type in the sender or receiver agreement.

To explain all of the properties of the individual adapters would exceed the scope of this book. Therefore, the next section focuses on a few special features of the RFC and IDoc adapters. Because the RNIF adapter and the CIDX adapter are conceptually different from all other adapter types, they are addressed separately in Section 6.5, Adapters for Industry Standards.

6.4.2 Special Features of the RFC and IDoc Adapters

The RFC adapter converts an RFC call to RFC-XML and sends it to the Integration Server. Conversely, the RFC adapter receives RFC-XML from the Integration Server and then generates an RFC at the receiver. Correspondingly, in communication with the IDoc adapter, the Integration Server sends and receives IDoc-XML.

This section does not explain how to configure the RFC and IDoc adapters to exchange messages with the Integration Server. Instead, it looks at how the adapters map the information to the configuration objects of the Integration Directory in an RFC or IDoc. It will become clear from this explanation just how you can configure the message exchange with these adapters in the Integration Directory.

Mapping Logical Systems to Communication Components

During configuration in the Integration Directory, you work with communication components. The Integration Server expects information in the message header about which communication component has sent the message and uses the configuration data to assign a receiver communication component. But how does the name of the communication component get into the message header?

In the previous section, you saw that you must configure a sender channel and a sender agreement for sender file, sender JMS, and sender JDBC
adapters to add to the message header. This isn't necessary in RFC and
IDoc adapters, because the adapters can determine the service name by
using an *adapter-specific identifier*. The following identifiers exist for RFC
and IDoc adapters:

▸ **SAP system ID and client**
SAP systems set the system ID (for example, U6X) and the client (for
example, 105) in the RFC or IDoc control record.

▸ **Logical system**
This field can be set freely by external IDoc senders. The field isn't
evaluated if SAP systems are communicating with the Integration
Server.

The RFC and IDoc adapters can access these identifiers and map them to
communication components as follows:

1. The SAP system ID, client, and logical system are available in the
sender SAP system and in the SLD. They are attributes of the business
system that you've configured (see Section 6.1.1, Settings in the System Landscape Directory). When a business system from the SDL is
assigned to another business system, the Integration Directory transfers the identifiers from the SLD to the Integration Directory. To view
which identifiers have been transferred from the SLD for the communication component, select SERVICE • ADAPTER-SPECIFIC IDENTIFIERS.

2. Sender SAP systems set the SAP system ID and the client in the RFC
or IDoc control record at runtime. External IDoc senders set the logical system.

3. RFC and IDoc adapters read the adapter-specific identifiers from the
runtime cache that is filled from the Integration Directory when activating the change list and compare them with the information from
the RFC or IDoc control record. The adapter determines the communication component name in this way and writes it in the message
header.

To map the identifiers to the communication component, it's sufficient
to have entered the business system in the SLD. Therefore, the adapter-

specific identifiers in the Integration Builder are read-only. By using the menu options from the first step, you can not only view the identifiers for the RFC and IDoc adapters, but also enter a DDID identifier for the marketplace adapter. This identifier cannot be entered in the SLD and fulfils the same purpose as the identifiers for the RFC and IDoc adapters.

Mapping IDoc Partners to SAP NetWeaver PI Parties

Section 6.3.1, From Internal to Cross-Company Communication, showed that the Integration Server normalizes identifiers from external business partners to the SAP NetWeaver PI party so that it only has to reference this SAP NetWeaver PI party in the configuration. In the IDoc world, you can use partner types for a message exchange using EDI; for example, logical system (LS), customer (KU), or vendor (LI). If IDoc communication is to take place using the Integration Server, the following differentiation is important:

▸ IDoc partners of type LS exchange messages with the Integration Server at the communication component level. In this case, the IDoc adapter leaves the communication party field in the message header empty. The mapping to the communication component was covered in the previous section.

▸ For all other IDoc partner types, the IDoc adapter generates an alternative identifier for the external party in the message header, according to the following rules:

▸ The name of the sender communication component (determined as described in the previous section) determines the issuing agency. Example: U8R_106.

▸ The name for the identification scheme is formed from the partner type and, optionally, the partner role, thus ALE#<Partner type> or ALE#<Partner type>#<Partner role>. Example: ALE#KU.

▸ The partner number of the IDoc is taken as the partner name. Example: 0000010053.

To map IDoc partners of this latter type to SAP NetWeaver PI parties, proceed as described in the Normalization to SAP NetWeaver PI Party section, in Section 6.3.1. Enter the alternative identifier generated by the IDoc adapter in the SAP NetWeaver PI communication party to which the IDoc partner is to be mapped. Select the identification scheme that should later be sent in the outbound processing of the Integration Server in the communication channel.

An additional factor to consider is that, unlike external business partners, partner types in IDoc communication are used for internal company scenarios. If you map IDoc partners to SAP NetWeaver PI parties, you must therefore assign a business system communication component to the SAP NetWeaver PI party by creating the business system communication component at the SAP NetWeaver PI party. (This is one of the few cases where a business system and communication party are required in the key in configuration.) In Figure 6.21, the business system service, U8R_106, is assigned to the IDocPartner SAP NetWeaver PI party. The key of this communication component therefore consists of both fields.

SAP NetWeaver PI party with business system

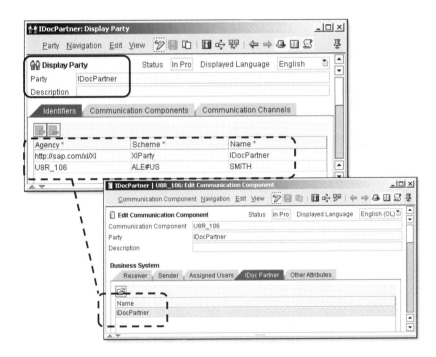

Figure 6.21 Business System with SAP NetWeaver PI Party for IDoc

The Integration Builder uses the alternative identifiers in the SAP NetWeaver PI parties to determine which SAP NetWeaver PI parties

Example

reference the service U8R_106 and lists them in the IDoc Partner tab of the service (in this example, IDocPartner).

In the example[6] shown in Figure 6.22, two IDoc partners with a partner type other than LS (logical system) exchange IDocs using the Integration Server.

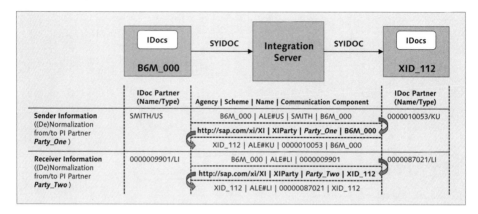

Figure 6.22 Case Example for (De)normalization with IDocs

In B6M_000, the sender party is registered as user SMITH, and in XID_112 it's registered as a customer with the customer number 0000010053. To map the sender parties to one another, proceed as follows:

1. Create a Party_One communication party in the Integration Directory and assign the business system B6M_000 to this party.

2. Enter the alternative IDoc partners for the sender under Alternative Identifiers for the Party_One communication party: B6M_000 | ALE#US | SMITH and XID_112 | ALE#KU | 0000010053. This enables the Integration Server to recognize during inbound processing that the message with the sender information B6M_000 | ALE#US | SMITH | B6M_000 belongs to the communication party Party_One | B6M_000 (normalization).

---

6 You can find this and other configuration scenarios on IDocs in the SAP Developer Network (SDN) at *https://www.sdn.sap.com/irj/sdn/howtoguides* via the menu path END-TO-END PROCESS INTEGRATION • ENABLING APPLICATION-TO-APPLICATION PROCESSES • HOW TO SAMPLE IDOC-XI SCENARIOS.

3. In the receiver channel for the connection, select the agency XID_112 and the scheme ALE#KU for the sender. As a result of this setting, the Integration Server writes the sender XID_112 | ALE#KU | 0000010053 | B6M_000 in the message header (denormalization).

In the same way, you must create a Party_Two communication party for the mapping of the receiver parties. Select scheme XID_112 | ALE#LI in the same receiver channel as in step 3.

The sender and receiver in this example are identified by different IDoc partners. To conclude this section, we draw your attention to a similar IDoc scenario: If the receiver in this example was an IDoc partner of type LS (logical system), you would have to delete the sender and receiver party from the message header for the receiver system XID_112. In this case, instead of denormalizing using the receiver channel, you would use a header mapping (receiver agreement) to map these fields to empty values. **IDocs without partners**

Once again, you can see that the functions in the Integration Builder support as many configuration scenarios as possible. Unfortunately, we can't describe them all in this book. Before you learn about the transport of configuration data in Section 6.6, Transports Between the Test and Production Landscapes, the next section addresses one final scenario: using the RNIF adapter to support the RosettaNet industry standard.

6.5   Adapters for Industry Standards

If two business partners want to exchange data with one another, they must use the same data exchange format. The business partners must also negotiate aspects such as data security and the data exchange procedure until they reach an agreement. Coordinating these issues can involve considerable costs, and consequently, an increasing number of industries are cooperating to agree on standards for data exchange.

In the high-tech industry, RosettaNet is a consortium of world-leading companies in the information technology, electronic component, semiconductor manufacturing, and telecommunication sectors. This self-funded consortium produces industry-wide, open e-business process **RosettaNet** standards for harmonizing processes between supply-chain partners worldwide.

Chem eStandards Like the RosettaNet standards for the high-tech industry, the Chem eStandards of *Chemical Industry Data Exchange* (CIDX) are available for the chemical industry.[7] CIDX, or — since early 2009 — *Open Applications Group* (OAGi), is a membership-based organization that provides standards for e-commerce in the chemical industry on behalf of the chemical sector. The CIDX adapter that is available in SAP NetWeaver PI 7.1 is based on the Chem eStandards encryption and security specifications that, with specific deviations, refer to an extended subarea of RosettaNet Implementation Framework Version 1.1. The following section discusses the RosettaNet and Chem eStandards and examines how they are supported in SAP NetWeaver PI.

6.5.1 RosettaNet Standards

RosettaNet has adopted the following specifications (presented here in a simplified version) to define standards:[8]

► **Partner Interface Processes (PIPs)**
RosettaNet models processes in a supply chain based on PIPs. A PIP specifies how business partners interact in different roles (for example, buyer and seller). This specification includes the sequence and content of the messages to be exchanged and the duration, security settings, and authentication of the interactions.

► **RosettaNet Implementation Framework (RNIF)**
PIPs are executed using the RosettaNet Implementation Framework. The RNIF specification determines the message exchange protocol at the transport, routing, packaging, and transaction level, irrespective of the content of the messages to be exchanged. There are two RNIF versions: 1.1 and 2.0. Accordingly, in SAP NetWeaver PI there are two RNIF adapters: RNIF 1.1 adapter and RNIF 2.0 adapter.

---

7   For more information, refer to the CIDX and OAGi websites: *http://www.cidx.org* and *http://www.oagi.org*.

8   For more information, see the RosettaNet homepage at *http://www.rosettanet.org*.

The RosettaNet standards do more than merely define a message protocol; a PIP also determines the sequence of multiple messages. Before we examine the implications of using RosettaNet with SAP NetWeaver PI, let's take a closer look at PIPs.

A PIP describes a business transaction that is part of a higher-level process. For organizational purposes, PIPs are divided into clusters and segments representing the corresponding business areas. Figure 6.23 shows an example for PIP3A4. Various PIPs are required to execute a higher-level process. Therefore, the complexity of a PIP is relatively low.

PIPs

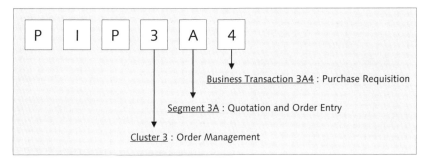

Figure 6.23 Naming Conventions for PIPs

RosettaNet defines the content of a PIP using *Document Type Definitions* (DTDs), which belong to the PIP. A PIP also describes the sequence of messages for the particular business case. There are two types of messages:

▶ **RosettaNet action messages**
These messages are defined and are part of the PIP. They contain the business data, for example, for a purchase order.

▶ **RosettaNet signal messages**
These messages are confirmations of RosettaNet action messages. As a rule, they are asynchronous.

The message sequence always follows the same pattern, specified in RNIF 1.1 and 2.0: There are synchronous and asynchronous *single-action* and *two-action* patterns. Figure 6.24 shows the model for the exchange of asynchronous messages. Communication parties that support RNIF must be able to assume the role of both initiator and responder.

Single-action and two-action patterns

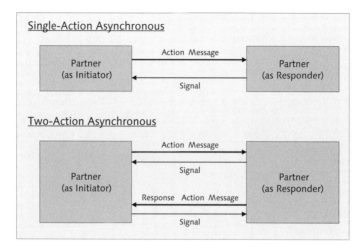

Figure 6.24 Asynchronous Single-Action and Two-Action Patterns

Keeping these basic points in mind, let's look at how SAP NetWeaver PI supports the execution of PIPs.

6.5.2 RosettaNet Support with SAP NetWeaver PI

RosettaNet communication with SAP NetWeaver PI

To start, let's clarify what it means for an SAP customer to have SAP NetWeaver PI support the RosettaNet standards. Figure 6.25 shows the implementation of RosettaNet communication with SAP NetWeaver PI as an extension of Figure 6.24.

▶ The business partner exchanges messages using RosettaNet standards. To do this, it communicates using the RNIF adapter of the Integration Server as if it were any other communication party that supports RNIF 1.1 or 2.0.

▶ A customer that uses SAP NetWeaver PI can offer a business partner message exchange using RosettaNet for certain SAP applications. The SAP application must meet the following requirements:

  ▶ It must provide interfaces that can be mapped to the interfaces specified by the corresponding PIP.

  ▶ It must provide the mapping programs required for this mapping.

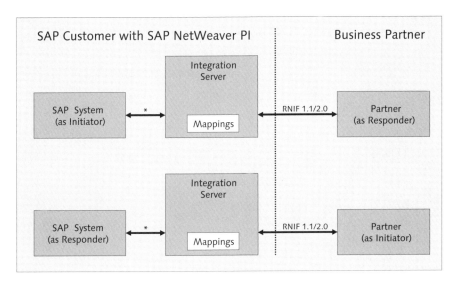

Figure 6.25   RNIF Communication with SAP NetWeaver PI

Any message protocol can be used between the SAP system and the Integration Server, but it must be converted to RNIF for the business partner. To date, SAP NetWeaver PI supports only asynchronous single-action or two-action process types.

Regarding the basic principle, additional design objects and the RNIF adapter are required to support a RosettaNet standard. It's SAP's responsibility to develop these design objects and ship them as SAP NetWeaver PI content of the Enterprise Services Builder. For this purpose, SAP offers its customers *SAP business packages*, which contain the following:

SAP business package for RosettaNet

▸ Integration scenarios for selected PIPs

▸ Interfaces and mappings of the SAP application that customers use to implement the RNIF communication for selected PIPs

▸ Communication channel templates, which considerably simplify the configuration of the RosettaNet scenario

Table 6.7 lists all PIPs that are contained in the current SAP business package.

PIP	Business Case
PIP0A1	Notification of Failure
PIP2A12	Distribute Product Master Notification
PIP3A4	Request Purchase Order
PIP3A7	Notify of Purchase Order Update
PIP3A8	Request Purchase Order Change
PIP3A9	Request Purchase Order Cancellation
PIP3B2	Notify of Advance Shipment
PIP3B12	Request Shipping Order
PIP3C3	Notify of Invoice
PIP3C4	Reject Invoice
PIP3C6	Notify of Remittance Advice

Table 6.7 PIPs of the SAP Business Package for Industry Standards

Now we'll use an example to illustrate how RNIF communication is modeled using integration scenarios in the SAP business package. Each PIP has three integration scenarios:

▶ One integration scenario in which the RosettaNet standard is modeled. This integration scenario is located in the software component version ROSETTANET 1.0.

▶ One integration scenario for modeling an SAP application in the role of initiator and one for the role of responder. These scenarios are located in the software component version ROSETTANET ERP 2.0, which references the underlying software component version ROSETTANET 1.0. This enables these scenarios to use the basis objects of the RosettaNet standard.

Figure 6.26 shows an example for PIP3B2 and an SAP application in the role of responder (R3 MM as Receiver). In the same way, SD in the second integration scenario (not shown), PIP3B2_Shipper, from ROSETTANET ERP 2.0 assumes the role of initiator.

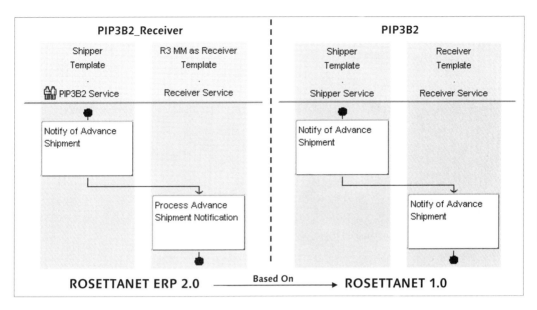

Figure 6.26 PIP3B2 as Integration Scenario

During configuration, you reference the integration scenario from the software component version ROSETTANET ERP 2.0 in each case. These integration scenarios reference the operation mappings for RNIF communication.

Now that we've provided a detailed description of the RosettaNet standards and their integration with SAP NetWeaver PI, the following section briefly discusses the support of standards in the chemical industry.

6.5.3 Chem eStandards

The Chemical Industry Data Exchange (CIDX), or — since early 2009 — Open Applications Group (OAGi), publishes standards for common data exchange in the chemical industry, the Chem eStandards. The CIDX adapter that is available in SAP NetWeaver PI 7.1 is based on the Chem eStandards encryption and security specifications. You can use the CIDX adapter to exchange messages between an Integration Server and a system that is compliant to Chem eStandards business transactions within a cross-company process.

To support this standard and to simplify the configuration, SAP provides scenarios with the corresponding design objects as *SAP business packages for CIDX*. These packages include the following objects:

▶ Integration scenarios

▶ Interfaces and mappings of the SAP application that customers use to implement the CIDX communication for selected scenarios.

▶ Communication channel templates, which considerably simplify the configuration of the CIDX scenarios

Similar to the scenarios for RNIF communication presented in the previous section, three integration scenarios are available for CIDX communication:

▶ One integration scenario in which the CIDX standard is modeled. This integration scenario is located in the software component version CIDX 1.0.

▶ One integration scenario for modeling an SAP application in the role of initiator and one for the role of responder. These scenarios are located in the software component version CIDX ERP 1.0, which references the underlying software component version CIDX 1.0. This enables these scenarios to use the basis objects of the CIDX standard.

The use of integration scenarios for generating the configuration objects is based on the configuration already presented for the RosettaNet standards.

For the scenarios of the two industry standards, one final point to mention is that all actions of the integration scenarios of ROSETTANET 1.0 or CIDX 1.0 reference abstract service interfaces. The reason behind this is that the RosettaNet methodology does not make any differentiation between outbound and inbound, and therefore the interfaces modeled in RosettaNet can be used for both directions.

This concludes the description of the configuration concepts. The next section considers how to transport configuration objects between Integration Directories.

6.6   Transports Between the Test and Production Landscapes

Section 3.1.3, Object Versioning and Transport, in Chapter 3 discussed transports between Enterprise Services Repositories. These transports are important for the organization of a development and a shipment landscape.

The Integration Directory contains the configuration for runtime. Therefore, we recommend that you test the configuration in a test landscape before transporting the configuration data to a production landscape. For this purpose, SAP NetWeaver PI provides the same transport options as for the Enterprise Services Repositories. Of course, there are some differences, because design and configuration objects serve different purposes and are organized in a singular way:

▶ **Transport units**
Because configuration objects aren't shipped, there are no software component versions in the Integration Directory. You can either transport all configuration objects or use a configuration scenario or the object hierarchy (see Figure 6.27) to specify a selection.

▶ **Versioning**
The transport between Integration Directories isn't concerned with keeping object versions of different Enterprise Services Repositories consistent. When an object is transported to a target directory, the Integration Builder always creates a new object version. Therefore, the import sequence is important.

▶ **Adaptations**
To avoid messages being sent from the production landscape to the test landscape, the Integration Builder limits the transportable attributes of the configuration objects. The adapter metadata from the Enterprise Services Repository specifies which attributes in the communication channel are transportable and which are not. (Non-transportable attributes aren't exported.) Once the import in the Integration Directory is complete, you have to revise the imported configuration. Therefore, the Integration Builder puts configuration objects in a change list after import. You can make any necessary changes to these objects before you release them for runtime.

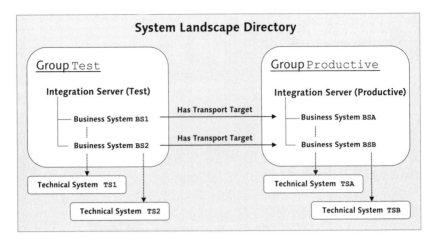

Figure 6.27 Mapping Business Systems Using Transport Targets

Conversions The transport environment converts some attributes of the configuration objects automatically. For example, the address of a non-central Adapter Engine is converted to the Adapter Engine of the Integration Server, because the non-central address is no longer valid in the target landscape. In addition, the names of the technical systems also change in the target landscape. It would be an arduous task to assign the new technical names to all business systems in the SLD. Instead, SAP NetWeaver PI provides a mechanism that automatically converts the names of business systems during transports to a target directory:

1. The system data in the central SLD refers to your whole system landscape. You enter the technical systems and business systems there, for both the source and target landscapes.

2. To keep business systems from the source and target landscapes separate, you define a group for each landscape in the SLD. You then create a business system group for the Integration Server of the landscape (in the Business Landscape area of the SLD). All business systems that are assigned to the Integration Server are automatically part of this group.

3. To convert the business systems, you must assign a business system from the target landscape group to each business system from the source landscape group. To do this, you specify the transport target

directly in the business system of the source landscape (see Figure 6.27).

The business systems BS1 and BS2 belong to the Test group. The business system BSA is entered in the SLD as the transport target for BS1, and BSB is entered as the transport target for BS2. The Integration Builder thus converts the names of the business systems from the Test group to the names of the business systems from the Production group during directory transports. This also works with more than two Integration Directories. You can therefore transport configuration objects from a test directory to a consolidation directory, and from there to a production directory, and convert the names of the business systems using the corresponding groups in the process.

The transports from the SAP NetWeaver PI design and configuration objects from the Enterprise Services Builder or the Integration Directory can be implemented in different ways:

▶ **File system**
When you transport via the file system, the contents from the source system are exported as a file, and this file is then imported to the target system. This option is suitable if you want to transport only individual objects from time to time and don't not want to build a complete transport landscape for this purpose.

▶ **Change Management Service (CMS)**
Using the *Change Management Service* (CMS) you can transport design and configuration objects between multiple systems via predefined transport landscapes. Here you can only transport objects from the SAP NetWeaver PI tools; Java and ABAP classes, client and server proxies generated using the proxy generation, ABAP programs, and other development objects that implement the actual application logic must be transported separately.[9]

---

9 You can find additional information in the configuration guideline on SAP NetWeaver PI at *http://help.sap.com* via the menu path, SAP NETWEAVER • SAP NETWEAVER PI/MOBILE/IDM 7.1 • SAP NETWEAVER PROCESS INTEGRATION 7.1 INCLUDING ENHANCEMENT PACKAGE 1 • SAP NETWEAVER PROCESS INTEGRATION LIBRARY • ADMINISTRATORS' GUIDELINE • CONFIGURATION OF SAP NETWEAVER • CONFIGURATION OF SAP NETWEAVER SYSTEMS • CONFIGURING PI (PROCESS INTEGRATION) • OPTIONAL CONFIGURATION TASKS.

▶ **Change and Transport System (CTS)**
If you want to transport all ABAP and Java objects, such as design and configuration objects, proxy classes, programs, and additional ABAP and Java development objects — which you created and configured in your scenarios — using a transport technology, you use the transport via the CTS.[10]

At this point, we won't offer a detailed description of the configuration of the individual transport variants; instead, refer to the links provided in the footnotes. This chapter provided a comprehensive description of configuration in the Integration Directory. The next chapter discusses the runtime components of SAP NetWeaver PI; you will learn that programming with proxies does not overwrite the configuration; rather, it enables you to enhance the configuration in a dynamic way.

---

10 For further information refer to the configuration guideline on SAP NetWeaver PI (see CMS) and the guide How To Configure Enhanced CTS for SAP NetWeaver Process Integration, in the SDN (*http://www.sdn.sap.com/irj/sdn/howtoguides*) for SOA middleware.

This chapter looks at the runtime components of SAP NetWeaver PI and describes how you can check them in monitoring. The focus of the chapter is on the Integration Engine and the Advanced Adapter Engine as the most important components of SAP NetWeaver PI and the proxy runtime as the runtime environment for programming with ABAP and Java proxies.

7   Runtime

In the previous chapter, you learned that you can use adapters to connect many different application systems to the Integration Server. Of course, each adapter has its own protocol and programming model in the application, which exceeds the scope of this book and therefore isn't included. Therefore, Section 7.3, Proxy Runtime, covers only the programming model for service interfaces from the Enterprise Services Repository. Because the interfaces here are based on Web Service Definition Language (WSDL), Section 7.3.2, ABAP Proxies and Web Services, explains the role played by proxies for Web services, and vice versa. However, to better understand how messages are processed, Sections 7.1 and 7.2 concentrate on the technical aspects of the Integration Engine and the Advanced Adapter Engine. Finally, Section 7.4 provides you with an overview of monitoring.

7.1   Integration Server and Integration Engine

All messages that are processed by SAP NetWeaver pass through the Integration Server or the Advanced Adapter Engine. The Integration Server is implemented in ABAP and uses its middleware technology; for example, the Internet Connection Framework (ICF). By contrast, the Advanced Adapter Engine is implemented on AS Java and uses its middleware technology. In this section, we provide an overview of the configuration of the Integration Engine (and the Integration Server) and take a look at message processing. Section 7.2 discusses the Advanced Adapter Engine and its configuration options. Unlike configuration in the Integration Directory, the technical configuration described in the following sections is predominantly the system administrator's task.

7.1.1 Basics

Clients

Once you've installed SAP NetWeaver Application Server, you create clients for the ABAP side. Each client can have the role of either a sender or receiver. Note the following two cases:

- You want to use the RFC or IDoc adapter to exchange messages with the Integration Server. In this case, the IDoc adapter and the Advanced Adapter Engine are responsible for messaging with the Integration Server.

- You want to use proxies to exchange messages with the Integration Server. In this case, a local Integration Engine on SAP NetWeaver AS ABAP handles messaging. When we look at the receivers and senders of messages in Section 7.1, we'll concentrate on communication using ABAP proxies

Configuration as the Integration Server

We now know that the local Integration Engine of the business system is responsible for messaging tasks when communicating with the Integration Server. To configure an SAP NetWeaver AS ABAP system as the Integration Server, you must specify a client in which the Integration Engine is configured as the central Integration Server. Therefore, the client for the Integration Server uses the same runtime component as clients to which you give the role of an application system: the Integration Engine. The difference is that besides the messaging logic for receiving and sending messages, you can use the Integration Engine that is configured as the Integration Server to call additional services (for example, routing and mapping). For each SAP NetWeaver AS ABAP system, there can be only one client in which an Integration Engine is configured as the Integration Server. Figure 7.1 shows an example. The local Integration Engines can exchange messages only by connecting to the Integration Engine that is configured as the Integration Server. If a client on SAP NetWeaver AS ABAP is configured as the Integration Server in a productive system landscape, you must not use any other Integration Engines on that AS ABAP.

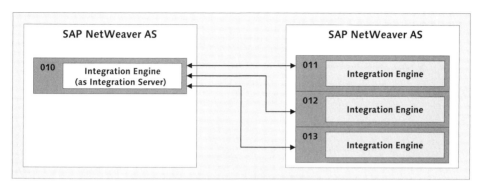

Figure 7.1 Integration Engines on SAP NetWeaver AS ABAP

In the original status of a client, the Integration Engine is configured neither as a local Engine nor as the Integration Server. To define the role of a business system, you must configure the global configuration data in the relevant client. By executing a configuration wizard, this configuration is automatically implemented for the central Integration Server after the installation of SAP NetWeaver PI within the scope of the post-installation tasks. If you want to configure a client with a local Integration Engine, you implement the steps manually. To do so, in Transaction SXMB_ADM, select the Integration Engine Configuration entry. The Integration Engine cannot function without the global configuration data. In the same transaction, you can construct *specific configuration data* to optimize the exchange of messages or to tailor it to meet your requirements. The global and specific configuration data is client-specific, and the transaction saves it in a customizing table.

Global and specific configuration data

The processing steps of the message are collected in a *pipeline* for each Integration Engine. Each processing step is handled by a pipeline element, which calls a pipeline service. In this way, pipeline services can be called by different pipeline elements. The composition of the pipeline element here is strictly defined by SAP. SAP NetWeaver PI runtime creates a separate instance of the pipeline for each message to be processed; this pipeline is then used exclusively to process the message until all pipeline elements have been worked through. The term *pipeline* is used

Structure of the Integration Engine

because the runtime processes the *sender pipeline*, the *central pipeline* (the pipeline for the Integration Engine configured as the Integration Server), and the *receiver pipeline* one after the other.

We'll end this section with a look at the structure of a message that is processed by the Integration Engine. The SAP NetWeaver XI message protocol of the Exchange Infrastructure is based on the Worldwide Web Consortium (W3C) note, SOAP Messages with Attachments.[1] The Integration Server expects a message, which has the structure shown in Figure 7.2.

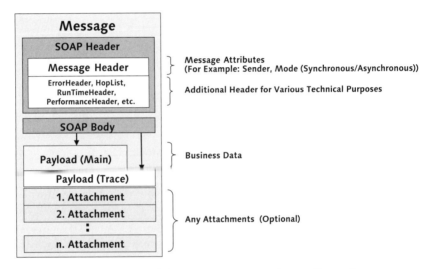

Figure 7.2 Message Format of the SAP NetWeaver XI Message Protocol

Therefore, all sender adapters convert a call or message from the sender to this format; the proxy runtime creates this format directly. The SOAP header of a message contains all of the important information that the Integration Server requires to forward the message, whereas the *payload* contains the actual business data. In proxy communication, you can also append an unlimited number of attachments to the message before it's sent. Attachments typically consist of non-XML data; for example, pictures, text documents, or binary files. The information in the message header must have the correct format for the message to be processed on

---

1 Refer to *http://www.w3.org/TR/SOAP-attachments*.

the Integration Server. The payload isn't touched unless the data needs to be mapped. When you view messages in message monitoring, you'll recognize the structure of the message from Figure 7.2.

Building on what you've learned so far, the next section describes how the Integration Engine processes messages.

7.1.2   Processing Steps of a Message

The way that the Integration Engine processes messages depends on the *quality of service* (QoS). Together, the proxy runtime (ABAP and Java), local Integration Engine, Integration Server, and Advanced Adapter Engine support the following qualities of service:

Quality of Service

▸ **Best effort (BE)**
Synchronous message processing; the sender waits for an answer before continuing with processing.

▸ **Exactly once (EO)**
Asynchronous message processing; the sender does not wait for an answer before continuing with processing. The Integration Engine or the Advanced Adapter Engine guarantees that the message is sent and processed exactly once.

▸ **Exactly once in order (EOIO)**
The same as EO quality of service except that the application can serialize messages by using a queue name. The Integration Engine or the Advanced Adapter Engine deliver the messages in this queue in the sequence in which they were sent from the sender system.

Because the local Integration Engine exchanges messages with the Integration Server when proxies are used for communication, all qualities of service mentioned above are supported for proxy communication. Which adapter supports which quality of service depends on the adapter. In this case, the messaging of the Advanced Adapter Engine ensures the specified quality of service.

To make things easier, we'll focus on message processing using ABAP proxies in the following example. We'll begin by looking at how the Integration Engine processes asynchronous messages. In both the EO

Asynchronous processing

and EOIO QoS cases, the Integration Engine accesses the *qRFC inbound scheduler* on SAP Web AS. The following qRFC queues are used:

▶ **Queues for sending and receiving messages**
For EO QoS, the Integration Engine distributes the messages to different queues. The various queues have fixed prefixes that correspond to the way they are used. The name suffixes are used to distribute the messages to different queues that are used the same way.

For EOIO QoS, all messages share a queue; the suffix of this queue must be set explicitly in the application program by a *serialization context* before the client proxy is called (see Section 7.3, Proxy Runtime). This means the EOIO queue acts as a blocker queue. For EO, the Integration Engine distributes the messages randomly. If an EO queue contains a message with errors, whether the message is removed from the queue depends on the type of error. Whether subsequent messages are more or less likely to terminate with the same error depends on the type of error, so the queue is either stopped (for instance, in the case of connection problems to the receiver), or the erroneous message is terminated with an error and taken from the queue so that subsequent messages can be processed.

▶ **Queues for returning acknowledgments for asynchronous messages to the sender**
To ensure that acknowledgments are sent back along the same path as the corresponding request message but in the opposite direction, the Integration Engine uses the hoplist of the message header and *backward pipelines*.

▶ **A queue that is specially reserved for unusually large EO messages**
By using specific configuration parameters, you can define the minimum size of messages that are processed separately in this queue.

Before you can exchange asynchronous messages at the sender, at the receiver, and on the Integration Server, you must first register the qRFC queues in Transaction SXMB_ADM. In the Integration Server, the queues are automatically registered when the configuration wizard is executed.

Figure 7.3 follows the processing of an asynchronous message. Let's start with processing in the local Integration Engine at the sender.

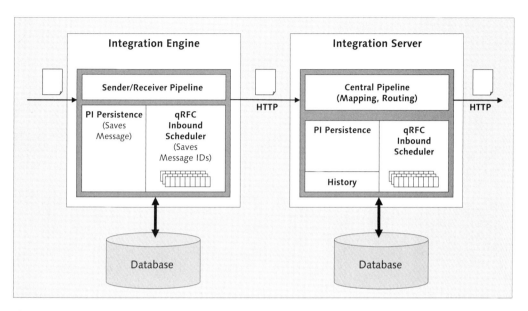

Figure 7.3 Asynchronous Message Processing

1. A proxy call in the application program (not shown in the figure) provides the local Integration Engine with the payload, attachments, and other details for the message header, which the Integration Engine uses to structure the message as illustrated in Figure 7.2. At the same time, a message ID is created for the message.

2. The Integration Engine persists the entire message by using an SAP NetWeaver PI persistence layer and schedules processing in the qRFC inbound scheduler via a function module. The function module merely references the message ID.

3. Processing of the application program continues after the next COMMIT WORK statement.

4. The qRFC inbound scheduler processes the scheduled function module calls by using the round-robin algorithm: The queues have the same time slot in the default setting; therefore, the scheduler takes the same amount of time to process each queue. If you require prioritized message processing, you can increase the time slot for particular queues and distribute messages to these queues via a filter.

Prioritized message processing

235

5. As soon as the qRFC inbound scheduler calls the scheduled function module, the latter reads the message from the persistence layer. The sender pipeline then sends the message by using HTTP.

The sequence of steps is similar at the inbound channel of the Integration Server, except for the following differences:

▶ On the Integration Server, the caller that sends the messages to the Integration Engine isn't the proxy from the application program, but the local Integration Engine at the sender.

▶ The qRFC inbound scheduler on the Integration Server schedules messages for processing in the central pipeline. The *history* is a table in which the Integration Engine saves the message ID and the status of the message at the end of each processing step. In this way, the Integration Engine can still guarantee the exactly once quality of service, even if the message has already been deleted or archived from the persistence layer.

▶ New message IDs are created only if multiple receivers are determined for the message during logical routing. In this case, the Integration Engine generates a new message with a new message ID for each receiver and then persists each one.

Commit handling The process repeats with the local Integration Engine at the receiver. When processing messages asynchronously, the Integration Engine works as much as possible like a tRFC (for EO) or a qRFC (for EOIO). Temporary application data and Integration Engine calls are written to the database together in an explicit COMMIT WORK. However, unlike tRFC or qRFC, different Integration Engine calls within a transaction are also sent in different messages. Each Integration Engine call generates a separate independent message. The logical unit of work (LUW) that encompasses the individual calls isn't transported to the target of the call.

Synchronous processing Unlike the course of action that occurs during asynchronous processing, synchronous calls aren't put in the queue for the qRFC inbound scheduler; instead, they act as blockers for the relevant callers (the application program and Integration Engine). If the request message is processed successfully at the receiver, a new message ID is generated for the response message. The connection between the latter and the original request message isn't lost, because the runtime references the message ID of the request message in the header of the response message (in the header field, RefToMessageId). As far as the database commit (DB_COMMIT) is concerned, the Integration Engine functions in exactly the same way as it does during a synchronous RFC call.

Additional Configuration Options

The following list provides an overview of how you can influence message processing in other ways:

▶ **Time-controlled message processing**
You can postpone the processing of messages with EO and EOIO QoS. To do so, you must define a filter for the messages concerned and a job that schedules processing of the filtered messages.

▶ **Prioritized message processing**
As already mentioned, for specific application cases, you can differentiate and prioritize by application cases the processing of messages with the EO or EOIO QoS. For this purpose, you configure filters based on sender and receiver IDs and assign a queue prefix. You can assign a higher or a lower priority to messages.

▶ **Message packaging**
To improve the performance of message processing, you can combine messages in packages and process them together. You can configure the package creation in the sender system and in the central Integration Engine. In the receiver system, you can only receive and save packages; they are then processed as single messages. Note that the plain HTTP adapter cannot process packages and that the Advanced Adapter Engine can receive packages but cannot create them. You use the RUNTIME/PACKAGING parameter in Transaction SXMB_ADMD to activate the message packaging. To adapt the message packaging to your requirements, you can change existing configuration types or create new ones and assign them to specific senders and receivers. You can also deactivate the packaging for specific receivers.

▶ **XML validation**
Using XML validation, you can check the structure of an SAP NetWeaver PI message payload that was received or is to be sent. To be able to use the XML validation, provide the XML schemas from the

Enterprise Services Builder in the file system and activate the validation either in the sender agreement or the receiver agreement, depending on whether you want to check a received message or a message to be sent. You can perform the XML validation both in the Advanced Adapter Engine and in the Integration Engine.

► **Logging**

Logging logs the status of the message to be processed prior to the first processing step (inbound message) and after each call of a pipeline service. The Integration Engine persists for the entire message and information about the processing status so that you can monitor message processing in message monitoring. Logging for asynchronous and synchronous messages is deactivated in the default setting. For synchronous messages, this means they cannot be found in the message monitoring if the processing was without errors.

You can activate logging in different grades: for an Integration Engine (at the sender, Integration Server, or receiver), for all Integration Engines, for specific pipeline services, or for a specific field in the message header. In the latter case, the logging information is saved in the message header even if logging is explicitly deactivated in the configuration settings.

► **Tracing**

At runtime, various SAP NetWeaver PI runtime components write information to the trace to document each processing step as it's executed. As described in Sections 5.2, Preconfiguration and Testing of Mapping Programs, 5.3.1, Java Mappings, and 5.4.3, Advanced Message Mapping Techniques, in Chapter 5, you can also write information to the trace during a mapping program. The level of detail of the message monitoring information that is written to the trace varies according to the trace level configured (0: no trace; 3: all processing steps traced). By default, the trace is written with trace level 1. Similar to logging, you can activate different grades of trace: for the Integration Engine, for all Integration Engines involved in message processing, and for a particular message in the message header.

► **Deleting and archiving messages and retention periods**

Correctly processed messages are deleted in the default setting. However, in Transaction SXMB_ADM, you can configure how long the

Integration Engine retains messages, and history entries, before they are deleted.

You must archive all messages that aren't to be deleted. Messages that have been modified or cancelled manually are archived automatically. To archive messages, first specify the interfaces of the messages that you want to archive and then schedule one job to write the messages to the archive and another to delete the archived messages. If you only want to delete the messages periodically, you simply need to schedule one job. These mechanisms stop the database tables from overflowing.

Now that you've received detailed information on the configuration of the Integration Engine, the following section discusses message processing in the Advanced Adapter Engine.

7.2   Advanced Adapter Engine

Using the Advanced Adapter Engine, you can connect the Integration Engine to SAP systems (RFC adapter) or non-SAP systems via adapters; for this purpose, various adapters are available to convert XML-based and HTTP-based messages to specific protocols and formats of these systems, and vice versa. You can also use the Advanced Adapter Engine to process messages locally: On the conditions described in Section 6.2.3, Integrated Configuration, in Chapter 6, you can improve the performance of the message exchange by configuring the scenario in such a way that the message is processed only in the Advanced Adapter Engine, without any involvement of the Integration Engine. To do so, the Advanced Adapter Engine provides mapping and routing locally. Section 6.2.3 discussed such a scenario using the Integrated Configuration configuration object in detail. The following sections focus on the runtime aspects of the Advanced Adapter Engine.

7.2.1   Basics

The Advanced Adapter Engine is a separate software component that is automatically installed on the Integration Server when you install SAP NetWeaver Process Integration. In this case, this is a *central* Advanced

Central and non-central Advanced Adapter Engine

Adapter Engine. You can also install the Advanced Adapter Engine separately on a different host. Then it's a *non-central* Advanced Adapter Engine.

Benefits of the non-central Advanced Adapter Engine

You can integrate multiple non-central Advanced Adapter Engines with the Integration Server, which can have various benefits that you should consider during the planning of the integration scenarios to be configured:

▶ **Isolate scenarios**
You can separate individual scenarios from one another; for example, to outsource time-critical scenarios to other Advanced Adapter Engines.

▶ **Prioritize scenarios**
You can give higher priority to individual scenarios by assigning more hardware resources to the corresponding Advanced Adapter Engine.

▶ **Distribute scenarios due to network or security aspects**
If the non-SAP systems to be connected are in different geographical regions or in other network zones, we advise that you use non-central Advanced Adapter Engines.

▶ **Isolate adapter types**
To improve the resource distribution, it may be beneficial to outsource certain adapter types to separate Advanced Adapter Engines.

With these configuration options, you can minimize interfering influences of parallel scenarios and improve the availability of critical scenarios.

Communication data in the SLD

From a functional perspective, both types of Advanced Adapter Engines, central and non-central, are equally suitable for message exchange. In contrast to the Integration Server, no further technical settings are required to process messages in the Advanced Adapter Engine. After installation, both the central and the non-central Advanced Adapter Engines automatically register in the connected SLD and store their data there; at runtime, this data is used to send messages to the correct address. You can then select the registered Advanced Adapter Engines in the Integration Directory when you create a communication channel; this way you specify which Advanced Adapter Engine is addressed in the scenario at runtime. The following sections discuss the processing of messages in the Advanced Adapter Engine.

7.2.2 Adapter Framework

The Adapter Framework is the central component for the Advanced Adapter Engine; it's based on AS Java and the Connector Architecture (JCA) of AS Java. The Adapter Framework provides interfaces to configure, manage, and monitor adapters. The configuration interfaces are used by both the SLD and the Integration Directory to manage data of the Advanced Adapter Engine, or to provide configuration data to the Advanced Adapter Engine. The Runtime Workbench uses the interfaces for managing and monitoring within the monitoring and administration of the Advanced Adapter Engine. The following sections provide more detailed information on this topic.

The Adapter Framework has its own queuing and logging services that enable an Adapter Engine operation without a direct connection to the Integration Server. These services are used for processing messages. Figure 7.4 is the basis for the following description of the processing of a message in the Advanced Adapter Engine.

Processing of messages

1. The adapter calls the module processor in the sender direction and transfers the message object either as an SAP NetWeaver XI message or in a different format. In the latter case, an adapter-specific module must convert the message into an SAP NetWeaver XI message.

2. Based on the sender information, the corresponding module chain is selected in the module processor for further processing. The Adapter Framework contains two default module chains: one for the sender direction and one for the receiver direction. You can supplement the default module chains with customer-specific modules. The module processor controls the processing of the message.

3. The last module in the module chain forwards the message to the messaging service, which in turn, sends the message to the Integration Server via HTTP.

4. A message from the Integration Server is received in the Adapter Framework by the messaging service. Based on the receiver information, the corresponding module chain is selected in the module

processor for further processing. Customer-specific modules can be called in this direction too.

5. The module processor controls the steps in the module chain and processes the modules according to the configuration in the communication channel. The last module in the module chain forwards the message to the adapter.

6. The adapter transfers the message to the connected system in the receiver direction.

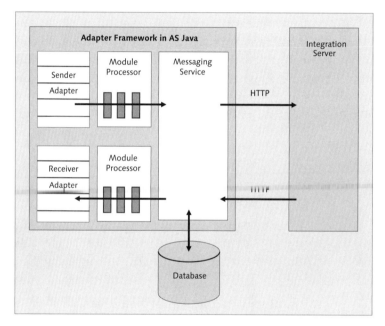

Figure 7.4 Message Processing in the Advanced Adapter Engine

This processing of a message, which either originates from the Integration Server or is sent to the Integration Server, corresponds to the technology that has been implemented since SAP NetWeaver XI 3.0. As of SAP NetWeaver PI 7.1, you can also process messages locally in the Advanced Adapter Engine. Recall that Section 6.2.3, Integrated Configuration, in Chapter 6 discussed the corresponding configuration using the Integrated Configuration configuration object.

The following describes the processing in the Advanced Adapter Engine in more detail. Figure 7.5 is the basis for the description of the local processing of a message in the Advanced Adapter Engine.

Local processing of messages

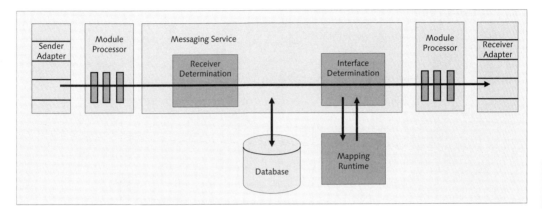

Figure 7.5 Local Message Processing in the Advanced Adapter Engine

1. The sender adapter calls the module processor and transfers the message object either as an SAP NetWeaver XI message or in a different format. In the latter case, an adapter-specific module must convert the message into an SAP NetWeaver XI message.

2. Based on the sender information, the corresponding module chain is selected in the module processor for further processing. You can supplement the local message processing with customer-specific modules too. The module processor controls the processing of the message.

3. The last module in the module chain forwards the message to the messaging service. The messaging service then calls the receiver and interface determination services for the local message processing. If a mapping is defined in the Integrated Configuration configuration object, the message is transferred to the mapping runtime to execute the mapping.

4. For the outbound processing, the messaging service transfers the message to the module processor for further processing; the module processor then processes the modules as specified in the configuration in the communication channel. The last module in the module chain forwards the message to the adapter.

5. The adapter transfers the message to the connected system in the receiver direction.

Now that we've provided a detailed description of processing a message in the Advanced Adapter Engine, the following section discusses further configuration options and provides some remarks on deleting and archiving messages in the Advanced Adapter Engine.

Additional Configuration Options

You have various options to influence message processing:

▶ **Message prioritization**
You can define rules for message processing in the Advanced Adapter Engine according to which specific messages are to be processed with different priorities (low, normal, or high). To define rules in *component monitoring* in the Runtime Workbench, you can use the header data of a message; that is, the sender partner and sender component, receiver partner and receiver component, and the interface. If no rule is found for an inbound message at runtime, it's processed with normal priority.

▶ **Availability times**
If you want to activate specific communication channels only at specific or recurring times, you need to plan availability times for these communication channels. This enables you to control communication channels automatically and independently of one another. You configure the availability times planning in the *communication channel monitoring* in the Runtime Workbench.

▶ **XML validation**
As already presented for the Integration Engine, in the Advanced Adapter Engine you can also check the structure of a received SAP NetWeaver PI message payload using the XML validation. To do so, the sender adapter first generates an SAP NetWeaver PI message and then implements the validation of the SAP NetWeaver PI payload. In the outbound processing, the XML validation is only performed in the Integration Engine; the receiver adapter does not provide this option. To use the XML validation in the Advanced Adapter Engine, provide the XML schemas from the Enterprise Services Builder in the

file system of the Advanced Adapter Engine, and activate the validation either in the sender agreement or in integrated configuration.

▶ **Archiving and deleting messages**
Correctly processed messages are deleted in the default setting. To do this, a deletion job is automatically generated in AS Java, which is executed once per day and deletes all correctly processed messages that are older than 30 days. However, in the SAP NetWeaver Administrator you can configure the SAP XI Adapter Java EE service so that it specifies for how long the Advanced Adapter Engine is supposed to retain messages in the database before they are deleted. You must archive all messages that aren't to be deleted. Manually modified or terminated messages are automatically archived; for this purpose, a daily archiving job is automatically generated. Note that this job is disabled by default and must be activated. To archive the correctly processed messages, use component monitoring in the Runtime Workbench to create archiving jobs for which you define rules with conditions that a message must meet to be archived by the job.

Now that you have a general understanding of the Advanced Adapter Engine, the following section more closely examines the programming model for proxy communication.

7.3   Proxy Runtime

Section 4.1, Developing Using the Proxy Model, in Chapter 4 gave reasons to use the outside-in approach. Starting with a service interface in the Enterprise Services Repository, you generate a proxy in an application system to enable messages to be exchanged with the Integration Server.

Figure 7.6 shows which runtime components enable proxy communication with the Integration Server:

Components in proxy communication

▶ **Proxies**
In terms of software logistics, proxies are part of the application. Therefore, you must compile and transport the proxy objects together with the application program. On a technical level, a proxy is a class (outbound) or an interface to be implemented (inbound).

▶ **Proxy runtime**
The proxy runtime is part of SAP NetWeaver PI. Note that the ABAP proxy runtime is a component of AS ABAP (Release 6.40 and higher) and that the Java proxy runtime must be installed together with SAP NetWeaver PI. From the data transferred to a consumer proxy, the proxy runtime creates the message to be sent or reads the received messages to call a corresponding provider proxy.

▶ **Local Integration Engine**
The local Integration Engine, which was introduced in the previous section, is also part of SAP NetWeaver PI. Along with the Integration Server, the Integration Engine guarantees messaging — the sending and receiving of messages, including the selected quality of service and status management for messages. When you're communicating using ABAP proxies, the Integration Engine is part of SAP NetWeaver AS ABAP. To communicate using Java proxies for an SAP NetWeaver XI 3.0–compatible interface on the EJB 2.0 standard, SAP ships a *messaging system* with SAP NetWeaver PI; the messaging system performs the tasks of the local Integration Engine on the AS Java server.

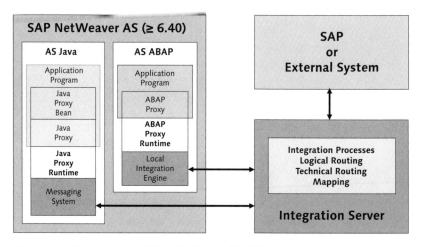

Figure 7.6 Communicating Using the Java or ABAP Proxy Runtime

In addition, the *Web Services Framework* runtime component is delivered with the SAP Java EE Engine. It's the runtime environment for Java proxies and was implemented based on the EJB 3.0 standard.

In the following section, you'll learn how to program with proxies in an application program. We'll start by looking at concepts that apply to both ABAP and Java proxy runtimes.

Sending and Receiving Messages

To send a message to the Integration Server, you must first define its contents and then send it using a proxy call. You define the contents in the application program by using the generated proxy objects. In Java, you use the access methods of the generated objects; in ABAP, you assign the required values to the generated structures and fields. Finally, you use a method call for the generated class to transfer the data to the proxy runtime, which then creates the message from the data (proxy call). The proxy runtime automatically writes the sender in the message header; the receiver information is extracted from the configuration in the Integration Directory.

The proxy call thus corresponds to the sending of a message. If, at design time, you created a synchronous service interface, the program will stop until a response message is received, and the proxy runtime will transfer the values of the message to the application program via the return parameters. There are, of course, no return parameters in asynchronous communication. In the default setting, the proxy runtime delivers such messages by using the exactly once quality of service, which means it's immaterial in which inbound and outbound queues of the Integration Engine the messages are processed. The Integration Engine distributes the messages to different queues to optimize performance. However, if the exactly once in order quality of service is selected, the messages are all processed in one queue to ensure that they are processed in the order in which they were received. You must enter the queue name in the application program of the proxy runtime as a *serialization context* prior to the proxy call. The Java proxy runtime transfers asynchronous messages directly to the messaging system, whereas in the ABAP application program, you bundle together asynchronous messages in multiple proxy calls and then send the messages by using a closing COMMIT WORK statement.

Synchronous and asynchronous communication

Both the ABAP and Java proxy runtimes provide you with options for transferring information to the proxy runtime, or querying information at the receiver in addition to the payload. We'll discuss only the most important options:

▶ **Exactly once in order and acknowledgments**
In addition to the aforementioned serialization context for exactly once in order, the proxy runtime can also process *acknowledgments* for asynchronous messages, which enable confirmation of the receipt of a message (system acknowledgment) and successful processing of the message at the receiver (application acknowledgment). All receiver adapters mentioned in Section 6.4.1, Overview, in Chapter 6 support system acknowledgments; integration processes and proxy runtime also support application acknowledgments. The RNIF and Chemical Industry Data Exchange (CIDX) adapters are the only adapters in the Advanced Adapter Engine that also scenario-dependently support application error acknowledgments.

▶ **Setting the receiver**
You specify the receiver of a message in the application program. This does not replace logical routing in the Integration Directory; rather, it enhances it. The routing runtime sends a message to the specified receiver only if there is a valid routing rule in the receiver determination that specifies that the receiver must be taken from the message header.

▶ **Message attachments**
The proxy runtime enables any text or binary files to be appended to the message or queried at the receiver.

▶ **Querying the payload**
You can query the payload of the message, for example, to archive it.

▶ **Querying the message ID**
Once you've sent the message, you can query the message ID; for example, to write it to an application log.

Implementing the provider proxies At the receiver, the application developers implement the ABAP Objects or Java interface created by proxy generation. When the local Integration Engine forwards a message to the proxy runtime, the message header does not contain this interface but instead contains the service interface that was created at design time. The proxy runtime must determine the implementing class and the method to be called for this service interface.

Therefore, you must register receiver service interfaces with the proxy runtime. (You've already seen this briefly in Section 4.1.2, Proxy Generation, in Chapter 4.) Once the message has been processed successfully at the receiver, the ABAP proxy runtime triggers a COMMIT WORK. Before we provide more details in the subsequent sections, let's look at error handling in proxy communication.

Error Handling

The proxy runtime can react to two types of errors:

▶ **System errors**
These errors occur during transporting of the message, and are triggered by an SAP NetWeaver PI runtime component; for example, when no receiver could be determined. The sender must use the CX_AI_SYSTEM_FAULT exception class (ABAP) or SystemFaultException (Java) to catch this kind of error. At the receiver, the proxy runtime persists system errors for monitoring (asynchronous communication) or returns the error to the sender (synchronous communication).

▶ **Application errors**
These errors occur at the receiver and are application-specific. An example of such an error is when a query at the receiver cannot be answered, because the customer number given isn't known in the target system. This type of error is primarily important for synchronous communication; the runtime persists fault messages for monitoring in asynchronous communication.

You define the structure of fault messages in the Enterprise Services Builder. They always consist of a standard part and, optionally, an application-specific part. You put all of the essential information about the error in the standard part; for example, the error text, type of error, and possibly a URL to link to further information. You define the structure of the application-specific part via a data type that you assign to the fault message type. Proxy generation creates an exception class for each fault message type, which the sender uses to catch the error in the application program via a try-catch block. Figure 7.7 shows an example with a Java application as the sender. All exception classes have the same superclass: CX_AI_APPLICATION_FAULT (ABAP) or ApplicationFaultException (Java).

Fault message type

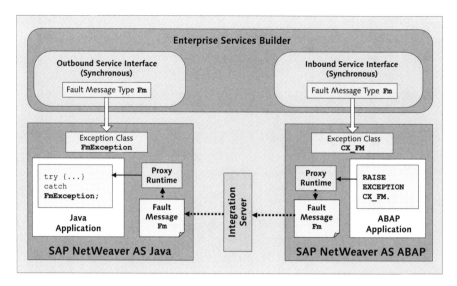

Figure 7.7 Error Handling with Fault Messages

7.3.1 Special Features for Java Proxy Communication

Section 4.1, Developing Using the Proxy Model, in Chapter 4 showed that already existing Java proxies can be regenerated for SAP NetWeaver XI 3.0–compatible interfaces on the EJB 2.0 standard. The new development of Java proxies is based on EJB 3.0, and supports the Web service standards. Of course, the differences in the programming model are also reflected in the different runtime behavior.

Java proxies with EJB 2.0

For existing SAP NetWeaver XI 3.0–compatible Java proxy implementations, the Java proxy runtime supports J2EE applications on the SAP J2EE Engine by using Enterprise JavaBeans 2.0. Java proxy generation creates the following classes for this purpose:

▶ Proxy classes that send or receive messages by using the Java proxy runtime and Java classes for the data types used.

▶ Bean classes as an outer shell that conforms to the J2EE standard. The bean classes call the proxy classes for communication. The bean classes are the home, remote, local home, and local interfaces commonly used in bean programming.

You program the message exchange in the J2EE application with the generated bean classes, which you then deploy along with the application, as you do with the Java classes.

Figure 7.8 shows the processing of an inbound message. As you've already seen, the proxy runtime must be able to determine the remaining service to be called from the service interface in the message header. Therefore, when dealing with J2EE applications, you must register a server bean and the name of the corresponding bean method in the *JPR registry* for each service interface. SAP NetWeaver PI provides a *proxy server* servlet to synchronously access the JPR registry in the J2EE cluster environment. You usually register interfaces just once during the initial configuration of the runtime; however, you can also register new interfaces or deregister existing interfaces at runtime. The proxy server rereads the registry each time it's changed, without having to be restarted. All commands that you send to the proxy server servlet have the following structure:

```
http://<host>:<port>/ProxyServer/<command>
```

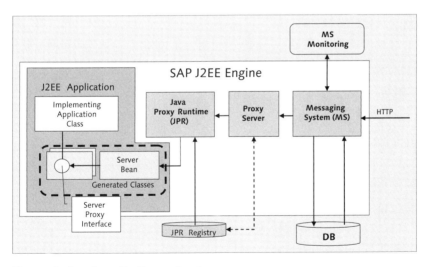

Figure 7.8 Java Proxy Runtime as Receiver

For example, the listAll command lists all registered service interfaces in alphabetical order. The jprtransportservlet command causes the proxy server servlet to perform a self-test.

Lastly, we'll mention a few general points regarding the Java proxy runtime:

► **Co-located beans**
Because the JPR supports EJB 2.0, you can use co-located beans. These beans are deployed in the same EJB container system and are executed on the same Java Virtual Machine (Java VM); performance is therefore improved. To differentiate co-located beans from remote beans, use the localejbs/ prefix.

► **Indirect outbound communication**
In addition to being able to be called by a J2EE application, the client proxy bean can also be called by a J2SE application. In this case, you must register the bean with the J2EE server by using the file jndi. properties.

Perhaps you're wondering to what extent proxies or SAP NetWeaver PI support the use of Web services, particularly because service interfaces are based on Web Service Description Language (WSDL). This point is discussed in more detail in the next sections. The harmonization described there with regard to programming or communication via Web services or SAP NetWeaver PI proxies is implemented both for Java and for ABAP proxies.

Java Web services with EJB 3.0 If Java proxies are implemented based on the EJB 3.0 standard, they are referred to as *Web service clients* in the outbound case, and as *Web services* in the inbound case. However, the changes aren't not limited to a pure renaming of the objects: The new programming model also provides new options for communication. In addition to sending messages via SAP NetWeaver PI, it's now also possible to directly exchange messages with the Web services via Web service protocols.

Section 4.1, Developing Using the Proxy Model, in Chapter 4 presented a concrete procedure for the service implementation, and provided details on the generated classes and methods. Therefore, this section only discusses the configuration of Java Web services and Java Web service clients. Once the Web service or the Web service client is deployed in the Java application system, and provided that you have administrator authorizations, you can start with the configuration using the SAP

NetWeaver Administrator. The specific procedure depends on the following factors:

▶ A distinction is made between the configuration of provider proxies (Web services) and consumer proxies (Web service clients).

▶ The configuration can be made centrally on the Integration Server or locally in the Java application systems. For this purpose, open the SAP NetWeaver Administrator on the Integration Server in the central mode (alias/nwapi) or in the application system in local mode (alias/nwa).

▶ Java Web services can be configured individually or as Web service groups. In the second case, the Web services are combined in business scenarios and can then be configured together.

Following this detailed description of the ABAP and Java proxies, we'll detail the connection between ABAP proxies and Web services.

7.3.2   ABAP Proxies and Web Services

On the subject of proxy communication, so far we've concentrated on the exchange of messages with the Integration Server. ABAP proxy generation supports two different scenarios:

▶ **SAP NetWeaver PI runtime**
Using the SAP NetWeaver PI runtime enables you to exchange messages by using the Integration Server. Here, you configure the receiver (or receivers) of the message centrally in the Integration Directory so you can access routing, mapping, and integration processes.

▶ **Web service runtime**
The Web service runtime is part of SAP NetWeaver AS ABAP. You can use the Web service runtime to call point-to-point services independently of SAP NetWeaver PI. The idea behind Web service runtime is that business partners publish a language-independent description of this service as a WSDL document. To call this type of service, generate an ABAP consumer proxy.

The following describes the ABAP proxy runtime from the point of view of SAP NetWeaver PI. It's assumed that proxy communication takes place via the SAP NetWeaver PI runtime, and we'll examine which

ABAP proxy runtime from the SAP NetWeaver PI perspective

253

enhancements are required to use the Web service runtime. The programming model is otherwise identical. Figure 7.9 shows both scenarios. If the integration logic of the Integration Server isn't required, you can, in principle, switch between the two runtime environments. In this case, the application can use only those functions of the SAP NetWeaver PI runtime that are also supported in the Web service runtime, and vice versa.

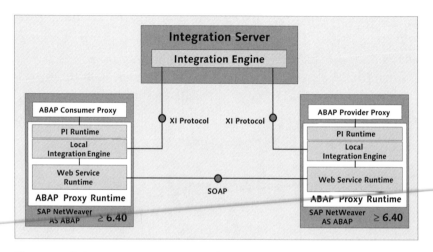

Figure 7.9 SAP NetWeaver PI Runtime and Web Service Runtime

Logical port When a proxy call is made using the SAP NetWeaver PI runtime, you don't need to enter a receiver, because all receivers are determined by the routing configuration in the Integration Directory. When communicating using the Web service runtime, use Transaction SOAMANAGER to configure the receiver in the sender system via a logical port, or use the Direct Connection configuration object, which was discussed in Section 6.2.5, Direct Communication, in Chapter 6. In addition to the address of the receiver, the port settings also contain options for logging and tracing, as well as security settings, for example. In the application program, you enter this port when you instantiate the proxy, for example:

```
CREATE OBJECT
    lo_clientProxy('LOGICAL_PORT_NAME').
```

Specification of the port when communicating using the SAP NetWeaver PI runtime is optional. If you do specify the port, in the XI Integration tab of Transaction SOAMANAGER, specify whether you want to use the SAP NetWeaver PI or Web service runtime in the definition of the logical port. If you don't specify the port during instantiation, the SAP NetWeaver PI runtime is selected.

If two communicating ABAP proxies don't require any of the services that are provided by the Integration Server, you can use the logical port to switch to the Web service runtime and thereby accelerate the rate of message exchange. In addition to the logical port, you also require a virtual interface and a Web service, which has been released in Transaction SOAMANAGER, for the generated provider proxy. To address the receiver at the logical port, enter the WSDL URL of the released Web service in the logical port.

Point-to-point connections

The only other difference between the programming models is the protocols that are available. Because the SAP NetWeaver PI runtime supports routing, there is, for example, a routing protocol available that enables you to set the receiver. You access the protocol the same way in both cases: Using the GET_PROTOCOL method of the proxy, you get a protocol instance that provides the required attributes and methods for the protocol. If the active runtime does not support the protocol, an exception is triggered.

Protocols

As illustrated above, you can switch from SAP NetWeaver PI communication using ABAP proxies to communication using Web services. However, the reverse isn't possible because service interfaces support only a subset of the range of WSDL commands, as mentioned in Section 4.1.1, Service Interface Development in the Enterprise Services Builder, in Chapter 4. For example, the SAP NetWeaver PI protocol expects a predefined structure for fault messages, whereas a fault message can have any structure in WSDL.

WSDL and service interfaces

In addition to a point-to-point connection using the Web service runtime or a connection using the SAP NetWeaver PI runtime, there is also a third option. Because the Integration Server can process SOAP messages, you can also call a Web service by using the Integration Server. The Integration Server receives the SOAP message from the caller and forwards it to a receiver in accordance with the configuration in the Integration Directory. Therefore, the receiver does not have to be a proxy. Because you

Enhanced Web services

can use the services of the Integration Server for this Web service call, it's known as an *enhanced* Web service. The following steps are required to define an enhanced Web service:

1. To be able to generate a WSDL description for the caller, you need a service interface. This can be either an outbound or an inbound service interface. The service interface isn't necessarily required for further configuration because it describes only the signature for the caller.

2. In the Integration Builder for configuration, follow the menu path TOOLS • DISPLAY WSDL. You create a WSDL description by entering the following details in the wizard:

   ▸ The address of the Integration Server or another Web server that is supposed to receive the Web service call.

   ▸ The service interface from the first step to publish the call signature via the WSDL document.

   ▸ Details about the sender of the SOAP message (party, service, and outbound interface). When the Integration Server receives the SOAP message, it needs these details to evaluate the configuration data. You enter the information about the sender in logical routing or operation mapping and in the collaboration agreements.

3. The caller can use the generated WSDL description to generate a consumer proxy and then send the SOAP message to the Integration Server by using the Web service runtime. You configure the receiver for the SOAP message on the Integration Server.

This concludes the overview of programming with proxies. The next section describes the options for message monitoring.

7.4 Monitoring

As you've already seen in this chapter, in addition to the sender and receiver systems, cross-system message exchange involves a series of runtime components. This section gives an overview of the options available for monitoring these runtime components.

The monitoring components are shown at the top of Figure 7.10. The *Runtime Workbench* is a Java-based tool that uses a Web interface to access all monitoring areas centrally; you open the Runtime Workbench from the SAP NetWeaver PI start page in the same way as the SAP NetWeaver PI configuration tools and the SLD. The Runtime Workbench uses existing monitoring components of SAP NetWeaver AS: the *Computer Center Management System* (CCMS), the *Process Monitoring Infrastructure* (PMI), and the Alert Framework. Among other things, process monitoring of the PMI enables you to monitor a continuous process that encompasses multiple components; therefore, the PMI isn't intended to support the monitoring of an integration process. This last point is discussed in more detail in Section 8.6, Monitoring the Execution of an Integration Process, in Chapter 8.

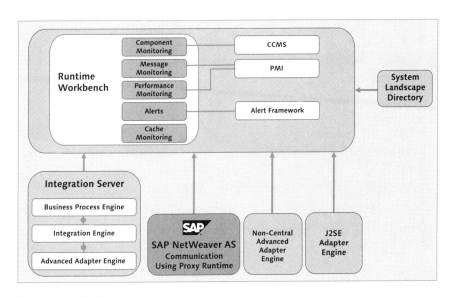

Figure 7.10 Monitoring Areas

Monitoring with the Runtime Workbench enables you to monitor all SAP NetWeaver PI runtime components (component monitoring), message processing both on the Integration Server and across all (end-to-end) SAP NetWeaver XI runtime components (message monitoring), and the speed and throughput of message processing (performance monitoring).

257

Additionally, administrators can use alerts to be informed about any errors that occur (Alert Framework).

Data for monitoring

For the purposes of end-to-end monitoring and performance monitoring, the Runtime Workbench evaluates data from the Process Monitoring Infrastructure (PMI). For this purpose, Configuration area of the Runtime Workbench, you must define the monitoring level of each component you want to monitor. All the other runtime components (Integration Server, Advanced Adapter Engine, proxy runtime) can determine their data without you having to make any configuration settings in the Runtime Workbench. In Cache Monitoring, you can also display the Integration Engine or Advanced Adapter Engine. In this way, you can display the value-mapping groups and determine which mapping programs or software component versions are in the cache.

Additional monitoring tools

You can call the various monitoring and configuration interfaces both in the Runtime Workbench and in SAP Solution Manager. *SAP Solution Manager* is installed as a separate central system, and it supports you throughout the entire lifecycle of your solutions — from business blueprint to configuration to production operation. SAP Solution Manager provides central access to tools, methods, and preconfigured content, which you can use for evaluation and implementation and in the live operation of your systems. In the *System Administration* work center, you can navigate to the various SAP NetWeaver PI tools and monitors, which are then called in the connected SAP NetWeaver PI system. The following section discusses in more detail the most important monitoring areas, which are available in the Runtime Workbench and in SAP Solution Manager.

Component Monitoring

Status overview

You use Component Monitoring to monitor all SAP NetWeaver PI runtime components. Figure 7.11 shows the status overview for the Integration Server. The Advanced Adapter Engine alerts users when there are warnings (yellow), when there is an error in the Integration Engines (red), when the status of the Business Process Engine and the mapping runtime is okay (green), and when the status of the non-central Advanced Adapter Engine is unknown (gray). A gray status means no information is available for the component in question; this is possibly because monitoring isn't activated for this component. To display more details, click on the status. Depending on the runtime component, you can do the following in the lower area of the Runtime Workbench: execute a self-test, call configuration data for the component, navigate to the communication channel monitoring, and send a test message to the component.

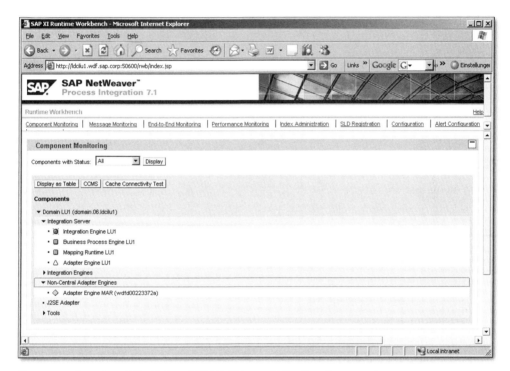

Figure 7.11 Overview of the Status of SAP NetWeaver PI Runtime Components

To resolve a component problem, start the CCMS, which is integrated in the Runtime Workbench via the SAP GUI for HTML. With the CCMS you can monitor all systems in your system landscape, call statistical information for your systems, start or shut down systems, and much more. Figure 7.12 shows the system status for the system on which the Integration Server is installed. The queues with the XBTS* prefix in client 105 of the qRFC inbound scheduler, which you first encountered in Section 7.1.2, Processing Steps of a Message, are blocked. You can navigate directly to the qRFC monitor from here to display more information.

CCMS

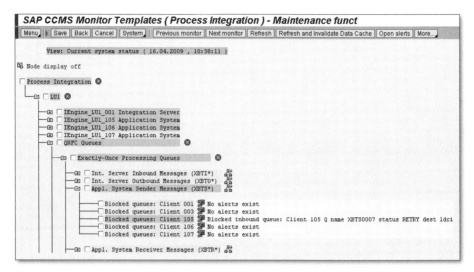

Figure 7.12 Working with the CCMS from the Runtime Workbench

Alerts   In the CCMS, you can define an automatic alert notification that informs administrators by email, pager, or fax about problems with a component. The next section examines the options for monitoring message processing offered by the Runtime Workbench and then takes a look at the alerts you can configure in the Runtime Workbench specifically for this purpose.

Message Monitoring

You monitor the processing of messages in message monitoring. The level of detail the information in message monitoring contains varies according to the settings you made in logging and tracing for the relevant runtime component. For example, in the default setting, synchronous messages that have been processed without errors aren't not shown in monitoring.

Selecting messages   Once you've selected Message Monitoring, you must restrict the number of processed messages. To do so, first select a runtime component and then select from where you want to display the messages. You can select messages directly from the database, have the system display an overview of a specific period of time, browse the archive for archived messages, and select indexed messages. For the search via an index, you need to use the Search and Classification Engine (TREX), and you must set up the indexing via the index administration in advance.

Now restrict the messages to be selected via the processing date and time and other fields in the message header. For example, by selecting the Status field, you can display all of the messages with errors for a particular period of time. In the list of messages that is then displayed, you can perform the following actions for individual messages:

▶ You can use the Resend option to manually resend messages with errors to the intended receiver, for example, if the receiver is temporarily not available.

▶ You can remove messages with errors from processing using the Cancel option, which then allows you to archive them.

▶ To display more information about a selected message in the list, select Details. Here you can view the message in the various processing steps of the pipeline by the Integration Engine.[2]

▶ You can use the Message Editor to edit the payload of an asynchronous message with errors. This enables you to adjust and reprocess messages that have led to an error in the runtime due to an error in the payload; for instance, in mapping.

▶ Because a message is passed between numerous runtime components in its journey from sender to receiver, you can also navigate directly to end-to-end monitoring from the list in message monitoring. The prerequisite for this is that you've activated the PMI in the Configuration area of the Runtime Workbench for all runtime components involved.

You can also call end-to-end monitoring directly in the Runtime Workbench. The following information is displayed whether you specify a sender or receiver:

End-to-end monitoring

▶ **Process overview**
The total number of processed messages (with errors) for all components. As soon as processing by a component results in one or more messages with errors, the status of the component changes from green to red.

---

2 The monitoring transactions in the Integration Engine can also be accessed in the system from Transaction SXMB_MONI.

▸ **Instance view**

The instance view shows the route of a particular message through the components involved (in other words, this pertains to the message instance). Figure 7.13 shows an example in which message processing was terminated on the way to the receiver.

In addition to performance data, the Statistics Data area shows the number of open messages, messages with errors, and successfully processed messages. To display these messages, click the respective status category. Using this same approach, you can also update the graphical overview for a message in the list (see Figure 7.13).

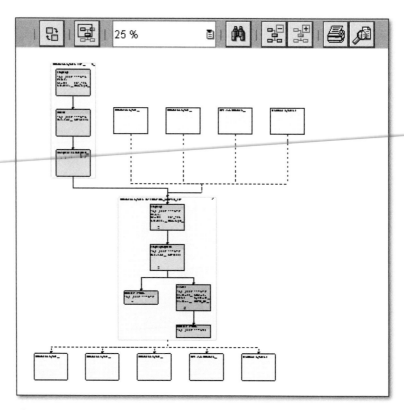

Figure 7.13 Overview in End-to-End Monitoring

To conclude this section, let's look at the notification options that are available to administrators when problems arise.

Alerts

Alerting in SAP NetWeaver PI uses the alert infrastructure (CCMS) of SAP NetWeaver AS; however, you can now also configure message-oriented alerts (notifications). To be notified by email, fax, or text message about an error during message processing, use the Alert Configuration in the Runtime Workbench. Put simply, the configuration converts a selected error code into a notification. Alerts are classified by alert categories.

Configuration

Figure 7.14 gives an overview of the configuration of alerts. The configuration enables alerts to be distributed to various users or user groups, who can subscribe to a particular category of alerts. The assignment of an alert to a user requires a few steps:

1. First, you need to define the alert itself. To do so, create an alert category with the following information:

User assignment

   ▶ The general attributes for the alert, for example, the maximum number of times it's supposed to be sent.

   ▶ In the notification text you can use *container elements* to include information from the message header in the alert.

   ▶ Finally, you assign a *user role for authorization* (a user role) This authorization is required by all users who want to subscribe later to the alert category in the *alert inbox* of the Runtime Workbench. If a user does this, the system automatically enters him in the fixed recipients list. Alternatively, you can assign the alert category to all users of a particular role. Independently of this, the users must also be assigned the aforementioned authorization role.

2. To convert error codes into alerts, you must define an *alert rule*. You describe the conditions under which an alert is to be triggered and then assign the rule to an alert category.

3. If an alert rule for an alert category is true, all users who have subscribed to the category in their alert inbox are notified. The alerts are always sent to the alert inbox, but they can also be sent to the receiver by email, fax, or text message (*personalization*). Time-dependent alerts are sent at a specific point in time; all other alerts are sent immediately. It's also possible to forward the alert to a substitute.

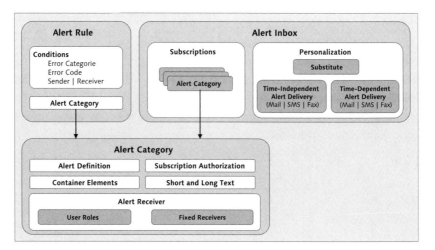

Figure 7.14 Configuring Alerts

This chapter ended with the configuration of alerts, and all aspects of stateless message processing have now been covered in Chapters 1 through 7. *Stateful* message processing means that information about a cross-system process is stored on the Integration Server. The next chapter discusses these integration processes.

SAP NetWeaver PI not only enables message exchange, but it also lets you use integration processes, which allow you to account for semantic connections between messages and control message processing accordingly; in other words, via Business Process Management.

8 Integration Processes

The previous chapters explained how you use messages to integrate application components. The systems exchange messages by using the Integration Server. The Integration Server ensures that the messages are transferred correctly but does not save any information about semantic connections between the exchanged messages or the status of the collaborative process. This stateless message processing is fine for most integration tasks. Chapter 10, Cross-Company Communication Using SAP NetWeaver PI, describes one such customer scenario where this is the case.

However, some situations require you to consider the semantic connections between messages and control the process flow accordingly. A practical example of such a requirement is the collection and bundling of messages. Related messages, such as purchase order items, are collected and assembled into a purchase order. The entire purchase order, instead of the individual purchase order items, is sent to the receiver. The opposite case can also arise: You need to partition a message into individual submessages and send them to different receivers.

Controlling processing in this way requires stateful processing of messages, where the status of the process or message processing is saved on the Integration Server. In SAP NetWeaver PI, stateful processing is realized by using integration processes. Chapter 9, Cross-Component Business Process Management at the Linde Group, describes a customer scenario using integration processes.

Stateful processing

8.1   What Is an Integration Process?

Step types An integration process specifies how messages are processed on the Integration Server at runtime. To define an integration process, you use a graphical editor to assemble the individual *steps*. The graphical editor provides predefined step types for this purpose. These include step types for processing messages, such as the *receive step* for receiving messages and the *send step* for sending messages. There are also step types for controlling the process flow, such as a loop or switch.

For each step, you define the relevant properties and the data that the step will process. For example, for a receive step, you specify the message that the step is to expect. The editor displays error messages and notes to enable you to identify problems and errors during definition.

Integration processes in SAP NetWeaver PI The definition, configuration, and execution of integration processes are completely integrated into SAP NetWeaver Process Integration: You define an integration process in the Enterprise Services Repository, you configure it in the Integration Directory, and it's executed at runtime. To define the process, you use the graphical process editor in the Enterprise Services Builder, as shown in Figure 8.1. In the Integration Directory, a wizard guides you through the configuration. The Business Process Engine, which runs on the Integration Server, is responsible for executing the integration process. Additional functions for monitoring the Business Process Engine are available in monitoring.

Predefined integration processes In real life, some integration process requirements arise repeatedly. To avoid having to start from scratch every time, SAP ships predefined processes for such cases. These are located in the Enterprise Services Repository under SAP BASIS • SAP BASIS 7.11[1] in the namespace *http://sap.com/ xi/XI/System/Patterns*. You can simply add the definitions of these shipped processes to your own processes and adapt and enhance them to meet your needs. These predefined processes are also a good starting point for defining integration processes if this is new to you. The majority of the figures in this chapter show these predefined integration processes.

---

1   For this purpose, select the software component version that corresponds to your SAP NetWeaver PI version.

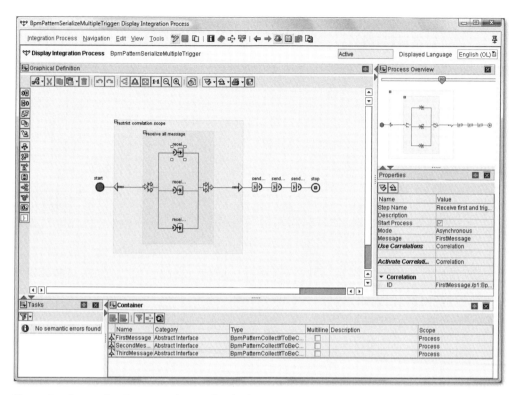

Figure 8.1 Integration Process in the Graphical Editor

8.2 Integration Processes and Other Processes

Processing business processes is also referred to as *business process management* (BPM). You can execute business processes within an application or system or across systems.

Business processes within applications usually require user interaction. The following is a simple yet typical example: An employee makes a leave request, which is forwarded to his manager. If the manager approves the request, the employee receives a corresponding notification, and the leave is updated in the system. If the manager rejects the request, the employee receives a corresponding notification and can edit the request. This type of process must usually consider the organizational structure: In this example, it's essential that the employee's manager or stand-in receives the leave request. To implement such processes that run within

Workflows within applications

applications in SAP NetWeaver, you use *SAP Business Workflow* to define workflows.

Integration
processes for
cross-component
processes

Unlike workflows, integration processes are executed not within an application, but across applications. Integration processes control the message exchange between systems but don't support user interaction. This is also referred to as *message choreography or cross-component business process management* (ccBPM).

SAP NetWeaver
Business Process
Management

You can create user-focused cross-application workflows using SAP NetWeaver BPM. Whereas in ccBPM the focus is on the orchestration of interfaces in an integration context, SAP NetWeaver BPM enables the development and operation of business processes that are typical for user interactions. This is also referred to as *service orchestration*.

Integration

SAP NetWeaver offers a comprehensive BPM approach, including pre-defined workflows, collaboration tasks, and cross-component integration processes. All three approaches are closely linked and integrated. If you want to enhance an existing integration process with a user interaction at a particular stage, you can start a workflow from the integration process. Conversely, a workflow can send a message to an integration process to start the integration process, for example. Likewise, a user-focused, cross-system process can call a workflow or integration process as a sub-process, for example. Now that you have a general understanding of the BPM approach in SAP NetWeaver, we'll redirect your attention to integration processes within SAP NetWeaver PI.

8.3   Designing an Integration Process

Before we look at how to define integration processes in detail, let's consider a few basic design aspects. This will make it easier for you to select the correct design elements later and translate your practical requirements into error-free integration processes.

Block-oriented
design

Similar to writing procedural programming languages, you use *blocks* to structure integration processes. A block can contain steps and additional blocks (Figure 8.2). The integration process itself is the outermost block of all blocks in the integration process.

This block structure helps you design a transparent and traceable process and automatically prevents certain design errors. In addition, the block structure has other functions; for example, to determine the visibility and validity of the data processed within a process. We look at these individual functions in more detail in the next sections.

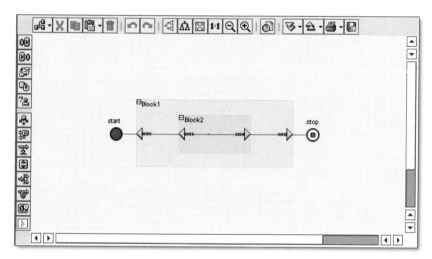

Figure 8.2 Process with Two Blocks

8.3.1 Data of an Integration Process

If a received message isn't to be simply forwarded, but processed in some way, the integration process must work with the data. For example, it must be able to receive, collect, and convert messages; increase counters; or check conditions. There are special step types for each of these tasks. To ensure that these step types process the various data elements correctly, you must describe which data is relevant in each case. To do so, you must define the data as container elements.

Container elements are comparable to variables in a programming language. You define the required container elements at design time; at runtime, they contain references to the respective data.

Container elements

In Figure 8.3, the selected receive step is to receive a particular message. We've defined the FirstMessage container element to describe this message. To enable the receive step to use this container element to receive the message, you enter the container element name as the Message property in the Properties area. At runtime, the FirstMessage container element references the corresponding message. In this case, the container element is defined globally (in the case of global container elements, "Process" is specified as the container in the Container area of the editor). This means it can be used in all blocks of the integration process. If the integration process is complex, it may be necessary to define local container elements, to exclude naming conflicts, for example. A local container element is visible in the block in which it's defined and in all lower-level blocks of the same block.

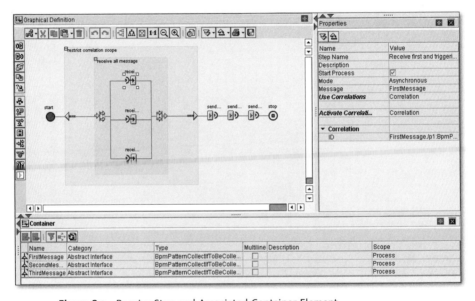

Figure 8.3 Receive Step and Associated Container Element

Categories and types of container elements

Various categories and types are available to enable you to describe different data. For example, if a container element is to reference a message at runtime, use the Abstract Interface category and specify the message type. If a container element is for a counter, select the Simple Type category and the corresponding xsd data type, which for a counter is xsd:integer.

You can also define a container element as a list of container elements of the same type. This is necessary if you want to collect messages in a container element; for example, in order to bundle them into a collective message at a later time. To define a list of this type, select the Multiline checkbox for the container element.

Multiline container elements

Once the data is defined as container elements, you can use it in the steps of an integration process. Enter the container element in the corresponding property of the step. If a receive step is to receive a message, enter the container element name that describes the message to be received as the Message property.

Using container elements

If a counter is to be increased or a list is to be created at runtime, you must set the value of the corresponding container element. You use a special step type to do this — the *container operation*. A container operation enables you to assign a value for a counter, for example, or append a message to a list of messages.

Setting values

8.3.2 Processing Messages

We've briefly discussed receive and send steps. Both step types receive or send messages in the integration process by using only abstract service interfaces. Altogether, all of the service interfaces used describe a process signature. Because you use container elements to access data in the integration process, you proceed in exactly the same way when you want to access message data. You use a container element of the type Abstract Interface, you specify the container element in the respective step, and in this way, you can access the content of the message in the step. Let's now look in more detail at the two basic step types for sending and receiving, and examine the other options for processing messages.

At runtime, an integration process is always started by a receive step, which pertains to exactly one message. In practice, however, you may want to start an integration process by using different messages. In this case, you assign several receive steps in parallel, as shown in Figure 8.3 in the previous section. To do this, you must insert the receive steps in a *fork*. Section 8.3.3, Controlling the Process Flow, describes this step type in more detail.

Receive step

Sending Messages from the Integration Process

In addition to one or more receive steps, an integration process usually contains at least one send step as well, which sends a received and processed message to a service (a business system, another integration process, or a service outside your own system landscape).

Receiver determination

There are different ways to determine the receiver of the message. The send step provides the following options for the Receiver From property:

▶ **Send context**
You normally configure the receiver determination in the Integration Directory and specify a send context in the send step. The send context enables you to address different receivers for the same service interface by assigning different send contexts for the respective steps. You reference the respective send context during configuration.

▶ **Receivers list**
In the send step, you can reference a foregoing receiver determination step that uses the receiver determination in the Integration Directory to compile a list of receivers. You can use a *ForEach* (discussed at the end of the next section) to distribute the messages to the various receivers.

▶ **Response to message**
A send step can respond directly to a previously received message. In this case, the receiver is determined from the message, and you don't need a receiver determination from the Integration Directory.

Asynchronous or synchronous

You can send a message from an integration process asynchronously or synchronously. If sending asynchronously, the send step does *not* wait for a response message from the receiver. If sending synchronously, the send step waits until the response message has been received from the receiver. In case of asynchronous communication, the *conversation ID* enables you to bundle messages semantically. You can evaluate the conversation ID in the course of processing; this enables you to map more complex communication patterns. If the order of messages is to be kept during transport by the Integration Engine (quality of service: exactly once in order), enter the queue to be used in the Queue Name (EOIO) field.

Correlating Related Messages

Often, several related messages are processed in an integration process; for example, a purchase order and a purchase order response, or a booking and a booking confirmation. You describe the relationship between these messages by using correlations. But why do you need correlations? Let's examine this question using an example.

You defined an integration process that processes ordering transactions: A receive step receives a purchase order, sends it to the corresponding receiver, and waits for a purchase order response. We'll refer to this process as an *ordering process,* and examine what happens when the process receives several messages for different purchase orders (see Figure 8.4):

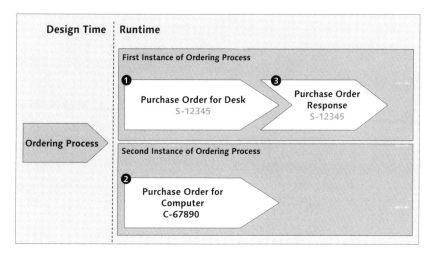

Figure 8.4   Ordering Process

❶ A purchase order for a desk arrives and starts the ordering process for the desk. The Business Process Engine generates a process instance, which holds the status of the ordering process on the Integration Server. Once the purchase order has been sent, the process instance waits for the purchase order response.

❷ A second purchase order arrives, this time for a computer. The Business Process Engine starts the ordering process again for the computer. It generates a second process instance of the ordering process.

Once the purchase order has been sent, this process instance also waits for the purchase order response.

❸ The purchase order response for the desk arrives.

How can you tell which of the two waiting process instances the purchase order response relates to? You would probably look for the purchase order number in the purchase order response and check which of the two instances contains a request for an article with this purchase order number.

Correlation The Business Process Engine does exactly this. All you have to do is describe the two messages involved and specify which element of these messages contains the purchase order number. In other words, you must define a *correlation*, which specifies how the Business Process Engine can identify related messages. To define a correlation, you enter the involved messages and the XML element in which the messages match. In more complicated cases, you can also use several XML elements to define a correlation. In this case, the values of all specified elements of the involved messages must match.

The correlation in Figure 8.5 is defined using the elements AgencyID and OrderNumber. Therefore, the two messages specified must have the same values for these two elements. The location of the two elements in the two messages is specified on the right side of the window (XPath specification).

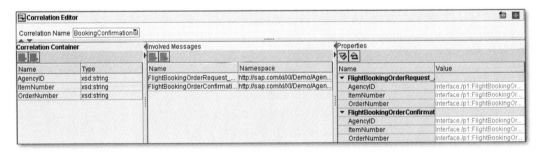

Figure 8.5 Defining a Correlation in the Correlation Editor

Activating and using correlations All that is left to do is define in which steps the correlation is to be used. In our example, the receive step that accepts the purchase order must *activate* the correlation, which means the system generates a unique key when a purchase order arrives and saves this key as the value of the correlation.

The receive step that gets the purchase order response *uses* this correlation. This means the system generates a unique key when a purchase order response with a purchase order number arrives, and compares this with the existing key. If the key matches the existing one, the message is assigned to the same process instance.

Transforming Messages

You've now seen how an integration process can receive and send a message. However, it's often insufficient to forward a message in its original format. For example, if the original message is a catalog and the receiver system can process only individual items, the original message must be divided so that the receiver system can process it.

If this is the case, you use a transformation step, which can separate a message into several messages or bundle several messages into a single message. You can also use a transformation step to convert a message for another interface. You define a corresponding operation mapping (see Section 5.2, Preconfiguration and Testing of Mapping Programs, in Chapter 5) for all of these transformations and specify it in the transformation step. Container elements of the Abstract Interface category provide the input data for the operation mapping and receive the generated data after its execution. Additionally, simply typed container elements can exchange data using mapping parameters.

Transformation step

8.3.3   Controlling the Process Flow

So far, we've concentrated on processes consisting of single steps executed one after the other. However, it's often necessary to execute steps more than once, or execute steps only when a particular condition is met. To model such situations, you can use loops and other control structures in an integration process that is similar to the way in which a programming language works. This is discussed below.

You saw in the description of the receive step that several receive steps can be arranged in a fork so that the process can wait for different messages at the same time. You can also use forks for any other steps that are

Fork

executed simultaneously; for example, for send steps that send independently to different receivers. In addition, you can specify whether the process has to complete all branches or just a specific number. Furthermore, you can define an end condition for the entire fork.

Switch
Similar to the fork arrangement of steps, you can define several processing branches with a *switch*. You specify a separate condition for each branch. In this case, processing does not continue in all branches simultaneously, as it does with a fork, but in the branch that first provides a `true` result for the condition. If none of the conditions are met, processing continues in the Otherwise branch, which is created automatically.

User decision
Via a *user decision* an administrator can influence the navigation to different processing branches manually at runtime. He can be provided with information from local variables for this purpose. You can specify the number of branches in the user decision individually during the definition of your integration process. For each branch created in the process definition, exactly one option is available for selection. When calling the user decision at runtime, the administrator receives a work item in *SAP Business Workplace*.

While loop
You've probably encountered loops in programming languages. Loops enable steps to be repeated within the loop. The steps in the loop are executed as long as the end condition for the loop produces a `true` result (while loop).

Executing Steps for Multiple Elements

Let's assume you have several processing steps that you want to execute not just for *one* message, but for several messages. To do this, you can define corresponding processing branches of a fork. However, this solution is rather complicated and requires you to know the number of messages at definition time. A preferable solution is to use blocks with dynamic processing.

Dynamic processing
In Section 8.3.1, Data of an Integration Process, you learned that you can define multiline container elements referencing container elements of the same type. Dynamic processing means that the Business Process Engine executes the steps within a block for all lines of a multiline container element of this type. For example, you can collect messages in a

loop and use a container operation to append them to a multiline container element.

If you want to process all elements of the multiline container element concurrently, use the *ParForEach* mode. For example, use this mode to send a message to multiple receivers in parallel.

ParForEach

In Figure 8.6, a send step within a block with ParForEach sends to all receivers in a receiver list in parallel. A subsequent receive step receives the response from each receiver.

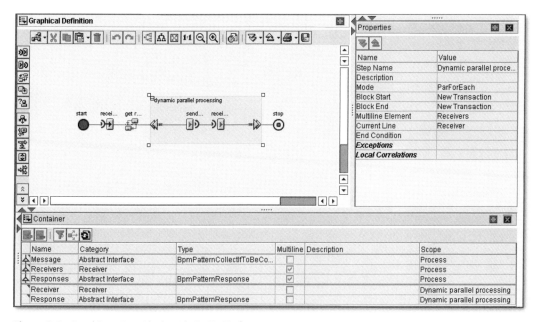

Figure 8.6 Send Step in a Block with ParForEach

If you want to process the individual elements of the multiline container element one after the other, use the *ForEach* mode. For example, use this mode to send a message to multiple receivers continuously.

ForEach

Note that there is a special feature in relation to correlations in dynamic processing. A correlation is usually valid for the entire process. If a request message and a response message are correlated via a purchase order number, as in Figure 8.5, only one purchase order number can be processed using this correlation for each process instance. However, in

Local correlation

dynamic processing, a separate purchase order number should be processed each time a block is executed. To do this, define the corresponding correlation as a local correlation, which means it's valid only for the block and can process a separate value for each block instance.

8.3.4   Time Control and Exception Handling

The time aspect is important when you're controlling integration processes. At the beginning of this chapter, you learned that the status of a process is saved. This means a process can wait several hours, days, or even weeks to receive a message without the process being canceled. However, it's often necessary for certain processes or process steps to be executed or completed at a specific time.

Exception handling is closely related to time control. An integration process can contain exception or error situations other than exceeding a deadline. You can define how the system is to react to such situations in exception handling.

Deadline Monitoring

If you want to monitor whether the Business Process Engine has executed selected steps by a particular moment, you define a deadline. To do so, insert the steps to be monitored in a block and then define a deadline branch for the block.

Figure 8.7 shows a block with deadline monitoring. If the block has not been completed 24 hours after generation, processing continues in the deadline branch; in this case, in the middle branch in the figure.

Deadline branch   A deadline branch is a processing branch that is executed when a deadline expires. You can put any steps in this branch; these steps are executed when the deadline expires. A deadline does not affect the other steps in the block. You can decide what should happen when a deadline expires.

If you want the process to be canceled, for example, add a control step for canceling the process to the deadline branch. If, on the other hand, you simply want a particular user to be informed, add a *throw alert* control step. This throws an alert for SAP Alert Management, which enables you to ensure that the user responsible is informed of the process status by email or text message, for example, so he can then take the necessary measures.

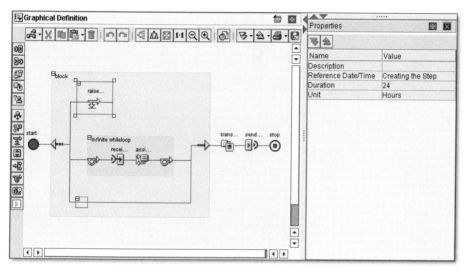

Figure 8.7 Block with Deadline Branch (Middle Branch)

Another time control aspect of an integration process is the start time of a step. You can define the start time of a step in an integration process by inserting a delay before the step. To do this, use a wait step, for which you define the delay as a moment or period of time.

Specifying the start time of a step

Exception Handling

The previous section presented an exception situation — the expiry of a deadline. An integration process can contain other exceptional or erroneous situations, such as system errors or exceptional business situations.

An example of a system error is when a message cannot be sent from a process. In this case, the process *can no longer* continue normally. An example of an exceptional business situation is when one of the involved receivers does not have a required material. In this case, the process *should* no longer continue normally. Instead, normal processing should be canceled, a warning given if necessary, or alternative processing steps executed.

Exceptions and exception handlers You account for such situations by defining exception handling when you define the process. First, you define an *exception* for the event that the process cannot or should not continue normally. Exceptions for system errors, for example, can be thrown by a send step or a transformation step. You throw exceptions for business errors with a control step. You then insert the control step at the corresponding point in the process definition and specify the name of the exception that is to be thrown.

If the system error occurs at runtime, or the process reaches the control step for the business exception, an exception is thrown. The exception triggers the process not to continue normally, but instead to continue in another processing branch — the *exception handler*. The active steps of the block for which the exception handler is defined are canceled, and processing continues in the exception handler instead. You can use all step types when defining the exception handler. This gives you great flexibility when defining the reaction to an exception. Once the exception handler has been processed, the process continues normally after the block.

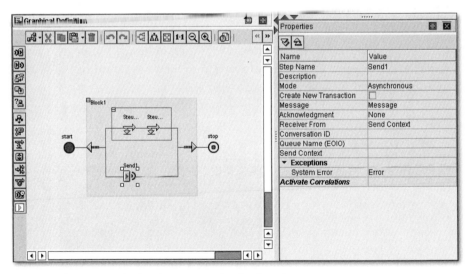

Figure 8.8 Block with Exception Handler Branch

In Figure 8.8, a system error causes the send step in the lower processing branch to throw the exception Error. This exception is assigned to the exception handler (upper processing branch). If a system error occurs during sending at runtime, processing continues in the exception handler. The first control step throws an alert for SAP Alert Management; the second control step cancels the process.

8.3.5 Default Setting of the Runtime Behavior

A transaction[2] is a sequence of processing steps that is executed either completely or not at all. When you complete a currently running transaction, the work item running in the background is completed as well, and the current status of the process is saved in the database. When you resume the processing, the process status is read from the database and a new work item is created. If a transaction cannot be executed completely, the system rolls back all processing steps within the transaction. Therefore, the length of the transactions is a decisive factor for the number of work items to be created for each process instance and the database accesses. By keeping the number of transactions low, you can increase the performance of the process processing. Conversely, the main memory requirement increases with the more extensive transactions. You can influence the transaction behavior during the process development.

Transaction behavior

The individual step types exhibit a different transactional behavior. You distinguish the following:

▶ Step types that don't require a new transaction. This primarily includes process control elements, such as *switches*, *loops,* and *forks*.

▶ Step types that always automatically generate a new transaction. This involves steps where the process must wait; for instance, *receive steps*, *wait steps*, or *user decisions*.

▶ Step types where the transaction behavior can be set by the process developer, for instance, *blocks*, *transformation steps*, or *send steps* that don't wait for an acknowledgment.

The queue assignment controls the transfer of messages to the process instances at runtime. You have the option to use this process property to parallelize the processing of messages in the Integration Engine and

Queue assignment

---

2 The transaction control for integration processes isn't a central transaction manager for a system landscape. The transaction control cannot roll back processing steps outside the Integration Server.

to thus increase the message throughput. You can enter the following values in the Queue Assignment parameter: "One Queue," "Multiple (Content-Specific)," or "Multiple (Random)."

It's obvious that the selection of the queue assignment depends on the correlations used in the process and thus on the respective process definition. Therefore, it's the task of the process developer to make an appropriate preselection. Based on this preselection, the administrator configures the actual runtime behavior (see Section 8.5.3, Configuring the Inbound Processing).

8.3.6 Importing or Exporting Integration Processes

If you want to use SAP NetWeaver PI to execute integration processes that you've developed using third-party software, you can import them to the graphical editor. Therefore, you don't have to define new processes but can add existing processes to the Enterprise Services Repository by using a wizard. The opposite is also possible: You can export integration processes and use them in other systems.

BPEL   The graphical editor supports the exchange formats BPEL4WS 1.1 (Business Process Execution Language for Web Services) and WS-BPEL 2.0 for import and export. The BPEL standard is managed by the Organization for the Advancement of Structured Information Standards (OASIS).

8.4   Additional Design Concepts

As an enhancement of the design elements mentioned, you're also provided with additional design concepts in the Enterprise Services Builder; specifically, monitoring process, step group, and alert category.

8.4.1   Monitoring Process

You use monitoring processes to monitor the business process flow. They allow you to automatically respond to specific events or missed deadlines of the process. The process to be monitored doesn't have to be created as an integration process explicitly but can be distributed across multiple applications. In other words, monitoring processes support the *business activity monitoring* (BAM) in SAP NetWeaver PI. Monitoring processes and integration processes are identical from a technical point of view.

8.4.2 Step Group

The bundling and reuse of frequently used processes is a proven principle in software development. To bundle process steps, you create step groups as independent objects in the Enterprise Services Builder. You can create frequently required sequences of steps once and use them several times; you thus have the option to structure integration processes. Note that the step groups are inserted once in the development phase of the integration process. Changes to a used step group don't affect the process logic of the integration processes that already use this step group.

8.4.3 Alert Category

Figure 8.8 in Section 8.3.4, Time Control and Exception Handling, shows an example of how you can use alerts to inform users about the process status. To be able to use alerts within the scope of a process, you require an alert category. You can create the alert category as an independent object both in the alert server using Transaction ALRTCATDEF and in the Enterprise Services Builder. The advantage is that you can define an alert container that you can use to dynamically add data from the integration process to the short text of the alert.

8.5 Configuring Integration Processes

The configuration of integration processes does not much differ from the configuration of other collaborative processes. Therefore, we won't discuss the entire configuration topic in this section; rather, we'll focus only on the special features.

8.5.1 Overview

At runtime, the Business Process Engine uses the services of the Integration Engine to send and receive messages. This interplay is shown in Figure 8.9:

❶ The Integration Engine receives a message from any sender. In this example, the Integration Engine uses a receiver determination in the Integration Directory to determine an integration process as the receiver. If the interface determination references an operation mapping, the Integration Engine executes the referenced mapping programs.

❷ After outbound processing, the Integration Engine forwards the message to the Business Process Engine. The Business Process Engine first determines whether the message is correlated with other messages and whether a matching instance of an integration process is waiting for the message. Of course, the message can also start a new process. You can influence the concrete runtime behavior of the individual process instances (see Section 8.5.3, Configuring the Inbound Processing).

❸ If the Business Process Engine reaches a send step during execution of the process, it transfers the message to the inbound channel of the Integration Engine, where the same steps are performed as in the first step.

❹ Finally, the Integration Engine determines a receiver that isn't an integration process and forwards the message accordingly.

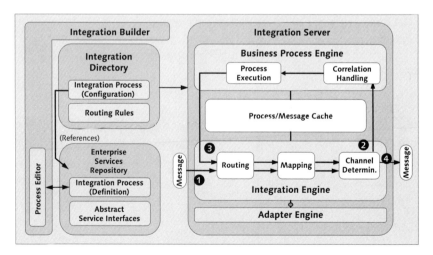

Figure 8.9 Integration Engine and Business Process Engine

As you saw in Section 8.3.2, Processing Messages, you need the receiver determination from the Integration Directory when sending messages (unless the message is to be returned as a response to a message received during the process). You configure the receiver of the message that you're sending from the integration process in the Integration Directory in the normal way. To do this, specify the integration process as the sender service in the receiver determination and assign one or more receivers to it. But what do you do if the receiver you want to use is dependent on the send step in the process? In this case, you use the send context of the send step to differentiate between different send steps of the same integration process. Let's use an example to illustrate this point.

Send context in receiver determinations

The integration process in Figure 8.10 has a fork with three send steps. You want to send a message to different receivers, depending on which branch is processed at runtime. To account for this in the configuration, you assign a different send context to each send step, for example, Parallel1, Parallel2, and Parallel3.

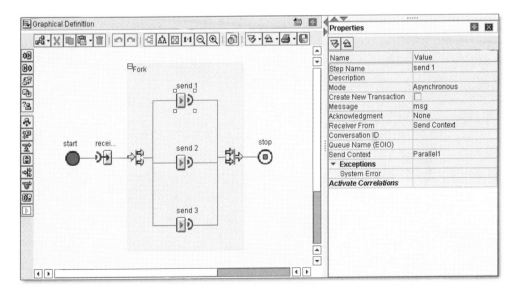

Figure 8.10 Parallel Send Steps with Individual Send Contexts

You then use the send context in the condition in the receiver determination to reference the respective send step of the integration process (see Figure 8.11). To reference a process step, use the technical context object

ProcessStep. Context objects are discussed in Section 4.3.3, Accessing Message Fields by Using Context Objects, in Chapter 4.

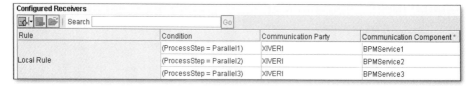

Figure 8.11 Configured Receivers in the Receiver Determination

Now that we've provided an overview of the dependencies between the Integration Engine and the Business Process Engine, the next section discusses the configuration process flow using integration scenarios.

8.5.2 Configuration Using Integration Scenarios

As you saw in Chapter 6, Configuration, it isn't necessary to define an integration scenario in the Enterprise Services Repository. However, using an integration scenario does make configuration considerably easier, because you can use a configuration wizard when using an integration scenario in the Enterprise Services Repository.

Creating an integration scenario

We recommend the following procedure for defining a corresponding integration scenario in the Enterprise Services Repository:

1. Define an action for each use of a service interface in the integration process.

2. Create the integration scenario.

3. Insert the actions in the corresponding application component in the integration scenario.

Figure 8.12 shows an example integration process, and Figure 8.13 shows the corresponding integration scenario. The integration process receives messages in a loop, bundles them into a collective message, and sends it. The first action in the integration scenario represents the sending of the messages by the sender, the second represents the receiving and bundling of the messages in the integration process, the third represents the sending by the integration process, and finally, the fourth represents the receipt of the messages in the receiver system.

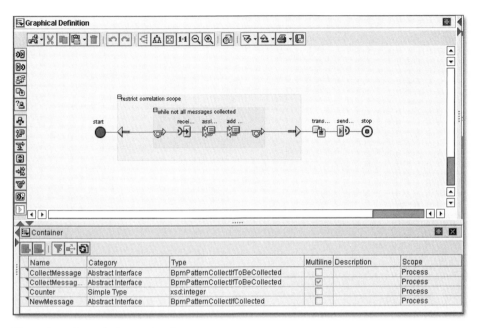

Figure 8.12 Example Integration Process

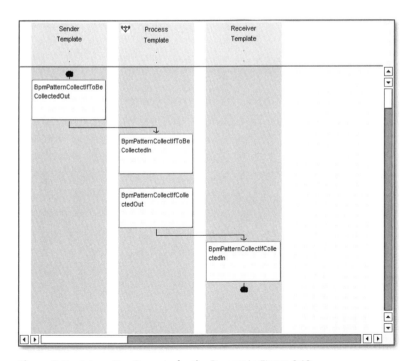

Figure 8.13 Integration Scenario for the Process in Figure 8.12

Configuration in
the Integration
Directory

Once you've created the integration scenario, you can start the actual configuration in the Integration Directory. You must take the following steps:

1. Create a service without a party for the integration process.

2. Define a service without a party for each business system of the integration scenario. In this example, for instance, you must define a service for the sender system and one for the receiver system.

3. Create a configuration scenario that references your integration scenario from the Enterprise Services Repository.

4. You can now call the integration scenario configurator, which guides you through the necessary steps (Figure 8.14).

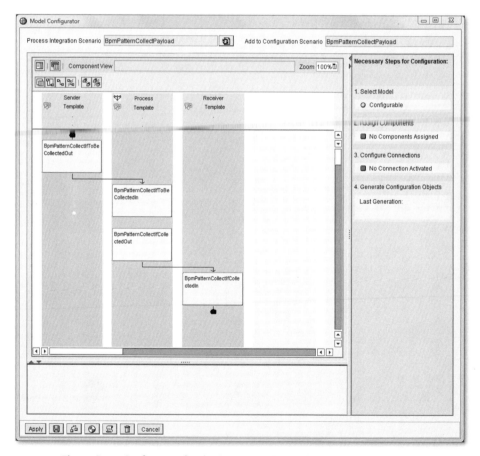

Figure 8.14 Configurator for the Scenario in Figure 8.13

You saw the integration scenario configurator in Section 6.1.2, Configuration Using Integration Scenarios, in Chapter 6. Therefore, we'll skip the steps in the configurator and turn our attention to the monitoring of integration processes in the next section.

8.5.3 Configuring the Inbound Processing

The inbound processing is a runtime component that sends messages to the ready-to-receive integration processes or starts new instances of integration processes if required. You have the option to set the parameters in such a way that they increase the throughput of messages and ensure the transfer of messages to the process instance. You configure the inbound processing via Transaction SWF_INB_CONF (Figure 8.15).

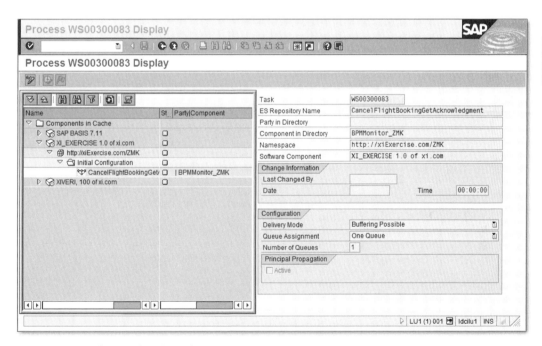

Figure 8.15 Configuring the Inbound Processing Using Transaction SWF_INB_CONF

The delivery mode determines whether messages that are to be sent to an integration process are supposed to be transferred to the process instance directly (mode: Without Buffering) or buffered (mode: Buffering   Delivery mode

289

Possible). We recommend that, if possible, you use the inbound processing without buffering. Select the setting with buffering only if you cannot ensure that a corresponding receive step is active for the messages at runtime.

Queue assignment Based on the preselection of the process developer (see Section 8.3.5, Default Setting of the Runtime Behavior), the system administrator can configure the concrete queue assignment. The following settings are available:

▶ **One queue**
The transfer of messages to the process instances is carried out via a single queue per process type. This variant works for any process definition.

▶ **One configurable queue**
The transfer of messages to the process instances is also carried out via a single queue that you configured individually. This can be assigned to a specific server in time-critical process types, for example, and also works for any process definition.

▶ **Multiple queues (content-specific)**
The transfer of messages to the process instances is carried out via multiple queues per process type. This way, you can parallelize the processing and increase the message throughput. You can use this variant if the process definition contains one correlation that does not change during the lifecycle of the process instance.

▶ **Multiple queues (random)**
Here as well, the transfer of messages to the process instances increases the message throughput via multiple queues. Use this variant only if no correlation was created within the scope of the process definition.

The following section discusses the special features in monitoring integration processes. Because the Business Process Engine runs on the same client of SAP NetWeaver AS that is configured as the Integration Server, the following options pertain to this client.

8.6　Monitoring the Execution of an Integration Process

At runtime, the Business Process Engine executes an integration process. You can monitor the execution of integration processes by using the monitoring functions of the Business Process Engine. Of course, you can also use the monitoring options in SAP NetWeaver PI as described in Section 7.4, Monitoring, in Chapter 7.

8.6.1　Analyzing the Runtime Cache

If an integration process has not been started, you can check whether a runtime version of the process has actually been generated. The runtime version of an integration process is generated from the definition of the integration process in the Enterprise Services Repository, and the entries for the service and party in the Integration Directory. This is done as soon as you activate the change list in the Integration Directory.

You can use Transaction SXI_CACHE to determine whether the runtime version was generated. If it was not, you can update the runtime version. This transaction gives you detailed reports of errors that have occurred. If you want to analyze the runtime version further, you can display it either in XML format or as a graphical representation in the Process Builder. You can also save the XML representation as a file if you want to send it to SAP support.

8.6.2　Process Monitoring

Many transactions are available for analyzing and monitoring integration processes. The starting point for accessing these transactions is Transaction SXMB_MONI_BPE. This transaction gives you access to other transactions for selecting, diagnosing, and restarting processes after an error. Most of these transactions take you to the workflow log, where you can perform a detailed analysis.

The Business Process Engine and the Workflow Engine of SAP Business Workflow are closely related. At runtime, the Business Process Engine uses the integration process to generate work items corresponding to

Process Builder

the steps of the integration process. You can display these work items in the Process Builder, and see at a glance how far the process has been executed and where problems may have arisen.

Workflow log In addition to the graphical display in the Process Builder, you can also display the workflow log as a view with technical details. In addition, you can display and analyze the details for each step of the execution, and branch to the work item container and navigate to the processed messages.

8.6.3 Message Monitoring

In message monitoring, you can use Transaction SXMB_MONI to display a selection screen where you can filter all messages that are processed by the Business Process Engine. You can navigate from the message to the workflow log, which displays all steps or work items and their status. In addition, you can display the work item container if you want to analyze a message before and after processing by a particular step.

This brings us to the end of the conceptual part of the book. In the second part of the book, you'll learn how SAP NetWeaver PI is used in the context of three customer scenarios. The next chapter continues the discussion of integration processes, using an appropriate practical case study to further illuminate the concepts we've introduced.

The Linde Group scenario had already been implemented using release 3.0 of SAP NetWeaver Exchange Infrastructure. Thanks to the downward compatibility of SAP NetWeaver PI, the scenario can also be executed in new releases of SAP NetWeaver PI.

9 Cross-Component Business Process Management at the Linde Group

This release-independent example represents a typical customer application. The Linde Group uses cross-system business process management (ccBPM) to collect, sort, regroup, and merge XI messages.

> **Note**
>
> To show correlation with the previous chapters, we have updated key terms to reflect the terminology used in SAP NetWeaver PI.

9.1 Business Background of the Scenario

With its three brands, Linde, STILL, and OM Pimespo, and its strategic partner Komatsu, the Linde Group (business area Material Handling [MH]) is one of the largest manufacturers of industrial trucks in the world.

The authorized dealerships of Linde Material Handling (UK) Ltd. can create warranty claims decentrally on an SAP R/3 4.6C system. However, the warranty claims are processed on the central SAP R/3 Enterprise 4.70 system. The data is exchanged between the systems via SAP NetWeaver PI. The warranty claims scenario at the Linde Group consists of three communication steps:

The dealership associated with Linde MH (UK) Ltd. registers every forklift sold on the local SAP R/3 system at the Basingstoke (UK) branch; this

Registering the forklifts

data is later used to process the warranty claims. The data is sent through SAP NetWeaver PI to the central SAP R/3 Enterprise system via IDoc-to-IDoc communication (see Figure 9.1). The data container used is an IDoc of type ZFSSUB1, which is developed by Linde.

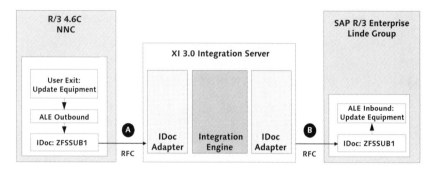

Figure 9.1   Registering the Forklifts

Creating the warranty claims

The dealerships in the UK (National Network Companies [NNC]) create every warranty claim in the SAP R/3 system at the Basingstoke branch. The warranty claims are sent to SAP NetWeaver PI, which forwards them to the central SAP R/3 Enterprise system (Figure 9.2). During the technical realization of the scenario, the emphasis was put on reusing as much of an existing file interface as possible. Therefore, a file containing the data for one or more warranty claims is saved on an FTP server every day for each dealership. The files are read by a sender FTP adapter, converted to one SAP NetWeaver PI message per warranty claim, and then sent to SAP NetWeaver PI. The XI messages are mapped to an XI message that is defined by the IDoc type ZWRANTY02. Finally, the message is sent to the central SAP R/3 Enterprise system via the IDoc adapter.

Returning the warranty claims

Once the warranty claims have been processed in the Linde Group's central SAP R/3 Enterprise system, the result is sent back to the local SAP R/3 system in the UK. In the process, all of the returned warranty claims for one day are collected and sorted and merged by dealership (Figure 9.3). Because this scenario uses an interesting example of a cross-component integration process, we'll look at it in more detail throughout this chapter.

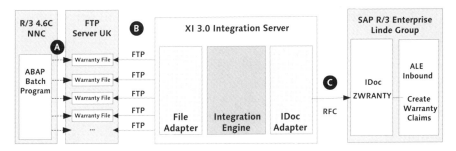

Figure 9.2 Creating the Warranty Claims

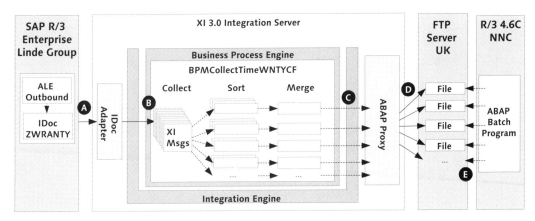

Figure 9.3 Returning the Warranty Claims

9.2   Technical Description

The return of the warranty claims can be divided into the sections described in the following.

9.2.1   Sending the Responses to the Warranty Claims

Once the warranty claims have been processed, one IDoc per warranty claim is sent from the Linde Group's central SAP R/3 Enterprise system back to the local SAP R/3 system in the UK as part of an application link enabling (ALE) scenario. The ZWRANTY02 IDoc type, which is Linde's enhancement of the basis IDoc type, WRANTY02, is used as the data container.

ALE scenario

295

9.2.2 Arrival of the Messages on the Integration Server

IDoc adapter

The IDocs of type ZWRANTY02 are first sent to the Integration Server by using the IDoc adapter. Acting as the link between the SAP R/3 Enterprise system and the Integration Server, the IDoc adapter has two tasks: It enables the technical connection between the IDoc/RFC protocol and the pipeline of the Integration Server, and it converts the data in the native IDoc format to an XML representation of the IDoc (IDoc-to-XML). The result is that the IDoc is converted to an XI message of type ZWRANTY02.

9.2.3 Cross-Component Business Process Management

Starting the BPM-CollectTimeWN-TYCF integration process

Once the Integration Server has received this XI message, it's forwarded to the BPMCollectTimeWNTYCF integration process by logical routing. The integration process can be divided into three sections that are processed sequentially:

1. Collecting the XI messages
2. Sorting the responses to the warranty claims
3. Merging and sending the messages

The following sections describe the processing steps in detail.

Collecting the XI Messages

The integration process is started by an XI message. The STARTINTERFACE service interface was defined and an ABAP proxy was created specifically for this purpose. The message ensures that the first part of the integration process — the collecting of messages — will begin exactly when this message is received.

Example step combinations

All IDocs of type ZWRANTY02 sent to SAP NetWeaver PI are caught and processed by the CollectWranty block (Figure 9.4). This block corresponds to the example step combination, BPMPatternCollectMessage. The *Collect* pattern is one of a series of example step combinations that are shipped together with SAP NetWeaver PI. The patterns provide examples of frequently occurring tasks to ease process modeling. The patterns are part of the SAP BASIS software component and are located in the integration processes of the namespace *http://sap.com/xi/XI/System/Patterns*.

Within this Collect pattern, all IDocs sent to SAP NetWeaver PI are individually put in an infinite loop by a receive step. A container operation then collects the messages in a multiline process container. The latter contains the contents of all IDocs received since the process started.

BPMPatternCol-
lectMessage step
combination

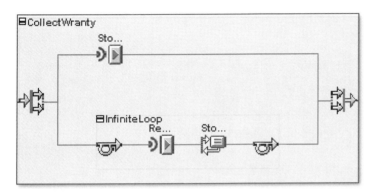

Figure 9.4 CollectWranty Block

Because the infinite loop with the receive step and the container operation was created as a branch of a fork in the CollectWranty block, it can be stopped by using a defined message (in this case, the StopInterface service interface). The StopInterface service interface is used only to stop the collection of IDoc messages at a specified time. It does not serve any other function. An ABAP batch process starts daily at 0:05 a.m. and sends StopInterface to the integration process via a proxy.

Fork

The XI message of type ZWRANTY02 is connected to the running integration process via a correlation, which consists of the date and the name of the message type. The Collect pattern causes all IDoc messages of this type to be collected every day until 11:55 p.m. and then transferred to the second section of the integration process.[1]

Correlation

---

1 IDoc messages that are sent to the Business Process Engine after the arrival of the end message enter a new instance of the integration process.

Sorting the Responses to the Warranty Claims

ForEach The second section of the integration process sorts the responses to the warranty claims collected in the first step by dealership. In this second section, a loop reads the IDoc data collected in the first step. This loop is created as part of the SortWrantyCfBlock block in the *ParForEach* mode (Figure 9.5). The loop reads the multiline element that was created in the first section and that contains the content of the collected IDocs. Each step in the loop fills a new container, which contains the data of the individual IDocs.

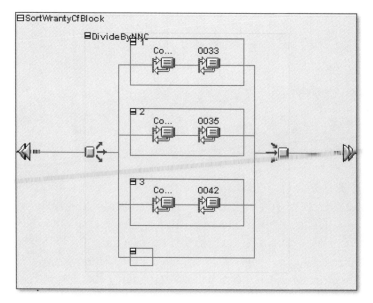

Figure 9.5 SortWrantyCfBlock Block

Switch Using the *Switch* process step, these containers are then distributed to the individual, dealership-specific branches. The messages are partitioned by using the partner number of the dealership, which is part of the container content. Each branch processes the messages that are intended for precisely one dealership.

Container operation A counter (Container Operation process step) determines the number of warranty claim responses accrued for a particular dealership (note that you're in a program loop here). Then, the second process step of the branch (Container Operation type) collects the individual, dealership-specific container content in a new container. At the end of the loop, these dealership-specific containers are transferred to the third section of the integration process before being sent.

Merging and Sending the Messages

The third section of the integration process starts with a process step of the Fork type (Figure 9.6). In this process step, each dealership has a separate branch to enable messages to be sent simultaneously. The Switch process step checks each branch to determine whether this process cycle contains any messages for the relevant dealership. The counter from the second section is used for this purpose.

Fork

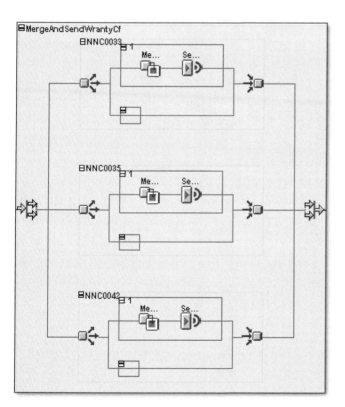

Figure 9.6 MergeAndSendWrantyCf Fork

299

Transformation

If there are one or more responses to warranty claims, the multiline elements of the container are put in one message for each dealership via a process step of the *Transformation* type. This is performed as part of a multi-mapping. If there are no messages for a specific dealership, the default branch of the switch, which contains no further process steps, is executed.

Sending

Finally, the responses to the warranty claims, which have been collected and put in a single message, are sent to the individual dealerships. Chapter 8 contains a detailed introduction to integration processes and process steps.

9.2.4 Message Outbound Channel

The send step in the integration process transfers the messages to the Integration Server pipeline. A receiver agreement determines the communication channel of type XI. This means that when the message leaves the pipeline, it's sent to the receiver via the XI protocol. In this scenario, the receiver is a local Integration Engine of SAP NetWeaver AS. From there, the messages are transferred to an ABAP proxy. The proxy creates a file on an FTP server for each outbound message; that is, for each dealership.

FTP

The decision to include the FTP server was made to incorporate a file interface that existed prior to the installation of SAP NetWeaver PI. By using a specific background job, the dealerships can import their messages to the R/3 NNC system from the FTP server and process them there.

This concludes the technical overview of the scenario. Now we'll take a more detailed look at the configuration steps necessary to define the scenario.

9.3 Implementing the Scenario at the Linde Group

The scenario is implemented in three sections, with each section building on the previous one.

1. First, the business systems that are involved in the integration scenario are created in the System Landscape Directory (SLD). Because Linde develops its own SAP NetWeaver PI objects within the scenario, certain software components must be defined in the SLD to accommodate these objects.

2. The building blocks of the integration scenario — such as data types, interfaces, mappings, and the integration process — are developed in the Enterprise Services Repository.

3. In the final step, the business systems created in the SLD and the building blocks of the integration scenario from the Enterprise Services Repository are assigned to routing rules in the Integration Directory. Once activated, these are then available in the SAP NetWeaver PI runtime to ensure that the messages sent to SAP NetWeaver PI are forwarded to the correct receiver.

The following sections present the individual steps of the implementation.

9.3.1 System Landscape and Software Catalog

Enterprise Services Repository objects are assigned to software component versions. They first need to be created in the SLD software catalog and then imported to the Enterprise Services Repository. All of the objects required for the warranty claims scenario at Linde were developed as part of the software component NNC, Version 1.0. This, in turn, is a part of Version 1.0 of the NNC product.

Software component versions

SAP Exchange Infrastructure uses the parameters party, service (or communication component), interface, and namespace to form the key for the routing rules that are to be defined. In the case of the service parameter, you can choose between business component (with or without a party), integration process, and business system. The business system represents a separate application system within the customer's system landscape and is therefore created in the SLD.

Business systems

Two steps are required to define the SAP R/3 Enterprise 4.70 business system in the SLD: The technical system D01 of type Web AS ABAP is created. This requires the installation number, the host of the central

301

message server, and the instance number to be entered. The system can be assigned additional application servers. In this scenario, client 200 was created on the technical system, and it was assigned to the product Linde MH.

D01BS200
Business System

Next, the D01BS200 business system can be defined. It's assigned to client 200 and the central Integration Server DXI.

XI_Proxy_Client
Business System

The XI messages in the outbound channel of the Integration Server are sent to the FTP server via an ABAP proxy; an additional client (100) was set up on the technical system (which also accommodates the Integration Server) for this purpose. This is assigned the XI_Proxy_Client business system, which is also used to send the messages for starting and ending the integration process (see Section 9.2.3, Cross-Component Business Process Management).

9.3.2 Design in the Enterprise Services Repository

Before development of the objects can begin, Version 1.0 of software component NNC must be imported to the Enterprise Services Repository from the SLD.

Software Component Version in the Enterprise Services Repository

Importing
interfaces

Because the warranty claims scenario includes the definition of message mappings based on IDoc structures, Linde enables the import of RFCs and IDoc interfaces from SAP systems. This means you can use existing RFC and IDoc structures from SAP systems rather than having to re-create them. In Figure 9.7, you can see the connection data to SAP system D01, client 200. The entry in the Message Server field has been blacked out for security reasons.

Namespace

New integration objects that are created in the Enterprise Services Repository are assigned to namespaces. The namespaces are defined in the Repository in the relevant software component version. By extending the company's Uniform Resource Locator (URL), you can ensure that a namespace is unique globally. The namespace *http://www.linde-mh.co.uk/XI/WarrantyClaims* is defined for all SAP NetWeaver PI objects that are created as part of the warranty claims scenario.

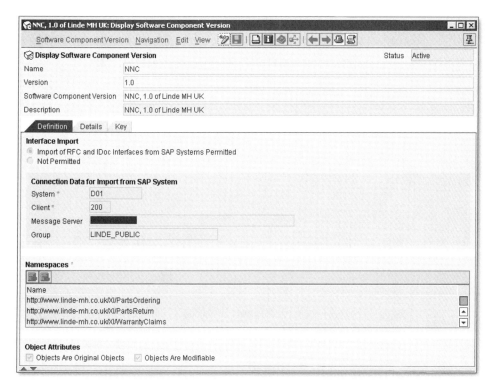

Figure 9.7 Connection Data and Namespaces of the NNC, 1.0 of Linde MH UK Software Component Version

Figure 9.8 Overview of Namespaces Created in the NNC, 1.0 of Linde MH UK Software Component Version

Because the D01 system is the Linde Group's development system, the object properties, Objects Are Original Objects and Objects Are Modifiable, are set. Once the changes to the software component version have

Object properties

been saved, the entries for the namespaces and imported objects are displayed in the overview tree (see Figure 9.8). Development of the objects can now begin in the Enterprise Services Repository.

Definition of Messages Involved in the Integration Process

Both IDocs and ABAP proxies are used to exchange messages with the integration process. For IDoc communication, the relevant structures are imported from the Linde Group's SAP application system. For ABAP proxy communication, the data structure is defined as a service interface in the Enterprise Services Repository. The following messages are involved in the integration process:

Importing IDoc structures

▶ **Importing the structure of the ZWRANTY02 IDoc**
The warranty claims are returned by using the ZWRANTY02 IDoc. Because the IDoc structure is required for the definition of mappings and as a template for abstract interfaces, it's imported from the SAP system D01.[2] Figure 9.9 shows how the structure of the ZWRANTY02 IDoc is displayed in the Enterprise Services Repository.

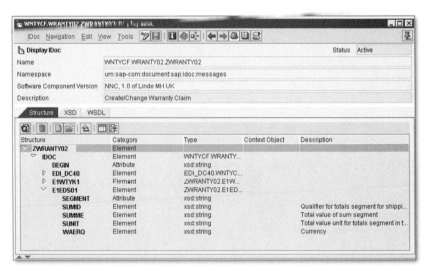

Figure 9.9 Message Structure of the ZWRANTY02 IDoc Type in the Enterprise Services Repository

---

2 The sender or receiver SAP system does not have to be identical to the system from which the structure is imported. However, the IDoc structure must be the same in both systems.

▶ **Defining the messages for starting and stopping the integration process**

Starting and stopping

The processed warranty claims must be collected and sorted by cross-component Business Process Management (ccBPM) within a defined period of time. Because, in this scenario, the start and end times for the integration process are controlled by a non-SAP system, you must define both a start and a stop message. Because both messages are sent to SAP NetWeaver PI from the business system, XI_Proxy_Client (as you'll see later), the service interfaces, StartInterface and StopInterface, are created with the attributes *asynchronous* and *outbound*. Figure 9.10 shows the StartMessage message type for the StartInterface interface, which is used to start the integration process.

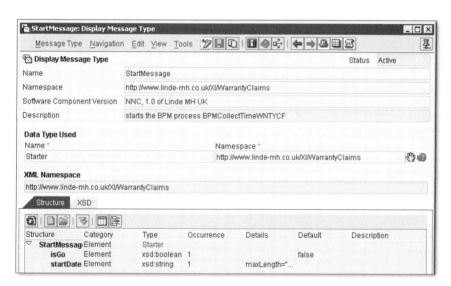

Figure 9.10 StartMessage Message Type

▶ **Service interface for sending collected and processed warranty claims**

Sending

After the warranty claims have been collected and sorted by the ccBPM process, they are sent to the local SAP system of the Linde dealership in the UK via an ABAP proxy. The asynchronous inbound interface, NNCWarrantyClaimsConfirmation_BPM, is defined in the Enterprise Services Repository for this purpose. Figure 9.11 shows the message type, NNCWarrantyClaimsConfirmation, which is referenced by the interface; it defines the structure of the messages that are sent to the dealership.

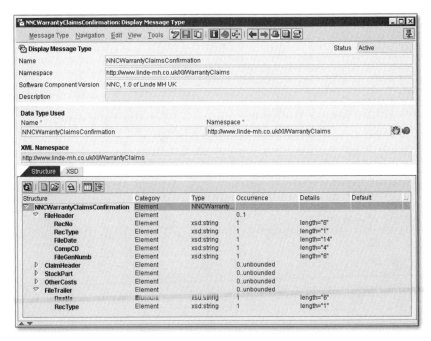

Figure 9.11 NNCWarrantyClaimsConfirmation Message Type

▶ **Signature of the integration process**

All service interfaces that are sent to or from an integration process define the signature of the integration process. In the case of our integration process, the signature is defined unambiguously by the service interfaces above: The integration process receives messages from the service interfaces, ZWRANTY02, StartInterface, and StopInterface, and sends NNCWarrantyClaimsConfirmation_BPM messages.[3]

---

3 As shown in Section 9.3.3, Configuration in the Integration Directory, you need to differentiate between the service interfaces of the sender and receiver services and the abstract interfaces of the integration process. Because no operation mapping is required in any of the four cases in this scenario, the structures are identical.

Now let's look at the individual configuration steps of the integration process in more detail.

BPMCollectTimeWNTYCF Integration Process

Figure 9.12 shows a graphical overview of the BPMCollectTimeWNTYCF integration process, with the three sections for collecting, sorting, and sending the messages. The configuration of the process steps 1 to n is explained in more detail in the rest of this chapter. Note that the current solution is implemented at three dealerships. This is indicated by the three branches in the sorting and sending sections.

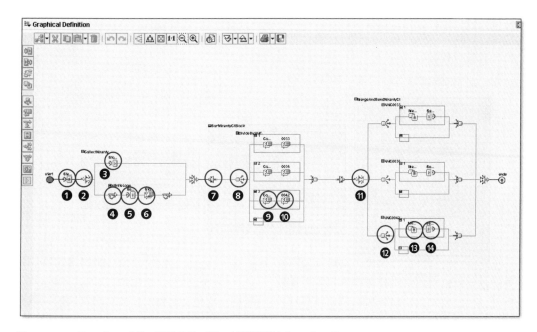

Figure 9.12 Overview of the BPMCollectTimeWNTYCF Integration Process

Defining the Correlations CorrelationA and CorrStartAndStop

To be able to selectively incorporate other messages in the process in additional receive steps, correlations need to be defined and activated. Figure 9.13 shows the entries for the CorrStartAndStop correlation used by Linde in the warranty claims scenario.

Once the correlation has been activated, the TimeStamp correlation container of the String type saves its key value. The correlation involves the messages, StartMessage_BPM_Abstract and StopMessage_BPM_Abstract. The fields of the messages that fill the correlation container at runtime — or whose contents will be compared with the contents of the correlation container to incorporate the message in the process — are defined in the properties. For the TimeStamp correlation container, the fields are startDate and stopDate.

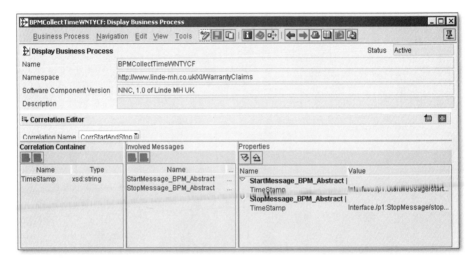

Figure 9.13   CorrStartAndStop Correlation

In the remainder of this section, you'll see that the CorrStartAndStop correlation is used to incorporate the stop message in the runtime instance of the integration process, whereas CorrelationA is used to receive IDocs of the ZWRANTY02 type.

Step 1: Start the Integration Process

Receive step   Integration processes can be started only by an XI message. Therefore, every integration process must have at least one receive step. Furthermore, the Start Process checkbox must be selected in the receive step. In the BPMCollectTimeWNTYCF integration process, this role is performed by the asynchronous receive step, StartCollect (Figure 9.14). The BPM-StartMessage container element is filled with the data from the start message. For this to happen, the container element must reference the abstract interface, StartMessage_BPM_Abstract. In the description of the configuration steps in the Integration Directory (later in this section), you will see how the StartInterface outbound interface, which is sent to SAP NetWeaver PI, is transferred to the abstract interface, StartMessage_BPM_Abstract.

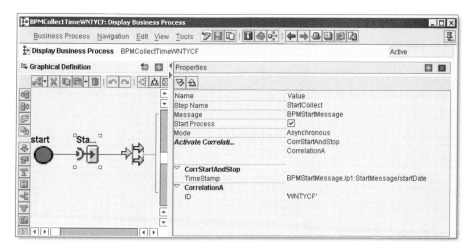

Figure 9.14   StartCollect Receive Step

Typically, the following cascading reference applies when an XI message is transferred to the container of an integration process: The container element to be filled references an abstract interface. This dependency is defined in the container definition of the integration process editor. This abstract interface must, in turn, be defined by an interface determination when an XI message is sent to the integration process.

In addition to starting the integration process and filling the container, the StartCollect receive step activates the correlations, CorrStartAnd-Stop and CorrelationA. The TimeStamp correlation container (of the CorrStartAndStop correlation) is given the value of the startDate field from the BPMStartMessage container (and therefore the StartMessage_ BPM_Abstract message), whereas the ID correlation container (of the CorrelationA correlation) is assigned the WNTYCF constant. These correlations are now the keys for future receive steps.

Activating the correlations

We already encountered the BPMPatternCollectMessage example step combination in Section 9.2.3, Cross-Component Business Process Management. Now let's look at exactly how it's used in practice in the integration process, BPMCollectTimeWNTYCF. In this scenario, the example step combination covers steps numbers two to six.

Step 2: CollectWranty Fork

Stopping criterion   The CollectWranty fork defines the stopping criterion for the receipt of the IDocs of the ZWRANTY02 type. In Figure 9.15, you can see that the number of necessary branches is 1. This means the fork will end and the integration process will move on to the next step as soon as one of the two branches is successfully processed.

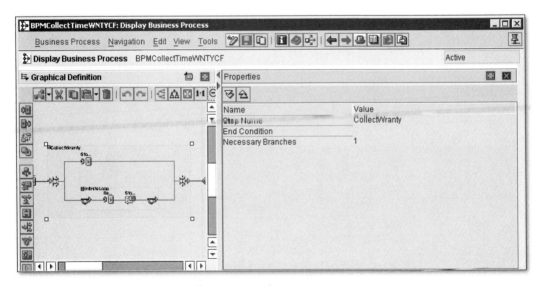

Figure 9.15   CollectWranty Fork

Step 3: StopCollect Receive Step

Figure 9.16 shows the properties of the StopCollect receive step. Again, the association with the abstract interface type message to be received is indirect: The BPMStopMessage container is created with a reference to the abstract interface, StopMessage_BPM_Abstract. The messages of this interface that are sent to SAP NetWeaver PI are only received by the process if the condition in the CorrStartAndStop correlation is satisfied. To satisfy the condition, the value in the stopDate field in the message must be the same as the value in the TimeStamp correlation container in an existing process instance.

The StopCollect receive step is on one of the branches of the Collect-Wranty fork. Consequently, it's capable of stopping the fork; indeed that is its task. Later, you'll that it's not possible for the second branch to be processed successfully. The StopMessage receive step therefore "switches off" the CollectWranty fork.

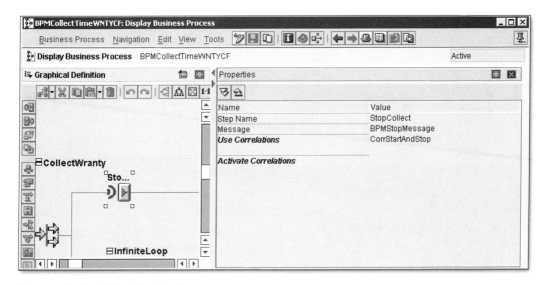

Figure 9.16 StopCollect Receive Step

Step 4: InfiniteLoop Loop

A loop in an integration process continues to be executed as long as the defined condition returns true. In this integration process, an infinite loop is created by ensuring that two constants are set equal to the value 1 (Figure 9.17).

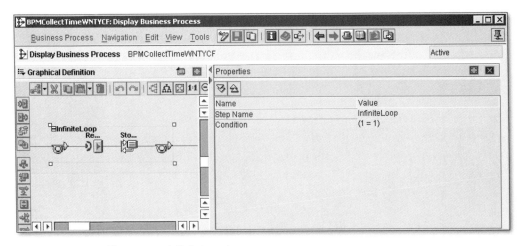

Figure 9.17 InfiniteLoop Loop

Step 5: ReceiveIDOCs Receive Step

Receiving IDocs

The ReceiveIDOCs receive step receives IDocs of the ZWRANTY02 type and transfers their contents to the WarrantyConfirmationIn container element. Here too, the link between the XI message and the container element is enabled by the fact that the container element references the abstract interface, WNTYCF_BPM_Abstract, in the container definition. The abstract interface, in turn, references the imported IDoc type, ZWRANTY02. In Figure 9.18, you can see that the receive step uses the CorrelationA correlation. It ensures that the only messages that enter the process instance are those in which the MESTYP field in the payload is equal to the WNTYCF constant (see also step 1). Because the receive step is in the infinite loop, IDocs can continue to be received until the end of the CollectWranty fork.

Step 6: StoreMessage Container Operation

Collecting IDoc contents

Each time the ReceiveIDOCs receive step receives an IDoc, it fills the WarrantyConfirmationIn container element. A container operation is used to collect the contents of each IDoc in a multiline container element before the next IDoc arrives and overwrites the container contents. This ensures that the contents of none of the IDocs are lost.

Figure 9.19 shows how such a collect step is created. It's important that the single-line container, WarrantyConfirmationIn, and the multiline container, WarrantyConfirmationInAllList, reference the same abstract interface and therefore have the same structure. The *append* operation then collects the data.[4]

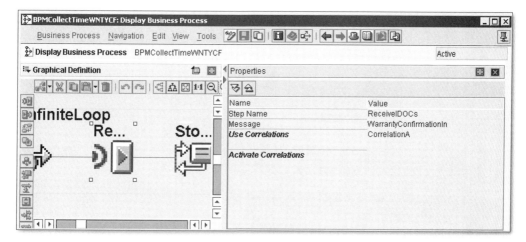

Figure 9.18 ReceiveIDOCs Receive Step

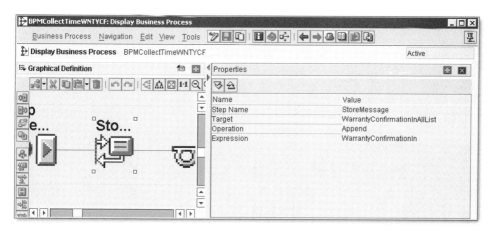

Figure 9.19 StoreMessage Container Operation

---

4 Remember that this process step is part of an infinite loop.

Step 7: SortWrantyCfBlock Block

Sort container contents

In the previous steps, the contents of all IDocs of the ZWRANTY02 type sent to SAP NetWeaver PI in the period of time between the receipt of the messages, StartInterface and StopInterface, were collected in the container element, WarrantyConfirmationInAllList. The contents of this container now have to be sorted by dealership. Again, this is achieved by using a loop, which in this case is defined by a block in the ParForEach mode (Figure 9.20). The loop runs through the individual lines of the multiline container element, WarrantyConfirmationInAllList, and transports its contents line by line to the WarrantyConfirmationInTemp container once for each loop. This container can now be operated on within the block.

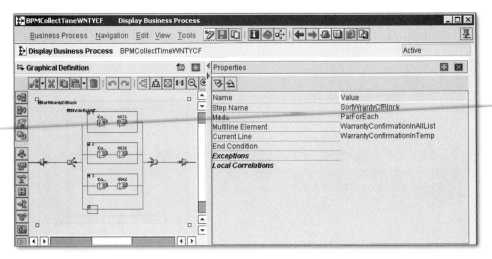

Figure 9.20   SortWrantyCfBlock Block

Step 8: DivideByNNC Switch

Figure 9.21 shows that within the loop, a specific branch is executed for each dealership. In this example, the sort mechanism was implemented for three dealerships. The branch criterion is defined by the PARNR field (party number) in the WarrantyConfirmationInTemp container.

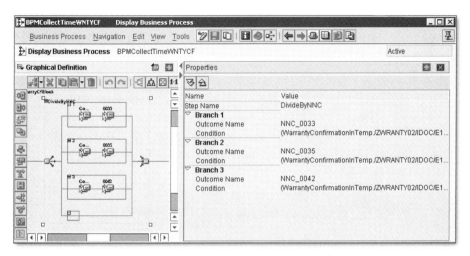

Figure 9.21 DivideByNNC Switch

Step 9: Count_0035 Container Operation

First, the number of warranty claims responses for each dealership has to be counted. This is done by container operations on each of the dealership-specific branches in the loop. A MsgCount_NNC_<PARNR> container element of the xsd:integer type is created for this purpose for each dealership. This container counts how many times the branch is executed.

Counting the warranty claims responses

Figure 9.22 shows how the step is defined for the dealership with the party number 0035. Each time the process step is called, the value 1 is added to the contents of container MsgCount_NNC_0035.

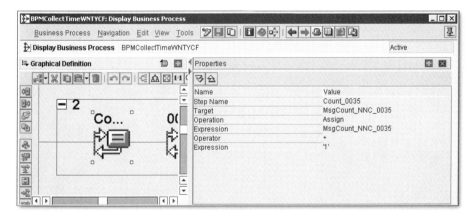

Figure 9.22 Count_0035 Container Operation

315

Step 10: 0035 Container Operation

Collecting the responses

Until now, we operated on the single-line container element, Warranty-ConfirmationInTemp, within our loop. Now, however, the warranty claims responses for each dealership must be collected in separate containers. This is done by using a container operation, similarly to collecting the IDocs in step 6. Each time a dealership branch is executed (for example, PARNR = 0035), the single-line container, WarrantyConfirmationInTemp, is appended to the multiline container, WarrantyConfirmation_NNC_0035 (see Figure 9.23).

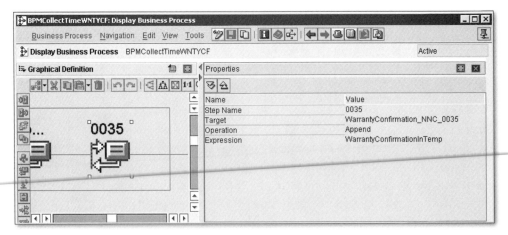

Figure 9.23 0035 Container Operation

Once all of the warranty claims responses have been distributed to the containers of the individual dealerships, they can be sent to each dealership as messages.

Step 11: MergeAndSendWrantyCf Fork

Sending the responses

In this example, the responses to the warranty claims are sent to three dealerships. A fork with three necessary branches is used to ensure that the containers with the sorted responses reach the correct dealership (see Figure 9.24).

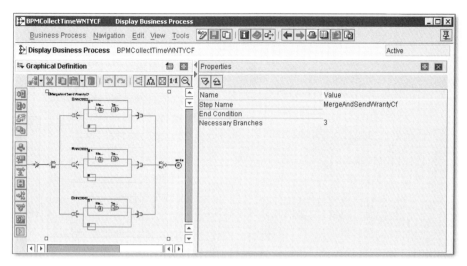

Figure 9.24 MergeAndSendWrantyCf Fork

Step 12: NNC0035 Switch

To ensure that no messages are sent to the dealerships without any warranty claims responses, the responses determined in Step 9 are queried for each dealership. The switch has two branches: If the MsgCount_NNC_0035 parameter does not equal 0, the upper branch is executed and the responses are sent to the dealership. However, if the counter equals 0, the "empty" lower branch is executed without any additional process steps. Figure 9.25 shows the settings required to define a switch for one dealership as an example.

Checking number of responses

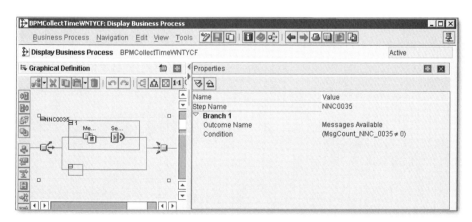

Figure 9.25 NNC0035 Switch

317

Step 13: Merge_0035 Transformation

Mapping Thus far in the integration process, all container elements that contain data about warranty claims responses reference the abstract interface, WNTYCF_BPM_Abstract, which is based on the structure definition of the ZWRANTY02 IDoc. However, the messages that are to be sent to the dealerships must have the structure shown in Figure 9.11, which means a mapping is required before the messages can be sent.

Aggregation In addition to the conversion of the structure, the contents of the container need to be aggregated. This is done with a *multi-mapping*. The WarrantyConfirmation_NNC_0035 multiline container from step 10 is applied to the transformation step. However, the container that leaves the step (Warranty-ConfirmationOut_0035) is a single-line container.

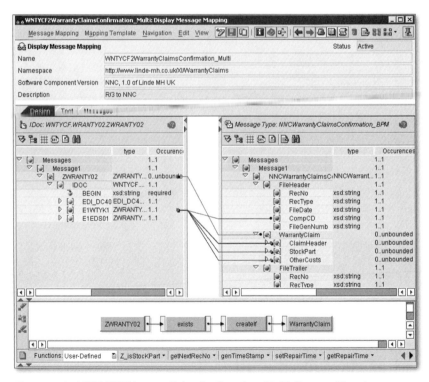

Figure 9.26 WNTYCF2WarrantyClaimsConfirmation_Multi Message Mapping

Figure 9.26 illustrates some dependencies of the message mapping created in the Enterprise Services Repository. This message mapping is called

318

from the operation mapping, WNTYCF2Warranty_ClaimsConfirmation_ BPM, as a mapping program.[5]

You now have everything you need for the transformation and can create the process step. Figure 9.27 shows the necessary settings. Note that you must enter the names both of the abstract interfaces and of the corresponding containers for the source and target messages.

Creating the process step

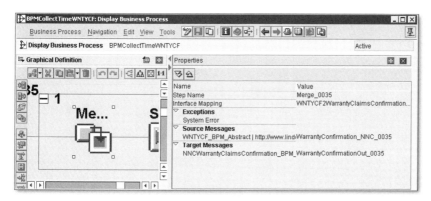

Figure 9.27   Merge_0035 Transformation

Step 14: Send 0035 Send Step

In the final step, the collected, sorted, and aggregated responses to the warranty claims are sent to the dealerships. Figure 9.28 shows the settings that are required. The contents of the WarrantyConfirmationOut_0035 container from the previous transformation step are sent asynchronously in the NNC_0035 send context. Therefore, the message is transferred to the pipeline of the Integration Engine, which then sends the message.

Sending the responses

Before you look at the settings in the Integration Directory, let's summarize the containers and their references that are involved in the integration process in the following overview table (Table 9.1). The container elements are shown chronologically in the order in which they appear in the integration process.

---

5 Note the changed terminology for *interface mappings*. As of SAP NetWeaver 7.1, they are referred to as *operation mappings*.

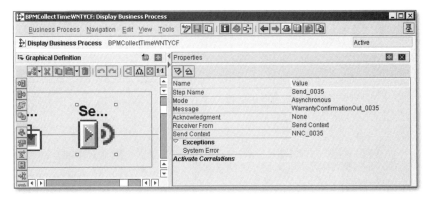

Figure 9.28 Send_0035 Send Step

Container Element	Abstract Interface	Message Type/IDoc Structure
BPMStartMessage	StartMessage_BPM_Abstract	StartMessage
WarrantyConfirmationIn	WNTYCF_BPM_Abstract	ZWRANTY02
WarrantyConfirmationInAllList	WNTYCF_BPM_Abstract	ZWRANTY02
BPMStopMessage	StopMessage_BPM_Abstract	StopMessage
WarrantyConfirmationInTemp	WNTYCF_BPM_Abstract	ZWRANTY02
WarrantyConfirmation_NNC_<PARNR>	WNTYCF_BPM_Abstract	ZWRANTY02
WarrantyConfirmationOut_<PARNR>	NNCWarranty ClaimsConfirmation_ BPM_Abstract	NNCWarrantyClaims Confirmation_BPM

Table 9.1 Containers and References in the Integration Process

9.3.3 Configuration in the Integration Directory

In this section, you've already seen what settings were made in the SLD and Enterprise Services Repository in Linde's SAP NetWeaver PI system. Therefore, all of the building blocks required for the scenario have been created and can now be assigned to the actual application systems. The necessary configuration steps, such as defining communication components[6], logical routing, and communication channels, are performed in the Integration Directory.

Configuration Scenario

With configuration scenarios, all of the configuration objects in the Integration Directory can be grouped into logical entities. In the Linde scenario, the NNC_WarrantyClaimConfirmation_To configuration scenario summarizes all of the Integration Directory objects that are required to send the responses to the warranty claims.

Communication Components

In SAP NetWeaver Process Integration, communication components represent the technical or business sources and targets of the XI messages. Therefore, they are the start and end points for all configuration steps. In the Linde scenario, communication components without a party of the integration process and business system type are used. (For a description of the different types of communication components, see Section 6.1.)

Section 9.3.1, System Landscape and Software Catalog, showed the steps that were necessary to create the business systems, D01BS200 and XI_Proxy_Client, in the SLD. Before they can be used to define logical routings, they first need to be imported into the Integration Directory from the SLD. While being imported, they are assigned to the configuration scenario, NNC_WarrantyClaimConfirmation_To, and are then added to the navigation tree under the relevant node (see Figure 9.29).

D01BS200 and XI_Proxy_Client Business Systems

Figure 9.29 Services of the NNC_WarrantyClaimConfirmation_To Integration Scenario

---

6 Note that *services* were renamed *communication components* in the course of the terminology changes.

BPMCollectTime
WNTYCF
Integration
Scenario

Section 9.3.2, Design in the Enterprise Services Repository, showed the steps that are necessary to create the BPMCollectTimeWNTYCF integration process in the Enterprise Services Repository. For the integration process to be able to receive and send XI messages at runtime, an integration process needs to be created in the Integration Directory. This, in turn, references the actual process definition in the Enterprise Services Repository. Note that both the integration process in the Enterprise Services Repository, and the integration process service in the Integration Directory, have the name BPMCollectTimeWNTYCF. However, these are two different entities. Figure 9.30 shows the reference to the integration process in the Integration Directory and the signature of the messages to be received. All services involved in the scenario are now defined, and you can begin to create the logical routings based on them.

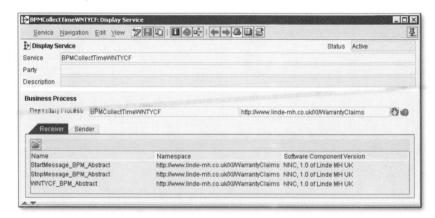

Figure 9.30 Receiver Interfaces of the BPMCollectTimeWNTYCF Integration Process

Logical Routing and Communication Channels

Section 9.3.2, Design in the Enterprise Services Repository, showed that the messages ZWRANTY02, StartInterface, and StopInterface are sent to the integration process, whereas the system for the Linde dealerships receives messages of the NNCWarrantyClaimsConfirmation_BPM type. These correspond to the abstract interfaces, WNTYCF_BPM_Abstract, StartMessage_BPM_Abstract, StopMessage_BPM_Abstract, and NNCWarrantyClaimsConfirmation_BPM_Abstract, of the integration process signature. Consequently, four receiver determinations and four interface determinations have to be created in the Integration Directory:

1. Sending the start message from the proxy client to the integration process service

2. Sending the responses from the application system to the integration process

3. Sending the stop message from the proxy client to the integration process

4. Sending the sorted and bundled responses to the proxy client

Receiver and interface determinations

In Figure 9.31, you can see the configuration settings that are required to ensure that the start message finds its way to — and is received by — the BPMCollectTimeWNTYCF integration process. The settings are as follows: If a message with the key fields[7] Service[8]: XI_Proxy_Client, Interface: StartInterface, and Namespace: *http://www.linde-mh.co.uk/XI/WarrantyClaims* is sent to the Integration Engine, it's forwarded to the theBPMCollectTimeWNTYCF receiver service (the integration process).

Sending the start message

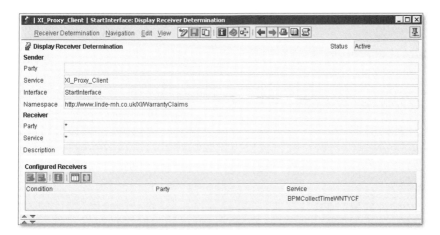

Figure 9.31   Receiver Determination for the StartInterface Outbound Interface

The newly determined receiver communication component is now part of the key and is used for the interface determination. Figure 9.32

---

7   These key fields are filled automatically by the sender ABAP proxy.

8   Here as well, note that *services* were renamed *communication components* in the course of the terminology changes.

illustrates how the StartMessage_BPM_Abstract receiver interface is derived from the newly formed key. Because the sender and receiver interface reference the same message type, no operation mapping is required. Because the receiver communication component is an integration process, no communication channel needs to be defined for it.

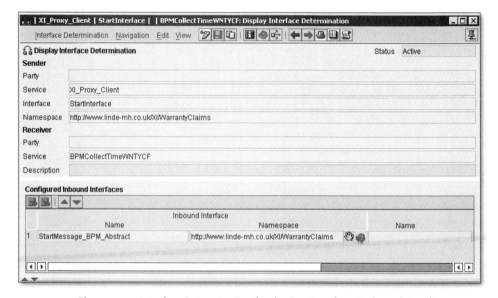

Figure 9.32 Interface Determination for the StartInterface Outbound Interface

Sending the responses
In Figure 9.33, you can see the settings for the receiver determination and interface determination for the IDocs of the ZWRANTY02 type that were sent to SAP NetWeaver PI from the D01BS200 business system. Note that only messages that have the key UK are sent to the BPMCollectTimeWNTYCF receiver service (the integration process). Neither an operation mapping nor a receiver agreement is required in this case.

However, it's still not guaranteed that the contents of the IDocs can also be transferred to the relevant container in the integration process. As described in Section 9.3.2, Design in the Enterprise Services Repository, the relevant receive step uses the CorrelationA correlation. The message is accepted by the integration process only when the condition in the correlation is satisfied.

With the exception of the interfaces, the configuration settings are the same as those used for the start message (see Figures 9.31 and 9.32). The message is also sent by the XI_Proxy_Client business system, and the BPMCollectTimeWNTYCF receiver communication component acts again as the receiver.

Sending the stop message

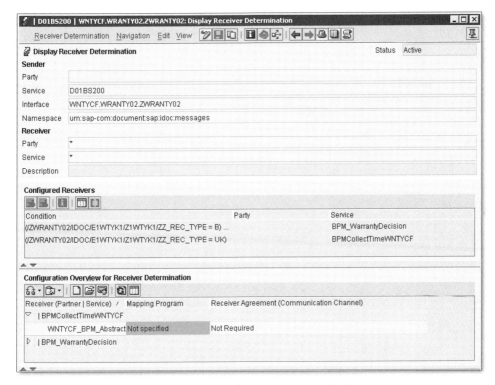

Figure 9.33 Receiver Determination and Interface Determination for the ZWRANTY02 Outbound Interface

A fourth logical routing is required to make the messages from the integration process available to the various dealerships. The receiver in this case is the XI_Proxy_Client business system, which is also used to send the start and stop message. Figure 9.34 summarizes the necessary settings.

Sending the sorted and bundled responses

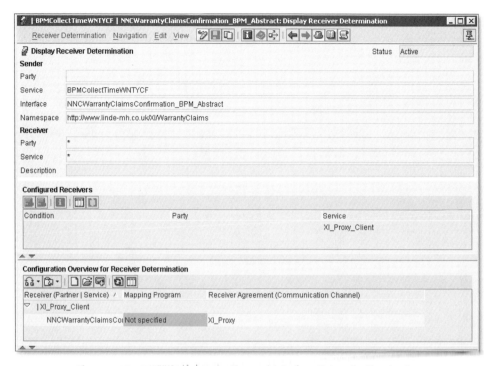

Figure 9.34 Receiver Determination and Interface Determination for the NNCWarrantyClaimsConfirmation_BPM_Abstract Outbound Interface

Unlike when the integration process acts as a message receiver, here a receiver agreement is required. The XI_Proxy receiver agreement contains a reference to a receiver communication channel of the same name. Figure 9.35 shows the settings required to send a message to the local Integration Engine of client 100. The entries for the target host and the service number have been blacked out for security reasons.

The ABAP proxy implemented on the Integration Engine receives the messages and makes them available on an FTP server UK (see Figure 9.33). These files are then imported into the local SAP R/3 system in the UK. The logical routings for the responses to the warranty claims have now been created. Once the changes are activated, SAP NetWeaver PI can be used to sort and merge the responses and then make them available to the Linde dealerships.

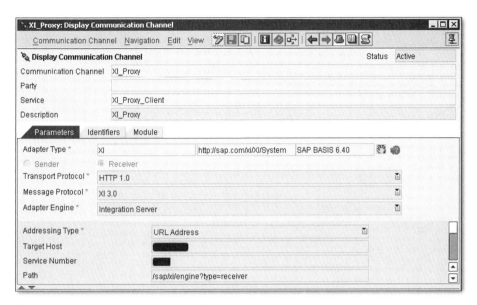

Figure 9.35 XI_Proxy Communication Channel

9.4 Summary

The Linde Group demands that all messages that contain individual responses to warranty claims be collected and returned to the respective dealership in the form of a dealership-specific message within 24 hours. SAP NetWeaver PI, with its integrated ccBPM function, provides the Linde Group with a tool for this purpose that enables the dependencies and associations between messages to be defined. Therefore, this scenario is a typical example of how cross-component business process management can be applied.

A global food manufacturer uses SAP NetWeaver PI as a central hub for exchanging business data with its partners. This chapter presents the implementation of the cross-company communication.

10 Cross-Company Communication Using SAP NetWeaver PI

As in the example in the previous chapter, this scenario was implemented based on a legacy release; however, it can also be implemented in more recent releases of SAP NetWeaver PI without any modifications. The terminology used in this chapter has been updated for better understanding.

10.1 Business Background of the Scenario

This SAP customer uses the Internet to exchange business data with its partners. SAP NetWeaver PI assumes the role of a central gateway for connecting the internal system landscape of the enterprise with the services of its business partners.

This chapter explains how connections are implemented between an SAP CRM 4.0 system and the UCCnet Data Pool Service. Particular attention is paid to those functions provided by SAP NetWeaver PI for business-to-business communication (B2B).

B2B communication

UCCnet enables product data to be published on the Internet, making it available to business partners at a central location. The product information is sent as catalog messages to UCCnet, where it's saved in a standardized format. This enables potential business partners to access the catalog data. The UCCnet Data Pool Service enables information to be collected

UCCnet

at a central location and made available in a standardized form, providing a foundation for electronic commerce.

10.2   Technical Description

This example focuses on integration that goes beyond the boundaries of the SAP customer's internal system landscape. Therefore, this chapter concentrates on the following components and functions of SAP NetWeaver PI:

Integration scenario

1. **B2B functions in the Enterprise Services Repository**
   In SAP NetWeaver PI, you can use integration scenarios to model cross-application collaborative processes. These integration scenarios are like blueprints, representing sample message flows between applications. You assign actual business systems and services to these blueprints to create logical routings in the Integration Directory. To enable the parameters required for B2B communication to be set automatically, select the External Party with B2B Communication checkbox under Communication Type when you define the application component in the integration scenario (see Section 3.3.1, Mapping Application Components to Systems, in Chapter 3).

Party and service

2. **B2B functions in the Integration Directory**
   SAP NetWeaver PI enables you to use not only business systems, but also parties and communication components as logical senders and receivers for XI messages. In general, when a business message is sent to a partner, no information is available about its system landscape. The interfaces provided by the partner are bundled into logical units; that is, the communication components. The communication components are published and can be addressed during B2B communication. You make the corresponding entries for maintaining these services in the Integration Directory.

   Conversely, the sender party (in this case, the SAP NetWeaver PI customer) may not want to reveal internal system information to its business partners. Here, too, it's possible to replace the information about the sender party's *own* business system with the neutral parameters *party* and *communication components* (see Section 6.3, Configuring Cross-Company Processes, in Chapter 6).

3. **Integration scenario configurator**
   Once you've created the integration scenarios in the Enterprise Services Repository, you can use them to derive configuration rules in the Integration Directory. To do this, you link the integration scenarios created in the Enterprise Services Repository with the communication components of the Integration Repository. The integration scenario configurator tool is available to guide you through the necessary configuration settings (see Section 6.2.1, Configuration Using Integration Scenarios, in Chapter 6).

4. **UCCnet adapter from iWay**
   The UCCnet adapter from iWay has two tasks during the connection of the UCCnet Data Pool to SAP NetWeaver PI. First, it establishes the technical connection between the two systems. Second, it converts the enhanced SOAP protocol of SAP NetWeaver PI to the proprietary data format of UCCnet Data Pool Services. The UCCnet adapter is bi-directional; it can send XI messages to the UCCnet Data Pool and receive UCCnet messages and forward them to the SAP NetWeaver PI runtime.

   From a technical point of view, the UCCnet adapter is a resource adapter in the Java Connector Architecture (JCA)[1] and can therefore be inserted in the Adapter Engine of SAP NetWeaver PI. For this purpose, iWay provides adapter metadata, which is saved in the Enterprise Services Repository of SAP NetWeaver PI. The actual adapter instance is implemented in the Integration Directory using the adapter metadata (see Section 10.3.4, Generating Integration Directory Objects Automatically). Figure 10.1 contains an extract from the metadata of the UCCnet adapter showing the specifications for the possible transport and message protocols of the UCCnet adapter.

---

1 The Java Connector Architecture is part of the J2EE specification.

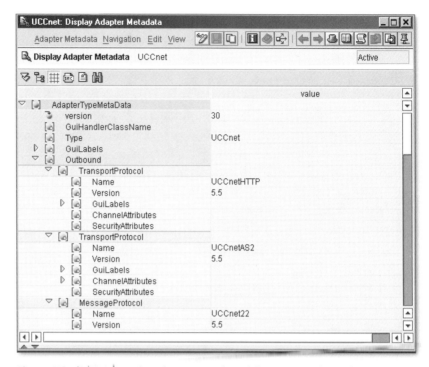

Figure 10.1 Extract from the Adapter Metadata of the UCCnet Adapter from iWay

10.3 Implementing the Scenario

This section gives a detailed description of the steps required to define the UCCnet scenario at the SAP NetWeaver PI customer site.

10.3.1 Components of the UCCnet Scenario

Figure 10.2 shows an overview of the components involved in the UCCnet scenario. Note that the catalog messages aren't sent directly from the CRM application to the Integration Server, but via an IBM Web-Sphere message queue and the SAP NetWeaver PI Java Message Service adapter (JMS) before reaching the Integration Engine. The UCCnet adapter from iWay sends the data to the UCCnet catalog service. Messages with errors aren't sent to UCCnet, but to the internal file system of the SAP NetWeaver XI customer (the *garbage collector*). The response messages from UCCnet reach the SAP CRM system via the RFC adapter.

332

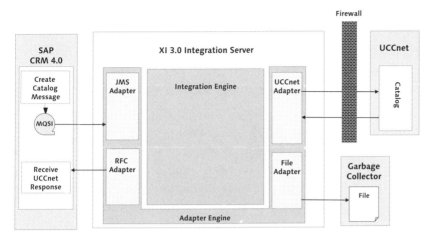

Figure 10.2 Components of the UCCnet Scenario

10.3.2 Development and Configuration Objects

To describe the UCCnet scenario at the SAP NetWeaver PI customer site, the following concentrates primarily on the settings in the Enterprise Services Repository and Integration Directory. From a technical point of view, the required settings in the System Landscape Directory (SLD) are the same as those of the Linde scenario in Chapter 9, Cross-Component Business Process Management at the Linde Group. Therefore, we won't go into further detail here.

Unlike the Linde scenario, however, this implementation uses a *top-down approach* to create the *Integration Repository objects*. This means the integration scenario is the starting point for developing the objects, and the first step is to define the message flow with the help of a graphical tool, the *integration scenario editor*. The next step is to create the required Repository objects. The description of the settings in the Integration Directory at the SAP NetWeaver PI customer site focuses on the B2B functions, the configuration of the iWay UCCnet adapter, and the use of the integration scenario configurator.

Top-down approach

10.3.3 Top-Down Approach to Create Design Objects

Enterprise Services Repository objects must be assigned to software component versions and namespaces. Therefore, the first step is to define the software component versions in the SLD and import them to the Enterprise Services Repository. Two software components are created for the UCCnet scenario.

Software Components GL_CPE and NA_UCCNET

The GL_CPE software component contains all of the Repository objects related to XI messages sent or received by the customer's SAP CRM system. It's based on the software component version SAP BBPCRM 4.0 shipped by SAP. Figure 10.3 shows how Version 1.0 of the GL_CPE software component is displayed in the Enterprise Services Repository. The Details tab displays the namespaces that are inherited from the SAP software component version, SAP BBPCRM 4.0.

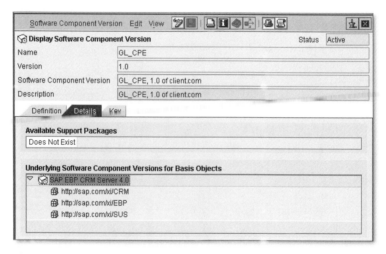

Figure 10.3 Version 1.0 of Software Component GL_CPE

The NA_UCCNET software component contains all of the objects related to the UCCnet Data Pool Service. According to convention as defined by the customer, all objects that relate to both sides of the communication (integration scenarios and mappings) belong to the NA_UCCNET software component. Once the current versions of the software components have been imported to the Enterprise Services Repository, and the namespaces have been defined, development of the objects can begin.

Integration Scenario NA_CPE_UCCNET

The NA_CPE_UCCNET integration scenario is a graphical representation of all actions and message flows that are involved in the SAP NetWeaver PI customer's UCCnet scenario. It's a theoretical blueprint for the actual configuration settings to be made later (see Section 3.3, Modeling Using Integration Scenarios, in Chapter 3). This blueprint is defined using logical application components instead of existing services and systems.

The CPE application component represents the SAP CRM application. Therefore, the GL_CPE 1.0 product is assigned to it, which contains the software component version of the same name.

CPE application component

The UCCNET component represents the UCCnet Data Pool Service. Because this is an application provided by a business partner, the External Party with B2B Communication checkbox is selected under Communication Type. The 🏛 icon appears in the header data for the application component. UCCNET references the product version NA_UCCNET 1.0 with the software component version of the same name.

UCCNET application component

The GarbageCollector application component represents a generic receiver for messages with errors.[2] Like the UCCNET application component, GarbageCollector uses Version 1.0 of the product, NA_UCCNET.

GarbageCollector application component

Once the individual application components have been created, the development of the *actions* can begin. Actions represent elementary function units of an application and pertain to the sending and receiving of XI messages. They are displayed as white rectangles in the integration scenario (see Figure 10.4).

Actions

Because the top-down approach has been chosen for the design of Repository objects, the actions are initially created just as shells. They are assigned service interfaces corresponding to their function later in the design process.

The SUBMIT_CATALOG and RECEIVE_UCCNET_RESULT actions are created for the CPE application component, which represents the SAP CRM function at the SAP NetWeaver PI customer site. Note that the SUBMIT_CATALOG action represents a generic send step. It encompasses all functions that send messages to UCCnet.

CPE actions

---

2 Messages with errors are not sent to UCCnet; instead they are collected in a file and processed manually.

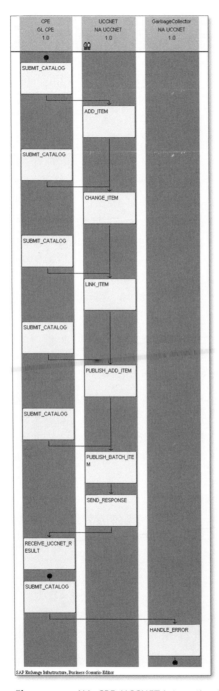

Figure 10.4 NA_CPE_UCCNET Integration Scenario

The SUBMIT_CATALOG action corresponds to the actions ADD_ITEM, CHANGE_ITEM, LINK_ITEM, PUBLISH_ADD_ITEM, and PUBLISH_BATCH_ITEM, of the UCCNET application component. The SEND_RESPONSE action sends the response messages from UCCnet to the RECEIVE_UCCNET_RESULT action of the CPE application component. The GarbageCollector application component contains only the HANDLE_ERROR action.

Table 10.1 gives an overview of the actions created in the UCCnet scenario and the corresponding service interfaces.

UCCNET actions

Actions and service interfaces

Action	Service Interface	Direction
SUBMIT_CATALOG	UCCNetCatalogMessageOut	Outbound
ADD_ITEM	UCCNetItemAddIn	Inbound
CHANGE_ITEM	UCCNetItemChangeIn	Inbound
LINK_ITEM	UCCNetItemLinkIn	Inbound
PUBLISH_ADD_ITEM	UCCNetItemPublishAddIn	Inbound
PUBLISH_BATCH_ITEM	UCCNetItemPublishBatchIn	Inbound
SEND_RESPONSE	UCCNetResponseOut	Outbound
RECEIVE_UCCNET_RESULT	CPE_GET_XI_RESULT	Inbound
HANDLE_ERROR	UCCNetUnprocessedItemsIn	Inbound

Table 10.1 List of All Actions and Service Interfaces Used in the UCCnet Scenario

Figure 10.5 shows the specific settings for the ADD_ITEM action as an example. The Create New Object function in the action editor was used to define the asynchronous inbound interface, UCCNETITEMADDIN, for the action.[3]

---

3 Because the SAP NetWeaver PI customer uses only XSLT mapping technology, it's not imperative that you save the exact structure of the XI message as a message type in the Integration Repository. However, you must specify a message type in the definition of a service interface. Therefore, dummy message types are used here.

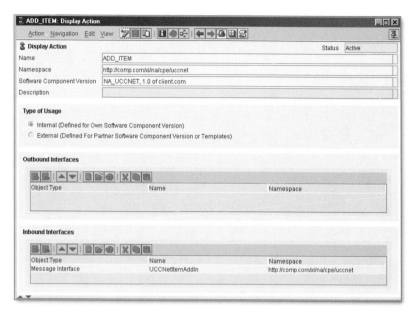

Figure 10.5 ADD_ITEM Action

Adding actions
and generating
connections Once the actions and the service interfaces to be used have been created, they can be added to the respective application component of the
integration scenario. Then you can define the connections *between* the
actions. Refer to Figure 10.4 to see how the actions and their connections
are arranged. Note that catalog messages don't have to pass through the
entire process flow shown in the figure when they are sent. In the real
integration process, it's more likely that in each case only *one* message
is sent to the UCCnet Data Pool Service, which then sends a response
message to the SAP NetWeaver PI customer's SAP NetWeaver CRM system. The various connections of the SUBMIT_CATALOG action represent
alternative communication paths. Creating all actions and their connections in one integration scenario does have certain advantages, as you
can see in the section on configuring the scenario.

Figure 10.6 shows an example of a connection. The SUBMIT_CATALOG
action communicates with the ADD_ITEM action. The entries under
Connection Type tell you that this is an asynchronous connection to a
partner outside the SAP NetWeaver PI customer's own system landscape
(B2B Connection). The steps required to define the assigned mappings
are described in detail in the next section.

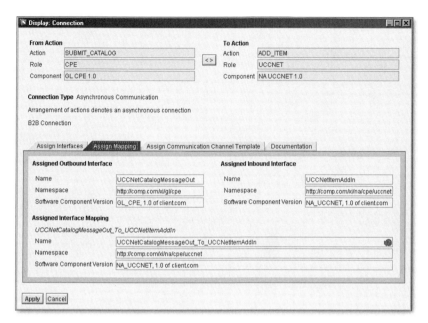

Figure 10.6 Connection of the Asynchronous Communication Type Between the SUBMIT_CATALOG and ADD_ITEM Actions

Imported Archives and Operation Mappings

The SAP customer has decided to use XSLT technology (Extensible Stylesheet Language Transformation) for the mappings in the UCCnet scenario. To be able to use this technology, the corresponding XSLT files are first defined outside SAP NetWeaver PI. Once the XSLT files have been bundled into a Java archive (*jar*), they can be added to the Enterprise Services Repository as an imported archive. Figure 10.7 shows the imported archive, UCCNET_XSLT_Mappings, containing the XSLT files.

Imported archives

The individual mapping programs of the imported archive can now be used to define the operation mappings in SAP NetWeaver PI. As you saw in the previous section, the message structures of the two applications, CPE and UCCnet, are different. In addition, each individual action on the side of the UCCnet application expects its own message structure. Therefore, a separate operation mapping must be defined for each connection between two actions in the integration scenario. The operation mapping itself references the respective XSLT program that connects the source message and the target message. Figure 10.8 shows how the CPEUCCi01

Operation mapping

339

mapping program of the XSL type (that is, XSLT) relates the messages of the UCCNetCatalogMessageOut outbound interface to the messages of the UCCNetItemAddIn inbound interface.

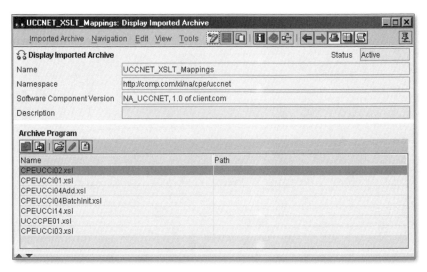

Figure 10.7 UCCNET_XSLT_Mappings Imported Archive

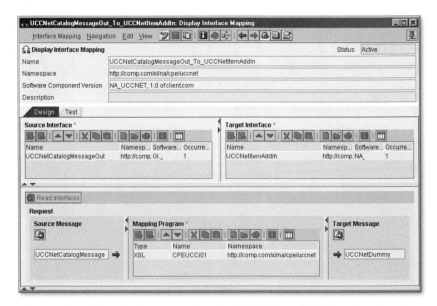

Figure 10.8 UCCNetCatalogMessageOut_To_UCCNetItemAddIn Operation Mapping

This defines all of the required Enterprise Services Repository objects for the UCCnet scenario. The integration scenario configurator can now be used to derive the corresponding configuration objects.

10.3.4 Generating Integration Directory Objects Automatically

The previous section looked at the NA_CPE_UCCNET integration scenario, which is required for the SAP NetWeaver PI connection between the customer's SAP CRM system and UCCnet. The next step is to use this blueprint for the integration process to derive the necessary logical routings. To do this, the *communication parties*, *communication components*, and *communication channels* that are involved in the scenario must be defined. These are then used to replace the theoretical application components in the integration scenario and thus define the configuration.

Communication Party

Communicating beyond the boundaries of a customer's system landscape requires not only communication components, but also the Communication Party parameter to identify the sender and receiver addresses. In this example, the two communication parties GL_COMP_T1 and NA_USA_UCCNET_T1 have been created. They represent the SAP NetWeaver PI customer and the UCCnet organization in B2B communication.

Figure 10.9 illustrates the GL_COMP_T1 party object, which represents the SAP NetWeaver PI customer in B2B communication. Under Identifiers, the first line shows the name automatically assigned for the party by SAP NetWeaver PI (Agency: *http://sap.com/xi/XI*, Scheme: XIParty), which is the same as the object name. In addition, the alternative identifier 4623530132435 (Agency: 009, Scheme: GLN) has been created. This is a Global Location Number (GLN), which identifies the SAP NetWeaver PI customer uniquely in the EAN (International European Article Numbering) or the UCC (Uniform Code Council) in the U.S.

GL_COMP_T1 communication party

Besides the identifiers, you can also see the EBUY and CPE communication components that are assigned to the communication party. The CPE communication component is discussed in the next section.

341

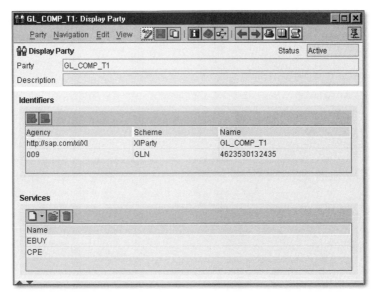

Figure 10.9 GL_COMP_T1 Communication Party

Communication Components

In SAP NetWeaver PI, communication components can be created as a *business component*, a *business system*, or an *integration process*. Note that when you define communication scenarios that go beyond the boundaries of your enterprise's system landscape, you must create the communication components twice. You define them first as a business component, which is assigned to the communication party that represents your own enterprise. Under this name, the communication component represents a specific internal function to the system environment outside the enterprisc's boundaries. You also define this communication component as a business system, which represents the communication component within the system landscape. In this scenario, the CPE business component and the CG1002LS business system represent two sides of the same coin.

Figure 10.10 shows the communication component represented by the CG1002LS business system. The interfaces used in the communication component (in this case, the inbound interfaces) are displayed automatically once the corresponding configuration settings have been made.

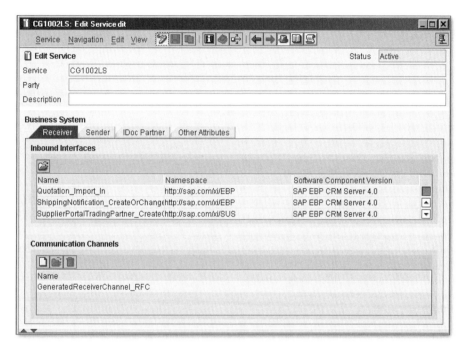

Figure 10.10 CG1100LS Communication Component of the Business-System Type

If messages with errors occur in the UCCnet scenario, they aren't sent to UCCnet, but are collected in a file system within the SAP NetWeaver PI customer's system landscape. The NA_UCCNETGARBAGE-COLLECTOR_S business component has been created for this purpose.

Messages with errors

In addition to the internal company services, another communication component must be created to receive and process the catalog messages on the side of the NA_USA_UCCNET_T1 communication party. The CATALOG_PUBLISH business component performs this function. Table 10.2 summarizes all of the communication components involved in the UCCnet catalog scenario.

Communication Component	Type	Description
CG1002LS	Business system	Represents the SAP CRM system CG1 within the SAPPI customer's system landscape
CPE	Business component	Address of the SAP CRM system CG1002LS in B2B communication
CATALOG_PUBLISH	Business component	UCCnet service for publishing catalog information
NA_UCCNETGARBAGECOLLECTOR_S	Business component	Generic service for processing error messages

Table 10.2 Communication Components of the UCCnet Scenario

Communication Channels

The technical parameters for connecting application systems to SAP NetWeaver PI are defined in the *communication channel* Integration Directory object. As you can see in the component overview of the scenario in Figure 10.2, communication channels must be created for the following adapters:

► Sender adapters: JMS, UCCnet

► Receiver adapters: UCCnet, RFC, file

Configuring the sender JMS adapter

Let's look at the configuration of the JMS and UCCnet adapters as an example. Figure 10.11 shows the technical parameters for establishing a connection to an IBM WebSphere message queue. Section 6.4, Adapter Configuration, in Chapter 6 contains an overview of the general adapter parameters. Note that you must install the corresponding JMS driver before you can use the JMS adapter. The driver software is available from the respective vendor (in this case, IBM).

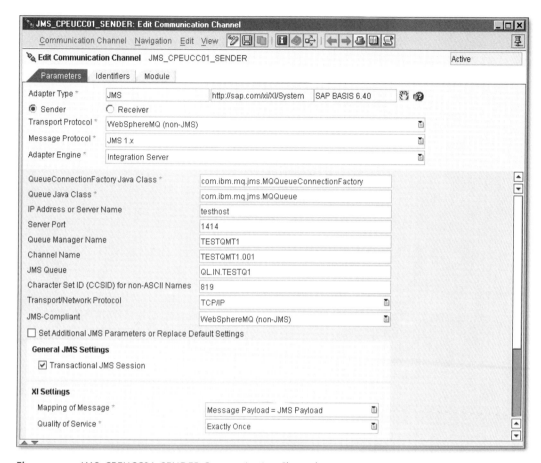

Figure 10.11 JMS_CPEUCC01_SENDER Communication Channel

Section 10.2, Technical Description, explained how the potential parameters for an adapter are made available in the Enterprise Services Repository in the form of adapter metadata. Let's now examine how these potential parameters are used for an actual adapter instance. Figure 10.12 shows some of the parameters used for the adapter in this particular scenario. For example, the transport and message protocols from the adapter metadata are shown in input help. Below this you can see the general parameters that are required to connect the adapter to the UCCnet Data Pool Service.

Configuring the
UCCnet adapter

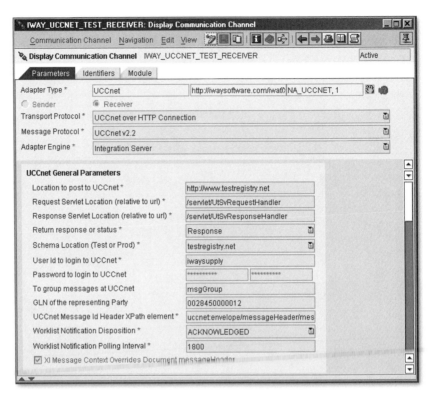

Figure 10.12 Parameters of the IWAY_UCCNET_TEST_RECEIVER Communication Channel

The enterprise-specific GLN number was defined as an additional identifier when the GL_COMP_T1 communication party was created (see Figure 10.9). Because various identifiers can be created for the different business contexts at an enterprise, it's necessary to specify which of these identifiers is to be used for each scenario. This is done in the Identifiers tab in the communication channel. It's specified here that this GLN number is to be used to identify the enterprise in the UCCnet Data Pool in this B2B scenario (see Figure 10.13).

Creating the logical routing automatically
Both the sender and receiver communication components and their communication channels are defined in this way. The template for the integration process (the integration scenario) is available in the Enterprise Services Repository. The integration scenario configurator uses both parts to create the logical routing automatically.

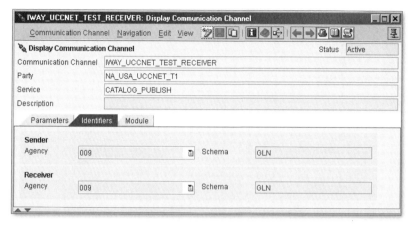

Figure 10.13 Identifiers of the IWAY_UCCNET_TEST_RECEIVER Communication Channel

Integration Scenario Configurator

The SAP NetWeaver PI customer uses the integration scenario configurator to create the Integration Directory objects. The benefit of the integration scenario is twofold: It simplifies the definition of logical routings, and it provides a graphical documentation for these logical routings.

Let's look at the individual steps of the automated process:

1. **Select the "NA_CPE_UCCNET" integration scenario**
   Once you've started the integration scenario configurator (via the menu path TOOLS • APPLY MODEL FROM ES REPOSITORY), you must first select the process integration scenario type and the integration scenario that you want to configure (in the UCCnet scenario of the SAP NetWeaver XI customer, this is NA_CPE_UCCNET). The task is to create a configuration scenario with the same name in the Integration Directory.

2. **Select component view**
   Because there can be several component views for one integration scenario, you must select the relevant one. In the UCCnet scenario, only one component view exists at the time of generation, as shown in Figure 10.14.

347

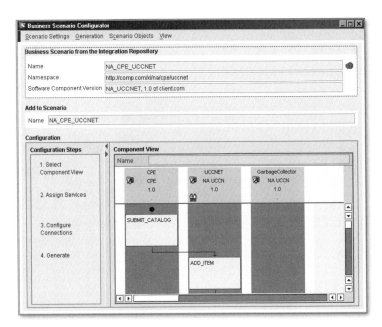

Figure 10.14   Component View of the NA_CPE_UCCNET Integration Scenario

3 Assign communication components

The next step is to assign the communication components maintained in the Integration Directory to the application components of the NA_ CPE_UCCNET integration scenario. In Figure 10.15, you can see that the real business system, CG1002LS, performs the function of the theoretical role CPE when messages are exchanged within the customer's system landscape.

Section 10.3.3, Top-Down Approach to Create Design Objects, explained that information about the business system should not be communicated outside the boundaries of the SAP customer's system landscape. Therefore, once the message leaves the SAP NetWeaver PI pipeline, the technical name of the business system (CG1002LS) must be replaced by a neutral name for the party (GL_COMP_T1) and communication component (CPE). This function is configured in the Business Components for B2B tab.[4] Figure 10.16 shows the settings required to define this assignment.

---

4   Note that business *services* were renamed *business components* in the course of the terminology changes.

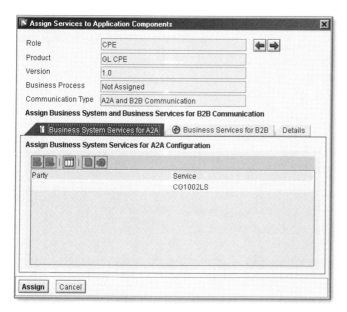

Figure 10.15 Assigning the CG1002LS Business System to the CPE Application Component

Figure 10.16 Assigning the CG1002LS Business System with the GL_COMP_T1 Party and CPE Service to the CPE Application Component

4. **Configure connections**

Once a service has been assigned to all application components, the individual connections can be configured. To understand the required settings, let's look at the connection between the SUBMIT_CATALOG and ADD_ITEM actions (see Figure 10.14).

Assigning connections and communication channels

Once the communication components are assigned to the application components, the party-service combinations, GL_COMP_T1 – CPE (sender) and NA_USA_UCCNET_T1 – CATALOG_PUBLISH (receiver), are displayed as the default values in the Connections from the Service Assignment tab (see Figure 10.17). You assign the predefined communication channels that are to be used for this connection for the respective communication components.

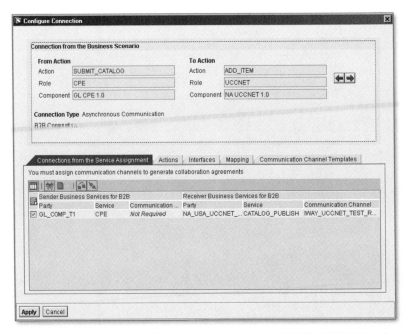

Figure 10.17 Configuration of Connection Between the SUBMIT_CATALOG and ADD_ITEM Actions

Assigning actions, interfaces, and mappings

The actions, interfaces, and mappings that are involved in the connection are listed again in the Actions, Interfaces, and Mapping tab. These are for information purposes. You use these tabs to view and check the settings made in the Enterprise Services Repository.

5. **Generate**

Once all of the connections are configured, you can start automatic generation of the logical routing. To do this, make the settings shown in Figure 10.18.

Under General Settings, you specify whether you want to generate the objects immediately or execute a simulation run. You then define the scope of the generation. In the UCCnet scenario, the Receiver Determination, the Interface Determination, and the Sender/Receiver Agreement are to be generated automatically. The generated objects are to be added to the Standard Change List.

Figure 10.18 Settings in the Integration Scenario Configurator for Automatic Generation of Logical Routing

Created Objects

When you click Start, all receiver determinations, interface determinations, and sender/receiver agreements are generated automatically. Figure 10.19 illustrates the receiver and interface determinations for the catalog messages sent from the SAP NetWeaver CRM system. The XPath expressions were later added to the receiver and interface determinations manually.

Once all of the change lists are activated, the configuration objects are available in the SAP NetWeaver PI runtime environment. The SAP customer can now automatically create, change, assign, and publish the catalog information defined in its SAP CRM system in the UCCnet Data Pool Service.

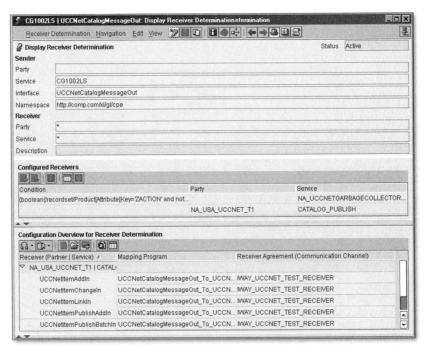

Figure 10.19 Automatically Generated Receiver and Interface Determinations for the UCCNetCatalogMessageOut Interface of the CG1002LS Communication Component

10.4 Summary

SAP NetWeaver PI enables the global foodstuffs manufacturer to publish its product data on the Internet, making it available to its partners at a central location. The integrated B2B functions conceal the SAP customer's internal system information from partners, reducing the risk of attacks from the Internet. The certified UCCnet adapter from iWay enables SAP NetWeaver PI to connect directly to the UCCnet Data Pool Service.

The integration scenario configurator makes creating configuration objects in the Enterprise Services Repository a fast and easy process. Integration scenarios from the Enterprise Services Repository are used as templates that provide detailed graphical documentation for the configuration.

This chapter presents another practical example in detail: the design, implementation, and configuration of a Web service at Boehringer Ingelheim, a pharmaceutical-affiliated group of research companies.

11 Implementation of a Web Service Scenario at Boehringer Ingelheim

SAP NetWeaver Process Integration 7.1 provides the option of communication via the Web service runtime. At Boehringer Ingelheim, a central Web service was implemented that can be addressed from both SAP systems and non-SAP systems.

11.1 Business Background of the Scenario

Boehringer Ingelheim is a worldwide affiliated group of companies that researches, develops, produces, and markets in two the main business areas of human pharmaceuticals and animal health. This results in an active global business that must adhere to a wide range of legal guidelines; among others, EC regulations 2580/2001 and 881/2002 on measures to combat terrorism. These regulations stipulate that businesses with sanctioned persons and institutions are liable to prosecution. For enterprises like Boehringer Ingelheim, this primarily means that address data of the persons involved must be checked when documents such as purchase orders are created.

To implement this check, the German federal publishing house, Bundesanzeiger Verlagsgesellschaft mbH, is one of the institutions that publishes a list of sanctioned addresses and names. This list is referred to as the *sanction list*. At Boehringer Ingelheim, the check of addresses against this sanction list is carried out with the SAP GTS system (*SAP Global Trade Services*). To ensure that this function can be used by all systems,

Check against
sanction lists

353

including non-SAP systems, the check is supposed to be provided via a Web service.

The phases for implementing the Web service consist of modeling, interface design, implementation, and configuration. The following sections provide a detailed description of the tasks that arise in the individual phases.

11.2 Technical Description

The example described here presents the design, implementation, and configuration of a Web service. This description details the following components and functions of SAP NetWeaver PI 7.1:

▶ **Modeling in the Enterprise Services Repository**
Various models are available for modeling business processes in SAP NetWeaver PI. The *process components models* are used to model the data with which the process component works and the service interfaces that are supposed to be provided. Interactions with other process components are presented in *integration scenario models*. The integration scenario model is the starting point for the *process components interaction model* that contains details on the communication between the various process components.

Global data types and service interfaces
▶ **Interface design in the Enterprise Services Builder**
Data types, message types, and service interfaces are defined in the Enterprise Services Builder for the design of the interfaces. The data types are defined based on global data types. They are then used in message types that, in turn, are stored in the inbound and outbound service interfaces.

▶ **Implementing proxies**
The design objects in the Enterprise Services Builder are used to generate and implement proxy objects in the application system.

▶ **Configuring the Web service in SOA management**
After the provider proxy is implemented, it's available as a Web service in the configuration and can be configured; in doing so, you specify the transport and authentication settings.

▶ **Publishing in the Services Registry**
After the Web service configuration is completed, it can be published in the Services Registry, including all settings relevant for the Web service runtime. From the Services Registry, all other systems can call this information and use it to create the consuming applications.

▶ **Testing the Web service in the WS Navigator**
From the Services Registry, the configured Web service can be called in the Web Services Navigator (WS Navigator) for testing.

▶ **Configuring in the Integration Directory**
To be able to call the Web service via the Integration Server, the logical and technical routing is maintained in the Integration Builder. The communication is carried out via a communication channel of the WS type.

Communication channel of the WS type

Now that you've been exposed to a brief overview of the steps for implementing the Web service scenario, the following sections discuss these steps in more detail.

11.3   Implementing the Web Service

The implementation of a Web service starts with the process modeling in the Enterprise Services Builder. The models are used as the basis to create the data types, message types, and service interfaces, from which you generate the proxy objects. After the proxy is configured as the Web service, it can be published and tested. To be able to address the Web service via the Integration Server, you need a configuration in the Integration Directory.

11.3.1   Modeling in the Enterprise Services Builder

A model-driven development of the enterprise services is an important goal of service development according to a service-oriented architecture for business applications. For this purpose, the Enterprise Services Builder provides a modeling environment via which you can create various models. Section 3.2, Modeling the Collaborative Process, in Chapter 3 discussed this modeling environment.

The process component with which you describe parts of the value chain of a business application is a central modeling object. The various model types focus on a precisely defined aspect of process components to help you understand the overall process from different perspectives. To do this, you use three basic models that are described in the following sections as examples.

Process Components Model

Process components

Each process component describes a uniquely defined part of the value chain. Initially, you use the *process components model* to model the data with which the process component works and the interfaces that are supposed to be provided.

Two process components are involved in this scenario. One component triggers the check of addresses that are contained in a newly created document. Another component on a different system checks these addresses against the sanction list.

GPAdressenManagement process components model

For the first subprocess, the GPAdressenManagement process components model was created in the Enterprise Service Builder in the software component version, BIDE_GTS_COMPLIANCE 1.0 of *eu.boehringer.com*. The process components were then modeled in this process components model. The model describes via which operations and service interfaces other process components access data of this process component, and via which operations the process component accesses the data of other process components. As shown in Figure 11.1, you must select SAP ProComp Model as the model type when you create a process components model.

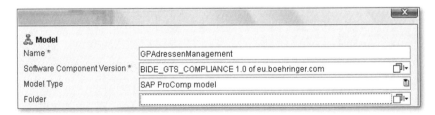

Figure 11.1 Creating the GPAdressenManagement Process Components Model

After you've created the model, you can implement the modeling in the work area. The Addresse (Address) object is created via the Business object icon (pink rectangle) from the modeling toolbar. The Belegmanagement (DocumentManagement) service interface is generated using the Service Interface icon (blue rectangle). In Figure 11.2, these two objects are shown in the work area of the modeling environment in the Enterprise Services Repository.

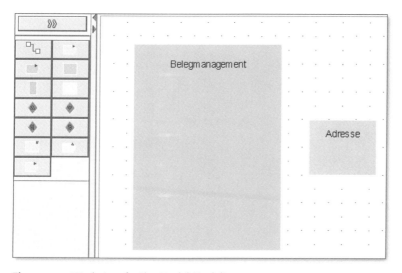

Figure 11.2 Work Area for the Model Modeling

Using the Operation icon (white rectangle), you define the PrüfeBeleg (CheckDocument) operation between the Addresse business object and the Belegmanagement service interface. Similarly, you define a second CheckAddress_out service interface with the two operations, PrüfeAdresseOhneAntwort (CheckAddressWithoutResponse) and PrüfeAdresseMitAntwort (CheckAddressWithResponse). These two operations are supposed to provide two check options — an asynchronous check without response and a synchronous check with response. Figure 11.3 shows both service interfaces and their defined operations.

Defining operations

357

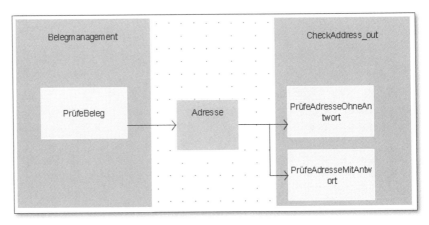

Figure 11.3 Service Interfaces with Operations

Defining relations
to other process
components Now you need to model the relation to the second process component that implements the address check. For this purpose, you use the Process Component icon from the modeling toolbar to create the GPBoykot-tlistenManagement component and link it with the two operations, PrüfeAdresseOhneAntwort and PrüfeAdresseMitAntwort. You establish the connection using the Connection icon ([icon]) in the modeling toolbar.

Figure 11.4 shows the complete modeled process components model, GPAdressenManagement. The model describes the GPAdressenManagement component that is involved in the process. It includes a service that can check a document using the Adresse business object. For this purpose, the Adresse business object uses two operations of the Check-Address_out service interface to establish a communication with another process component, the GPBoykottlistenManagement component. All further steps are then executed in this process component.

GPBoykottlisten-
Management
process compo-
nents model
To model a process components model for this second subprocess, another model of the SAP ProComp Model model type called GPBoykot-tlistenManagement was created. In this model, the ProcessComponent object from the modeling toolbar is used to define the GPAdressen-Management component, which represents the previously modeled subprocess. Additionally, as in the model of the other process components, you define the business object, service interface, operations, and connections.

358

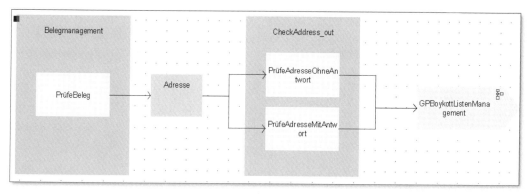

Figure 11.4 GPAdressenManagement Process Components Model

For the CheckSanctionList_in service interface, you define the two operations, FindeEintragMitAdresseKeineAntwort (FindEntryWithAddress-NoResponse) and FindeEintragMitAdresseMitAntwort (FindEntryWith-AddressWithResponse), which both access the Boykottliste (BoycottList) business object. The GPAdressenManagement process component can use these operations to check the Boykottliste object. Figure 11.5 shows the defined objects and connections for the GPBoykottlistenManagement process components model.

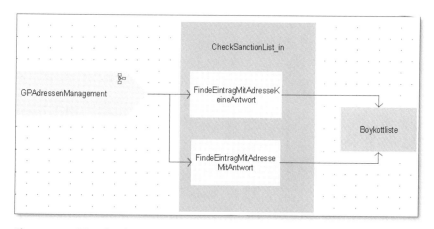

Figure 11.5 GPBoykottlistenManagement Process Components Model

To establish the connection between the two components, GPAdressen-Management and GPBoykottlistenManagement, the appropriate process

Defining connections

359

components model must be defined in the respective object Process Component. In the GPBoykottlistenManagement process components model, you maintain the connection to the GPAdressenManagement process components model in the context menu of the GPAdressenManagement process component via the menu path NEW • ASSIGNMENT. In the GPAdressenManagement process components model, however, you maintain the connection of the GPBoykottlistenManagement process component to the GPBoykottlistenManagement process components model.

Because the individual process components only describe individual parts of the overall process, they also interact. To illustrate these interactions, you work with the integration scenario model.

Integration Scenario Model

In the integration scenario model you illustrate all process components involved for the end-to-end scenario. It provides a general overview of the scenario to better understand the entire process and the interactions between the process components involved.

Creating the integration scenario model

In the present process of the address check against a sanction list in the SAP GTS system, the GPAdressenManagement components in SAP ECC (*ERP Central Component*) interact with the GPBoykottlistenManagement component in SAP GTS. For this process, as shown in Figure 11.6, the modeling environment in the Enterprise Services Builder was used to create an integration scenario model (model type SAP integration scenario model) called GPAdressenManagement-GPBoykottlistenManagement.

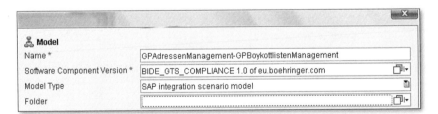

Figure 11.6 Creating the GPAdressenManagement-GPBoykottlistenManagement Integration Scenario Model

In the work area of the modeling area, you use the Deployment Unit icon (white rectangle) to create the two deployment units, ECC and GTS. The deployment units group all process components that are installed later in a system. The GPAdressenManagement process component is added to the ECC deployment unit, and the GPBoykottlistenManagement process component to the GTS deployment unit.

Defining
deployment units

You model the connection between the two process components using the Connection icon ( ); select Enterprise Service Interaction as the relation type. Figure 11.7 shows the modeled integration scenario model.

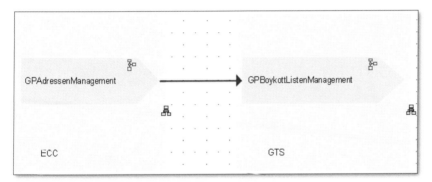

Figure 11.7 GPAdressenManagement-GPBoykottlistenManagement Integration Scenario Model

In the further course of modeling, the integration scenario model is the starting point for creating the process components interaction model.

Process Components Interaction Model

The integration scenario model defines the dependencies between the process components. Only the details for communication between the individual process components are still missing. This information is defined in the process components interaction model.

You can create the interaction model directly from the integration scenario model. For this purpose, select NEW • ASSIGNMENT in the context menu for the connection between the process components, and create a new model with the SAP ProComp interaction model model type in

Creating the
process
components
interaction model

the dialog that now appears. Figure 11.8 shows the basic structure of the process components interaction model to which you need to add the previously modeled objects. Here you select the objects you need for this scenario.

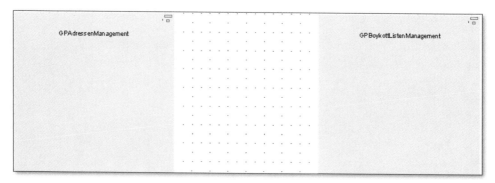

Figure 11.8 Basic Structure of the Process Components Interaction Model

Let's start with the GPAdressenManagement component. In the modeling toolbar, you use the Business Object icon (pink rectangle) to insert the defined business object, Adresse, and the Service Interface icon (blue rectangle) to insert the CheckAddress_out service interface to the GPAdressenManagement component. For the CheckAddress_out service interface, you use the Operation icon (white rectangle) to select the two operations, PrüfeAdresseOhneAntwort and PrüfeAdresseMitAntwort, whereas you can select the existing object via the help function when you rename the operations. Use the same steps to define the components for the GPBoykottlistenManagement process component; the Boykottliste business object, the CheckSanctionList_in service interface, and the two operations, FindeEintragMitAdresseOhneAntwort and FindeEintragMitAdresseMitAntwort, are added. Figure 11.9 shows the process components interaction model with all components that have been added so far.

Defining message types | After you've described the components, you need to add the message type objects, which then represent the message types used in the implementation. For this purpose, you use the Message type icon to create the BPAddressForCheckAsynch message type and to establish a connec-

tion from the PrüfeAdresseOhneAntwort operation of the GPAdressen-
Management component to the message type. A second connection is
created from the message type to the FindeEintragMitAdresseOhne-
Antwort operation in the GPBoykottlistenManagement component.

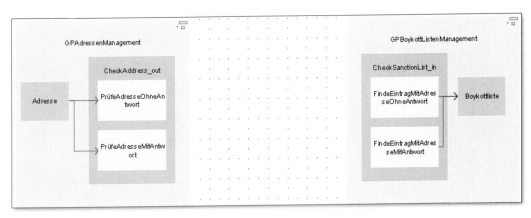

Figure 11.9 Defined Components in the Process Components
Interaction Model

A second message type, BPAddressForCheckSynch, is created for the synchronous query. For this message type you define a connection from
the PrüfeAdresseMitAntwort operation of the GPAdressenManagement
component to the FindeEintragMitAdresseMitAntwort operation of the
GPBoykottlistenManagement component. In the synchronous case, you
also must maintain a connection for the response. For this purpose,
you create the ReturnText message type and connect it with the same
operations. Once all connections are created, the model looks like Figure
11.10.

Based on the model, you can now create all objects to be implemented,
such as service interfaces, operations, and message types. To do so, you
select <OBJECT> ASSIGNMENT • CREATE ASSIGNMENT in the context menu
of the corresponding object and either create a new implementation
object or select an existing one. The following sections discuss in detail
the objects to be implemented.

Creating
implementation
objects

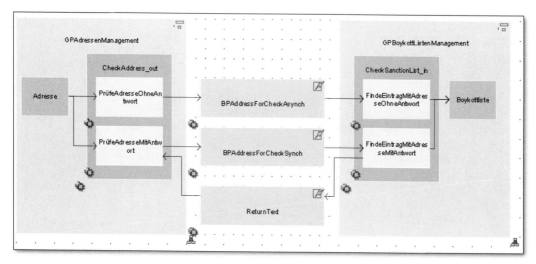

Figure 11.10 Process Components Interaction Model with Message Types and Appropriate Connections

11.3.2 Interface Design in the Enterprise Services Builder

As already mentioned, you can use the process components interaction model as the basis to directly create the service interfaces and message types. For the definition of the message type, data types are required, which Boehringer Ingelheim defined as global data types for reusability reasons.

Global Data Types as the Basis of Message Types

BI_GLOBAL
software
component version

In the SAP_GLOBAL software component version, SAP delivers global data types that must be copied to a separate software component version for release security reasons. This implementation example defined the BI_GLOBAL software component version was defined, which is supposed to be used for the global data types to be copied. This software component version was defined as a prerequisite version in the software component version, BIDE_GTS_COMPLIANCE, in the SLD. This ensures that the global data types from the BI_GLOBAL software component version can be used for defining the aggregated data types and message types in the BIDE_GTS_COMPLIANCE software component version. Figure 11.11 shows the configuration interface to be used in the SLD.

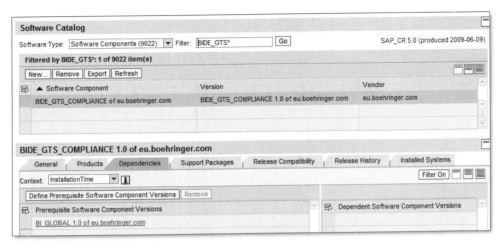

Figure 11.11 BIDE_GTS_COMPLIANCE Software Component Version with the Underlying BI_GLOBAL Software Component Version in the SLD

The global data types that were required for the definition of the aggregated data types and message types were, as shown in Figure 11.12, copied to the BI_GLOBAL software component version in the Enterprise Services Builder.

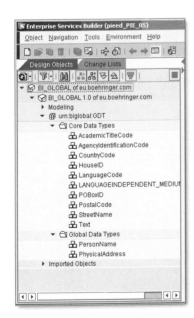

Figure 11.12 Global Data Types in the BI_GLOBAL Software Component Version

Defining message types

The global data types are used in the BIDE_GTS_COMPLIANCE software component version for the configuration of aggregated data types and the message types required for the scenario. As described in the previous section, the three message types described in the modeling step, BPAddressForCheckAsynch, BPAddressForCheckSynch, and ReturnText, are created from the process components interaction model and defined based on the global and aggregated data types. Figure 11.13 shows the BPAddressForCheckAsynch message type with the data types used. The message types are required in the subsequent configuration to be able to store them in the service interfaces.

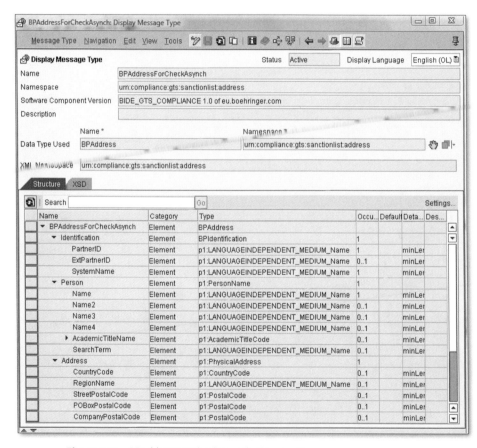

Figure 11.13 BPAddressForCheckAsynch Message Type

Service Interfaces

Because a provider and a consumer component are involved in the communication, two service interfaces, an inbound and an outbound service interface, are required for the communication.

CheckSanctionList_in inbound service interface

The CheckSanctionList_in inbound service interface that is specified in the modeling is created from the process components interaction model (as described in the previous section). It includes a synchronous and an asynchronous operation. Figures 11.14 and 11.15 show the two operations of the CheckSanctionList_in service interface.

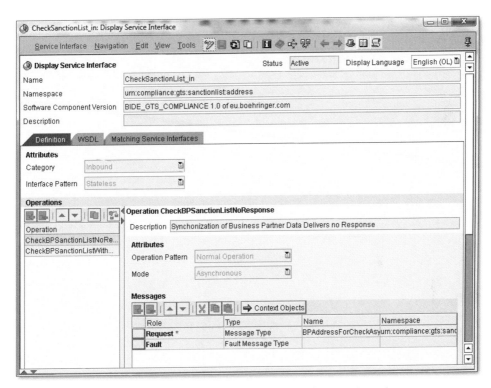

Figure 11.14 CheckSanctionList_in Service Interface with Asynchronous Operation with the BPAddressForCheckAsynch Request Message Type

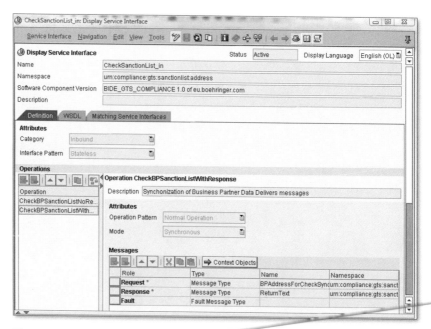

Figure 11.15 CheckSanctionList_in Service Interface with Synchronous Operation with the BPAddressForCheckSynch Request Message Type and the ReturnText Response Message Type

The BPAddressForCheckAsynch request message type is used in the asynchronous operation, the address check without response. In the synchronous operation, however, both a request and a response message type must be defined. For this purpose, the BPAddressForCheckSynch and ReturnText message types are selected using the input help.

CheckAddress_
out outbound
service interface

The CheckAddress_out outbound service interface is defined similarly based on the same message types; the only difference is that the category of this service interface is *outbound*, not *inbound*, because it's an outbound interface.

With the definition of the service interface, you've laid the foundation for the next step — the generation and implementation of the proxies. The following section describes these steps in more detail.

11.3.3   Implementing the Proxies

In the outside-in approach used here, the interface is defined in the Enterprise Services Builder and must then be transferred to the respective application systems. In these systems, the proxy generation is used to generate and implement a proxy: a provider proxy in the provider system and a consumer proxy in the calling system.

You start the proxy generation via the Object Navigator transaction (Transaction code SE80); the Enterprise Services Browser entry indicates the objects of the connected Enterprise Services Builder. You can double-click the respective objects to generate the proxy objects. You generate data elements from the core data types and structures from the aggregated and freely modeled data types. You create ABAP OO interfaces and classes in the ABAP Dictionary of the SAP system for service interfaces.

Proxy generation

Provided that the message types used reference data types from other namespaces, these data types must be generated explicitly in advance. In this example, data types from the BIDE_GLOBAL software component version were referenced from the aggregated data types and message types of the CheckSanctionList_in service interface. These data types must therefore be generated before you can generate the service interface and the aggregated data types. When you generate the aggregated data types, a reference is made to the data elements from the BIDE_GLOBAL software component version. To separate the proxy objects of the global data types and those of the application's implementation, they were generated in different packages.

In the generation of the proxy object for the CheckSanctionList_in inbound service interface, an ABAP OO class is generated that contains a method for each defined operation. The implementation of the Web service itself takes place in these two methods. An ABAP class with two methods is generated in the calling application system for the Check-Address_out outbound service interface. These methods are then called in the calling application to start the communication. Once the provider proxy is implemented in the GTS system, it's only available in the Web services configuration and can be configured there as a Web service.

Proxy implementation

11.3.4 Configuring the Web Service

To be able to use a provider proxy as a Web service, a Web service runtime configuration must be created for the proxy. Only then can it be called via the Web service runtime.

Configuring the proxy as a Web service

In this example, the CheckSanctionList_in service is supposed to be provided as a Web service in the SAP GTS system. To do so, in the SAP GTS system the Web service configuration is called using Transaction SOAMANAGER. Activating the Single Service Administration link in the Application and Scenario Communication tab starts the user interface for the Web service configuration. The search screen illustrated in Figure 11.16 appears, which provides the generated proxy, CheckSanctionList_in, as a service for selection.

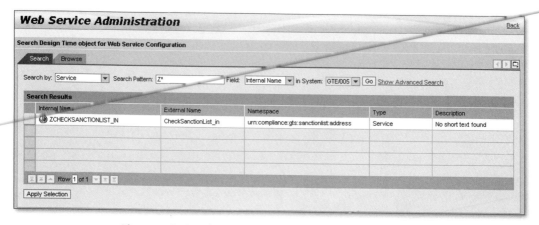

Figure 11.16 Search Screen for the Search for the CheckSanctionList_in Service

Selecting the service and clicking the Apply Selection button opens the service's administration view as shown in Figure 11.17. The empty field at the bottom right indicates that no endpoint has thus far been defined for this service.

Creating the endpoint

If you go to the Configurations tab, you can create such an endpoint as a runtime configuration for the service. You start the dialog for creating endpoints by clicking the Create Enpoint button. When you close the dialog, the configuration view of the new endpoint becomes visible (see Figure 11.18).

Figure 11.17 Administration View for the CheckSanctionList_in Service

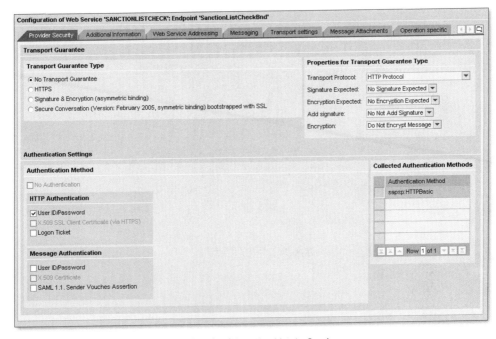

Figure 11.18 Configuration View for the CheckSanctionList_in Service

The transport guarantee and the authentication method are selected as the most critical settings here. After you save these settings, the service can be called as a Web service in the SAP GTS system. The overview shown in Figure 11.19 presents the newly created service and the associated binding.

Web service runtime settings

371

Figure 11.19 Administration View for the CheckSanctionList_in Service and the Associated Binding

Displaying the
WSDL document

You can use the Open WSDL document for selected binding link to display the generated WSDL document. The calling program requires the information in this WSDL document to be able to call the Web service. Among other things, here you can find the endpoint URL to call the Web service.

The Web service is fully functional and can be consumed by other applications. To simplify the search for Web services and to have them available at a central location, you can publish the service in the Services Registry, where it's available to all applications including the endpoint information.

11.3.5 Publishing the Services Registry

You can publish of services in the Services Registry using Transaction SOAMANAGER in the system in which the Web service had been configured -- in this example, the SAP GTS system. In the Technical Configuration tab, you can find the publishing function using the Publication Administration link.

Publishing the
Web service

In the publication administration shown in Figure 11.20, you must enter the name of the service and the Services Registry to which the Web service is supposed to be published. You then start the publication by clicking the Execute button. A log is displayed after the execution. The log shows whether the service and the associated endpoint could be published successfully in the Services Registry.

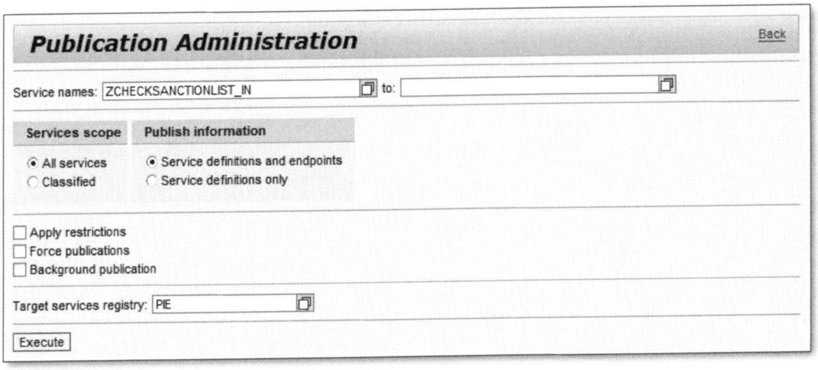

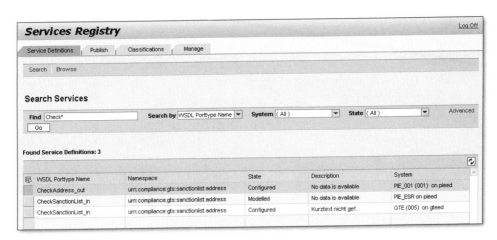

Figure 11.20 Publication Administration for the CheckSanctionList_in Service

As you can see in Figure 11.21, the CheckSanctionList_in service can be found as a configured service in the GTE SAP GTS system in the Services Registry.[1]

Figure 11.21 Services Published in the Services Registry

In the Services Registry you can now browse centrally for the service, and you can also test the service directly from the Services Registry via the Web Service Navigator.

---

1 The Services Registry is only installed in English in the system.

11.3.6 Testing the Web Services in the WS Navigator

From the Services Registry, you can directly navigate to the Web Services Navigator, where you can test the Web service with its runtime settings. After selecting the CheckSanctionList_in service in the search screen of the Services Registry, you can test the Web service, as shown in Figure 11.22, by clicking the Test button in the Endpoints tab. This starts the WS Navigator, and the Web service is then called with the target address stored in the service endpoint.

Figure 11.22 Endpoint Information on the CheckSanctionList_in Service in the Services Registry

Test environment The WS Navigator provides a test environment that enables you to select individual operations of a service and test them separately. After you've selected the operation, as shown in Figure 11.23, the system opens a test frame in which you can enter the values to be called.

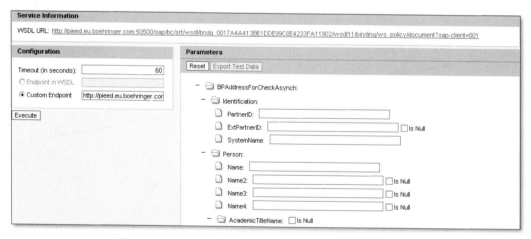

Figure 11.23 Test Environment for Testing the CheckSanctionList_in Service in the WS Navigator

374

After the Web service is called, the response to the call is displayed both in a browser-based interface and in XML format. In addition to the result, you can also view the server's complete HTTP response.

After the successful configuration of the Web service, you can implement the binding of the calling application. In general, you have two options here: the direct Web service call and the call via the Integration Server. The call via the Integration Server has the benefit that the sender can be any application. Both calls via technical adapters and calls via proxies are possible. The following section describes the configuration for the web service call via the Integration Server in more detail.

11.3.7 Configuration in the Integration Directory

To be able to call the Web service via the Integration Server, you need to configure the routing in the Integration Directory. In this example, the SAP ECC system with the IBE system ID functions as the sender. The receiver determination, the interface determination, and the receiver agreement are defined here.

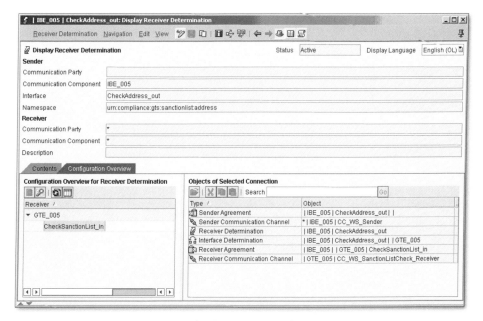

Figure 11.24 Receiver Determination for the IBE_005 Sender

Configuration of the routing

In Figure 11.24, you can view the receiver determination for the IBE_005 sender with the CheckAddress_out interface. The GTE_005 system is maintained as the receiver. In the configuration overview, you can view all objects of this connection; in the interface determination, you maintain the CheckSanctionList_in receiver; in the receiver agreement, you specify the communication channel to be used.

Communication channel of the WS type

Because a Web service is supposed to be called, the communication channel for the receiver must be of the WS type. In the communication channel, you make the technical settings for the call of the Web service (see Figure 11.25). These include, among other things, the transport and security settings. You must maintain the data of the Web service's provider system, in this case the GTE_005 GTS system, as the target host and the port.

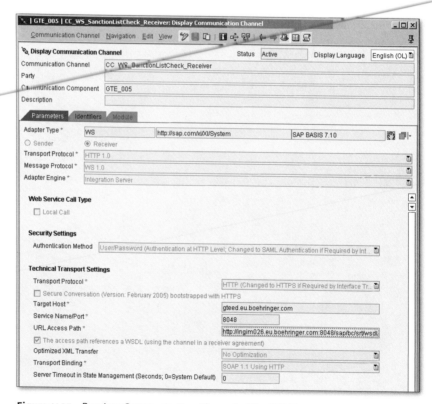

Figure 11.25 Receiver Communication Channel of the WS Type

The information for the authentication, however, isn't maintained in the communication channel, but in the receiver determination. Consequently, a communication channel can be used in different scenarios with different users for the communication.

The configuration of the SAP NetWeaver PI system is the last step in the configuration of the Web service scenario. The check against the sanction list can now be performed directly against the GTS system and as a call via the Integration Server.

11.4   Summary

With SAP NetWeaver PI 7.1, Boehringer Ingelheim can provide the central scenario of address check against sanction list as a Web service, and can address it both directly and via the Integration Server. This enables you to call the Web service from both SAP and non-SAP systems. The Web service adapters used provide comprehensive configuration options for reliable transfer based on the *Web Services Reliable Messaging* (WS-RM) standard protocol.

The modeling environment for the process model in the Enterprise Services Builder allow for a comprehensive modeling of business processes. Based on the modeled models, you can then create the configuration-relevant objects.

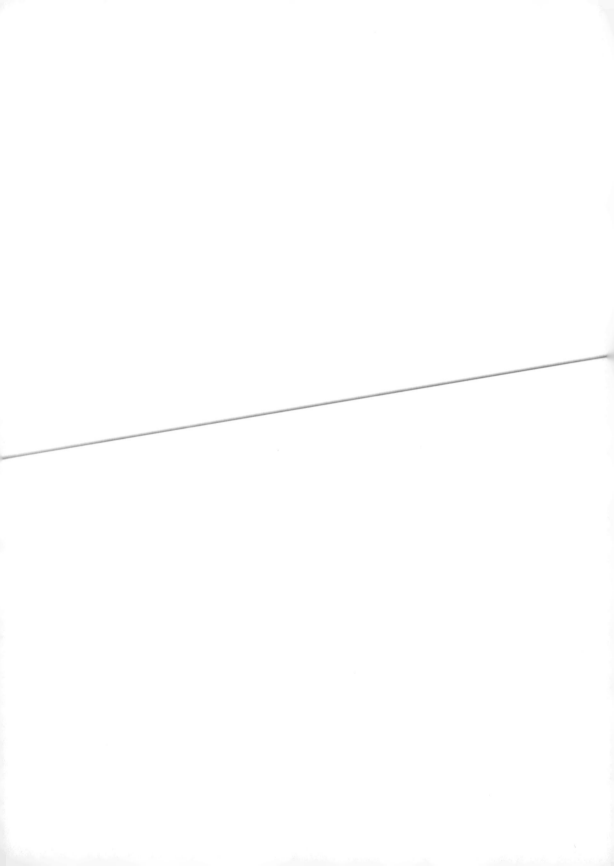

A   Glossary

This is a short glossary containing definitions of some of the most important terms in SAP NetWeaver PI. It is not a comprehensive list.

Abstract service interface   Interface without implementation in an application system. You cannot generate a proxy for this interface type. You use abstract service interfaces in integration processes, for example, to receive or send messages from application systems. Because abstract service interfaces are directionless, you can use the same abstract interface to receive or to send a message.

Acknowledgment message   A message sent to the sender to confirm that an asynchronous message has been processed successfully or that an error has occurred during message processing.

Action   An integration scenario object representing a function within an application component. It's not subdivided further. Actions focus on the exchange of messages between application components.

Adapter Engine   Runtime component for resource adapters used for integrating applications and systems using SAP NetWeaver PI. The Adapter Engine contains the Adapter Framework and has functions for messaging and queuing, security, and connectivity with the Integration Server. You can use this framework to add your own resource adapters or those of your partners.

Advanced Adapter Engine   With SAP NetWeaver PI 7.1, the Adapter Engine was enhanced with the option of message processing without the Integration Server, and it was renamed Advanced Adapter Engine. In the Integration Directory, the Integrated Configuration configuration object is used for this configuration. Using this configuration, the message processing for this scenario takes place in the Advanced Adapter Engine.

Application component   A component that represents a logical participant in an integration scenario and describes the business tasks and responsibilities of this participant in the scenario.

Business objects   Artifact of the process components architecture model for modeling data of a process component.

Business Process Engine   Runtime component for processing integration processes within the framework of cross-component business process management (ccBPM).

Business system   Logical sender or receiver that exchanges messages using SAP NetWeaver PI and that is entered in the System Landscape Directory (SLD). Business systems pertain to a system landscape.

Change list   User-specific list of objects in the Enterprise Services Builder and in the Integration Directory that are currently being edited.

Chem eStandards   Standard for communication within the chemical industry that are stipulated by the Chemical Industry Data Exchange. Information can be found on the CIDX and OAGi websites at *http://www.cidx.org* and *http://www.oagi.org*.

CMS Change Management Service. Transport technology of SAP to transport SAP NetWeaver PI design and configuration objects from the Enterprise Services Builder and the Integration Directory between systems.

Collaboration knowledge All contents of the Enterprise Services Builder and the Integration Directory.

Collaborative process An already existing or new process from the real business world that is supposed to be implemented via a message exchange with SAP NetWeaver PI

Communication agreement Specifies for a concrete sender-receiver pair which details defined in the communication profile are supposed to be valid for the message exchange.

Communication channel Defines the specific rules according to which messages are handled in inbound or outbound processing. In particular, in the communication channel you specify the type and the configuration of the adapter that is to be used in inbound or outbound processing.

Communication component Configuration object in the Integration Directory for addressing a sender or receiver. Communication components are usually provided by a communication party but can also be used without parties. Possible types are business systems, business components, and integration processes.

Communication party Configuration object used to logically address an enterprise of a collaborative process independent of the representation specified in the message header.

Communication profile Describes the technical options of the communication partners with regard to message exchange. It consists of an identifier, the communication components, interfaces, and communication channels.

Conceptual modeling Graphical mapping of the process flows of an enterprise from the operation perspective.

Configuration object Object in the Integration Directory. Object types include communication partners, various types of communication components, communication channels, receiver determinations, interface determinations, and sender and receiver agreements.

Configuration scenario Object for grouping configuration objects in the Integration Directory. If you created a configuration scenario, you can select an integration scenario from the Enterprise Services Builder and use it as a template for configuration.

Configuration time At configuration time, you configure a collaborative process for a particular system landscape in the Integration Directory so it can be evaluated by the Integration Server or the Advanced Adapter Engine at runtime.

Connection Part of an integration scenario that connects two actions in a process flow to one another.

Consumer proxy Runtime representative used by an application to send a message to the Integration Server or via the Web service runtime.

CTS   Change and Transport System. SAP transport technology used to transport ABAP and Java objects between systems.

Design object   Object in the Enterprise Services Builder. There are integration scenario, integration process, operation, mapping, and adapter objects.

Design time   Stage of development at which you define objects in the Enterprise Services Builder. You can ship these design objects and configure them for a particular scenario of a particular system landscape.

Direct connection   Configuration object in the Integration Directory that describes the direct assignment of a sender and an outbound interface to a receiver via the Web service runtime.

End-to-end monitoring   Function in the Runtime Workbench for monitoring the processing of individual messages within a preconfigured component set.

Enterprise service   Web service used for business processes.

Enterprise Services Builder   The repository used to describe all information to be shipped regarding the collaborative process, for example, integration scenarios, integration processes, interfaces, and mappings.

Identification scheme   An identification process that provides a context within which an object can be uniquely identified. Identification schemes are issued and managed by issuing agencies.

Identifier   A means of identification that consists of an agency, an identification scheme, and a code for identifying an enterprise.

Inbound interface   Superordinate term for interfaces that process messages at the receiver (for example, RFCs and IDocs) and inbound service interfaces for which you generate provider proxies in the application system.

Inbound processing   Processing step on the Integration Server for converting received messages in such a way that the Integration Engine of the Integration Server or the Advanced Adapter Engine can process them. Inbound processing varies according to the adapter type used.

Inside-out development   Generation of a formal interface description from an interface implementation.

Integrated configuration   Configuration object in the Integration Directory that describes message processing using the Advanced Adapter Engine.

Integration Directory   The directory used to configure the collaborative process.

Integration process   Design object in the Enterprise Services Builder for describing the stateful processing of messages on the Integration Server. You address integration processes as communication components in the Integration Directory.

Integration Server   Central runtime distribution engine for processing and forwarding messages.

Integration scenario A scenario that describes the collaborative process in the Enterprise Services Builder as an exchange of messages between application components.

Integration scenario model Object type of the Enterprise Services Repository for the graphical description of an executable process chain. The integration scenario model is part of the process component architecture model.

Interface determination Configuration object that describes the assignment of an outbound interface to an inbound interface and to an operation mapping.

Issuing agency Organization for managing and issuing one or more identification schemes to uniquely identify objects. The company Dun & Bradstreet, for example, manages the identification schema D-U-N-S for uniquely identifying company units.

Mapping Generic term for the transformation of a message regarding its structure and contained values.

Mapping program Program for transforming a message. Mapping programs in the Enterprise Services Builder are the message mappings created there, mapping templates, or imported XSLT or Java mappings.

Message An instance for exchanging data between senders or receivers and the Integration Server or the Advanced Adapter Engine. A message consists of a message header, the payload, and optionally any number of attachments (depending on the adapter type). The message header and payload are in XML format.

Message mapping Mapping program that you define using the graphical mapping editor in the Enterprise Services Builder.

Message type Language-independent interface object in the Enterprise Services Builder that defines the root element of a message.

Multi-mapping Mapping program for mapping m messages to n messages.

Namespace Qualifier for XML names to identify objects uniquely.

Non-central Advanced Adapter Engine Advanced Adapter Engine that is installed in a non-central server. The configuration is via the Integration Directory like for the central Advanced Adapter Engine.

Operation Function that provides a service interface. This level is used for the configuration of the message exchange.

Operation mapping Design object in the Enterprise Services Builder for defining the mapping programs for request, response, and fault messages that are to be executed for a source and target interface. For transformation steps in integration processes, you can also specify several asynchronous source and target service interfaces to merge or split messages using a multi-mapping.

Outbound interface Superordinate term for interfaces used by senders to send messages to the Integration Server or the Advanced Adapter Engine, for example RFCs, IDocs, and inbound service interfaces for which you generate consumer proxies in the application system.

Outbound processing Processing step on the Integration Server for converting a message in such a way that it can be processed by an external receiver, depending on the receiver adapter used.

Outside-in development Implementation of an interface using its formal description.

Payload The body of a message with the business data in XML.

PI content Process integration content. All contents of the Enterprise Services Builder.

Pipeline Defined sequence of Integration Engine services through which a message passes. The pipeline consists of individual pipeline elements, which call pipeline services.

Principal propagation The forwarding of user IDs from the sender via the Integration Server to the receiver in an SAP NetWeaver PI message.

Process component Self-contained part of a value chain.

Process component interaction model Object type of the Enterprise Services Repository for the graphical description of the communication between two process components at the message level.

Process component model Object type of the Enterprise Services Repository for the graphical description of business processes at the process component level. It describes the underlying data, service interfaces, and operations of a process component.

Provider proxy Runtime representative used by an application to receive a message using the Integration Server of SAP NetWeaver PI or via the Web service runtime.

Proxy Generic term for consumer or provider proxies.

Proxy generation Tool that uses service interfaces in the Enterprise Services Builder to generate proxy objects in an application system to exchange messages.

Proxy object Generated object in the application system, for example, a class, an interface, or a data type.

Quality of service Attribute of a message that determines how the sender delivers the message.

Receiver adapter Adapter that is called by the Integration Engine of the Integration Server or the Advanced Adapter Engine to forward a message to a receiver.

Receiver agreement An agreement that defines technical details for the communication between a receiver and the Integration Server.

Receiver determination Configuration object in the Integration Directory that describes the assignment of a sender and an outbound interface to one or more receivers.

Release transfer Transfer of objects of a software component version to another software component version of the same Enterprise Services Builder.

Request message Message from a sender to a receiver to make a request or transfer data to the receiver.

Response message   Message from a receiver as a direct response to a request from the sender.

RosettaNet standards   Standards stipulated by RossettaNet for communication in the high-tech industry. For more information, see the RosettaNet homepage at *http://www.rosettanet.org*.

Runtime Workbench   Central tool in SAP NetWeaver PI for monitoring message processing, runtime components, and performance.

SAP NetWeaver Administrator   (NWA) Central administration and monitoring tool provided by SAP for ABAP and Java systems in a browser-based user interface.

SAP Solution Manager   Central tool provided by SAP for accessing tools, methods, and preconfigured contents, which you can use for evaluation and implementation and in the live operation of your systems.

Sender adapter   Adapter for forwarding messages of a sender to the Integration Engine of the Integration Server or the Advanced Adapter Engine.

Sender agreement   An agreement that defines technical details for the communication between a sender and the Integration Server.

Serialization context   A string enabling a sender to group asynchronous messages. All asynchronous messages with the same serialization context arrive at the receiver in the same sequence that they were sent from the sender.

Service interface   Language-independent interface object in the Enterprise Services Builder for describing the signature of a caller or a receiver in WSDL.

Services Registry   Repository for Web services.

Software component version   Shipment unit for design objects in the Enterprise Services Builder. You import software component versions from the System Landscape Directory by using the Enterprise Services Builder.

Web service   Application that can be uniquely identified with a Uniform Resource Identifier (URI) and whose interface is defined using WSDL. Message exchange with Web services is based on XML.

WSDL   Web Services Description Language. Description language that is independent of platforms, programming languages, and protocol and is used for the exchange of messages on the basis of XML.

WS Navigator   Tool for calling and executing Web services.

XML   Extensible Markup Language. Although there are parallels to HTML, XML was developed to describe data, unlike HTML. The structure and type of data in an XML document are defined using XML Schema or a DTD (Document Type Definition). For a good introduction to different XML standards such as XML Schema, XSLT, XPath, DTD, SOAP, and WSDL, see *http://www.w3schools.com*.

XML validation   Message structure check at runtime in the Integration Server or the Advanced Adapter Engine.

B   The Authors

Mandy Krimmel studied engineering at the Humboldt University, Berlin, Germany. In 1998, she started her professional career at a research institute of the German Federal Land of Baden-Württemberg. There she assumed responsibility for the technical evaluation of various EU research projects. In 2001 she joined SAP's Active Global Support, where she worked in the area of SAP interfaces. Since 2003 she has been responsible for, among other things, the project management of integration tests, the enhancement of SAP NetWeaver PI demo applications, and the creation of technical guides for SAP NetWeaver PI in the area of Quality Engineering for SAP NetWeaver PI.

Dr. Joachim Orb completed his doctorate in meteorology at the Swiss Federal Institute of Technology, Zurich. In 1998, he started working at SAP Labs France, where his main focus was the development of SAP standard interfaces. In 2002, he joined SAP AG's SAP NetWeaver Regional Implementation Group (RIG) and was involved in the rollout of SAP NetWeaver in Europe. In 2010, he will begin work as a professor of computer science at the University of Applied Sciences, Offenburg, Germany.

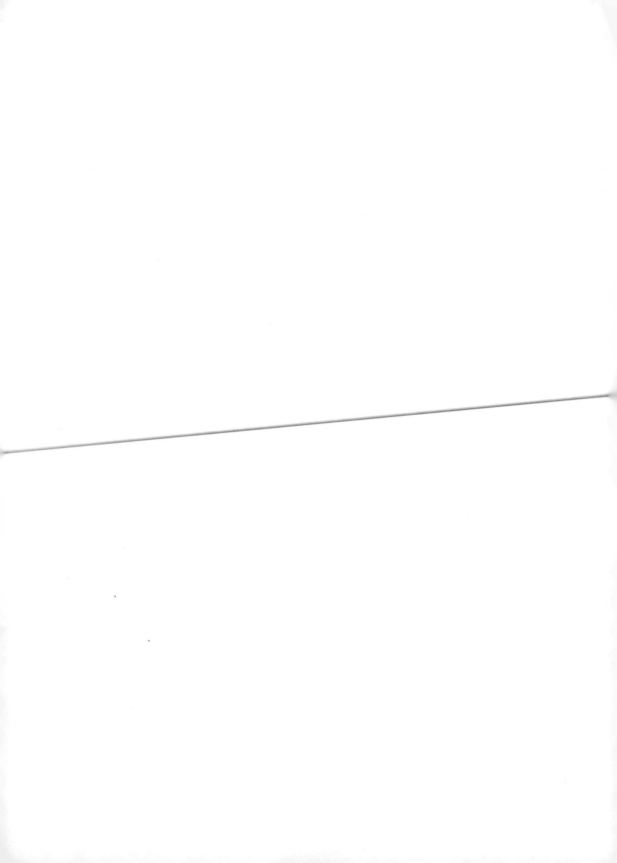

Index

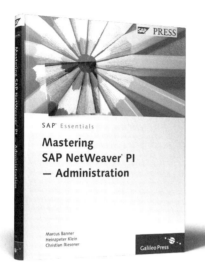

2nd edition, extended and updated for SAP NetWeaver PI 7.1

Benefit from exclusive tips on configuration, performance optimization, and monitoring

Learn everything about SOA integration and the Enterprise Services Repository

Marcus Banner, Heinzpeter Klein, Christian Riesener

Mastering SAP NetWeaver PI - Administration

This practical SAP PRESS Essentials guide will take you through all of the relevant administration tasks involving SAP NetWeaver Process Integration, helping you to identify and avoid the common pitfalls. The authors guide you through the configuration of Enterprise Services Repository and the System Landscape Directory. Exclusive insights help you to quickly learn the basics of configuring the System Landscape Directory and Change Management Service. Plus, you get a highly detailed introduction to the XI transport system. You'll learn about the crucial topics of authorizations and performance optimization. This second edition has been updated and revised, and is up to date for SAP NetWeaver PI 7.1. A new chapter covers the Enterprise Services Repository. With this unique guide, you'll profit immediately from the authors' wealth of practical experience, and you'll be fully prepared for the administration of SAP NetWeaver PI.

225 pp., 2. edition, 69,95 Euro / US$ 84.95
ISBN 978-1-59229-321-6

>> www.sap-press.com

Provides all functional details on the successor of CUA

Describes integration with SAP NetWeaver and SOA landscapes

Includes two detailed real-life scenarios

Loren Heilig

Understanding SAP NetWeaver Identity Management

Whether you're thinking about an identity management solution for your company, are currently implementing one, or are already working with SAP NetWeaver Identity Management, this book covers all important aspects for the selection, implementation, and operation of the solution. Take advantage of proven concepts and tips from the authors, and learn SAP NetWeaver IdM from A to Z.

approx. 320 pp., 69,95 Euro / US$ 69.95
ISBN 978-1-59229-338-4, April 2010

>> www.sap-press.com

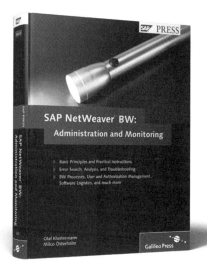

Basic Principles and Practical
Instructions

BW Processes, User and Authorization
Management, Software Logistics, and
much more

Error Search, Analysis, and
Troubleshooting

Milco Österholm, Olaf Klostermann

SAP NetWeaver Business Warehouse: Administration and Monitoring

With this book, you'll get a complete understanding of all administration
tasks that arise in a live SAP NetWeaver BW system, and you'll find
guidance on ways to solve any problems that might occur. Coverage
includes all topics relevant to administration and monitoring of SAP
NetWeaver BW, including basic principles, tasks, analysis, and
troubleshooting. Other key coverage topics include archiving and data
maintenance, the BI administration cockpit, report monitoring, SAP
support and much, much more.

600 pp., 2010, 79,95 Euro / US$ 79.95
ISBN 978-1-59229-330-8

>> www.sap-press.com

Setup, installation, configuration, and maintenance of the SAP database

Tried-and-tested administration solutions in connection with SAP NetWeaver Application Server

Including chapters about performance optimization and problem analysis

André Bögelsack, Stephan Gradl, Manuel Mayer, Helmut Krcmar

SAP MaxDB Administration

This book provides you with a detailed overview of the current MaxDB release 7.7. When necessary, it will also apply to earlier releases. The book deals with the internal structures of the database, and is based on the interaction with the SAP NetWeaver Application Server. The book will help you to quickly resolve errors in typical situations, explain in detail the typical administration tasks, and help administrators find performance bottlenecks. After reading this book, you will be prepared to own and administer MaxDB. The book is filled with step-by-step instruction, schematic diagrams, and helpful screenshots.

326 pp., 2009, 69,95 Euro / US$ 69.95
ISBN 978-1-59229-299-8

>> www.sap-press.com

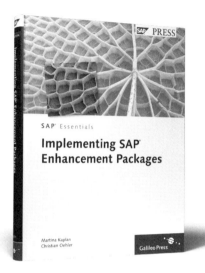

Shows how to install and activate enhancement packages via the switch framework

Explains how to successfully use all related EHP tools

Covers best practices for planning and running EHP projects

Martina Kaplan, Christian Oehler

Implementing SAP Enhancement Packages

With SAP NetWeaver 7.0 or SAP ERP 6.0, SAP has fundamentally changed the method of how you can import new functions to your running systems: Enhancement packages (EHP) can be activated in a more target-oriented, faster, and controllable way in the SAP system, via the switch framework. This book offers project guidelines for administrators on the use of SAP enhancement packages, including topics such as areas of use, planning, installation, project specifications, and best practices. It explains the planning of EHP projects (compared to common upgrade projects), provides details on the implementation of enhancement packages, and offers tips and tricks based on the authors' experiences.

approx. 200 pp., 69,95 Euro / US$ 84.95
ISBN 978-1-59229-351-3, July 2010

>> www.sap-press.com

Interested in reading more?

Please visit our Web site for all
new book releases from SAP PRESS.

www.sap-press.com